THE MIDDLE AGES

Renaissance and Reformation Times
The Middle Ages

By DOROTHY MILLS

The Book of the Ancient World
The Book of the Ancient Greeks
The Book of the Ancient Romans

THE
MIDDLE AGES

By DOROTHY MILLS, M.A.

HEAD OF THE HISTORY DEPARTMENT,
BREARLEY SCHOOL, NEW YORK

ILLUSTRATED

G. P. PUTNAM'S SONS
NEW YORK

MANUFACTURED IN THE UNITED STATES OF AMERICA AT THE VAN REES PRESS

To
MILLICENT CAREY McINTOSH

PREFACE

THE aim of this book has been to tell the story of the Middle Ages in such a way as to bring out the most characteristic features of the period and to emphasize those things in medieval life which have most significance for us today. It was not very difficult to begin the history with the fall of Rome, but it was a harder task to know where it should end. Reference is made in this book to the invention of gunpowder and to that of printing, to the fall of Constantinople and to the discovery of America, to the passing of feudalism and to the work of Wycliffe. When western Christendom was conscious that these things had taken place, the Middle Ages were at an end. It is the history that lies between them and the fall of Rome that is told here.

Medieval history is of necessity the history of many countries and of many movements and there is always a danger that it may become a disconnected narrative. It is hoped that this danger has been avoided by the Time Chart at the end of the book. The chart has brought into chronological order all the names and events referred to in the book.

Contemporary chronicles and other forms of medieval literature have been freely quoted, so that wherever possible the men and women of the Middle Ages might tell their own story. This could not have been done without the permission of authors and publishers to use copyright translations and versions of medieval literature. I am glad to take this opportunity to express my thanks to Messrs. G. Bell and Sons for passages from Henderson's *Documents of the Middle Ages;* to Messrs. Ernest Benn, Ltd., and Messrs. Little, Brown and Company for a passage from Bede Jarrett's *Social Theories of the Middle Ages;* to Messrs. A. and C. Black, Ltd., for passages from E. Lipson's *Introduction to the Economic History of England;* to Mr. B. C. Boulter and L'Edition d'Art H. Piazza for the translation and the original French of Charles d'Orléans' *Ballade;* to Messrs. Chatto and Windus for passages from the *Song of Roland,* Asser's *Life of Alfred, Early Lives of Charlemagne,* the *Vision of Piers the Plowman* and *The Babees Book,* and to Miss C. L. Skeat and Miss Edith Rickert for passages from the two latter books; to Messrs. J. M. Dent and Son for passages from Joinville's *Chronicle of the Crusade of St. Louis,* the *Wakefield Second Shepherd's Play* and Cecil Headlam's *Chartres;* to Messrs. Ginn and Company for passages from James Harvey Robinson's *Readings in European History,* Vol. I; to Greenberg, Publisher, for passages from W. C. Meller's *Knight's Life in the Days of Chivalry;* to Messrs. Henry Holt and Company for passages from Charles H. Haskins' *Rise of the Universities;* to Mr. Alfred A. Knopf for a passage from James Westfall Thompson's *Middle Ages;* to Messrs. Dodd Mead and Company and to John Lane, The Bodley Head, Ltd., for passages from E. G. Nash's *The Hansa, Its History and Romance;* to Messrs. Macmillan and Company for passages from *The Chronicles of Froissart,* J. R. Green's *Short History of the English People* and for Matthew Arnold's translation of the *Canticle of the Sun;* to The Macmillan

Company of New York for a passage from Henry Osborn Taylor's *Mediæval Mind*; to Mr. P. Nutt for passages from *The Crusade of Richard I*; to the Oxford University Press for passages from Charles Plummer's *Life of Alfred the Great*, Stubbs' *Select Charters*, J. Turral's *Source Book of British History*, R. B. Mowat's *New History of Great Britain*, Chaucer's *Prologue to the Canterbury Tales*, the *English Hymnal*, the *Germania* of Tacitus, and to Miss Joan Evans for passages from *Mediæval France* and *Monastic Life at Cluny*; to the Lady Abbess of the Pax House, West Malling, for passages from the *Rule of St. Benedict*; to Messrs. Methuen and Company for passages from the *Life of St. Francis by Thomas of Celano*, to the publishers and Miss Deanesley for passages from her *History of the Medieval Church* and to Miss Dymond for passages from her *Introduction to Medieval History*; to Messrs. G. P. Putnam's Sons for passages from Archer and Kingsford's *Crusades* and Justin H. Smith's *Troubadours at Home*; to Messrs. G. P. Putnam's Sons and William Heinemann of London for passages from Fr. Funck Brentano's *Middle Ages*; to Messrs. Charles Scribner's Sons for a passage from T. D. Hendrick's *History of the Vikings*; to the University of Pennsylvania Press for passages from Edward P. Cheyney's *English Towns and Gilds* in the Translations and Reprints Series.

I should also like to express my thanks for the help given me in the choice of illustrations at the Metropolitan Museum of Art, the Pierpont Morgan Library and for the translation of the script on the illustration of the *Arab Physician* given me by Mr. M. S. Dimand of the Metropolitan Museum.

The world of today is very different from that of the

Middle Ages, but it is a world whose roots lie in those distant centuries. It is my hope that those who read this book will desire to know more of what was one of the great periods of history.

DOROTHY MILLS

New York.

CONTENTS

PART I
THE EARLY MIDDLE AGES

PART II
THE UNITY OF THE MIDDLE AGES

PART III
THE LATER MIDDLE AGES

ILLUSTRATIONS

The illustrations in this edition are grouped at the end of the book, with the exception of the maps and plans.

A PAGE OF MEDIEVAL MUSIC. XIV Century

THE CHURCH OF SAN CLEMENTE, ROME

DIVISION OF THE SHEEP AND THE GOATS. Mosaic. VI Century
> A copy in mosaic of the VI century original mosaic in the church of S. Apollinare Nuovo, Ravenna. It is one of the scenes from the Life and Passion of Christ which decorate the walls of the nave. The subject is an allegory of the Last Judgment.

COURTYARD OF A PRIVATE HOUSE IN CORDOVA

CAROLINGIAN SCRIPT. X Century
> A Page from a Lectionary. Executed in the Benedictine monastery of St. Gall in northeastern Switzerland.

AN ALLEGORY OF THE MEDIEVAL CHURCH. XIV Century
> A Fresco in the Spanish Chapel in S. Maria Novella, Florence. Attributed to Simone Memmi.
>
> In the lowest right-hand corner is St. Dominic preaching first to infidels and then to heretics. He sets his dogs (Domini canes) at them as if they were wolves, and when the latter have been driven away, the rescued lambs are taken to lie at the feet of the Pope. Seated on a throne with the Duomo of Florence behind him, the Pope represents the Church. At his right sit the representatives of the spiritual

order, a cardinal, a bishop, priests and monks; at his left sit the representatives of the temporal order, the emperor, kings, barons, knights, and a group of laymen which includes artists and poets.

Above these groups are seen those who, in spite of St. Dominic's teaching, have given themselves up to worldly amusements, but they repent, confess their sins and then, led by St. Dominic, they approach the gate of Paradise. Angels receive them and crown them with flowers and St. Peter admits them to Paradise. There they join the company of prophets, saints and martyrs and with the Virgin and angels unite in adoration of Christ who is seated upon His throne.

ST. ANNE TEACHING THE VIRGIN TO READ. Early
XVI Century

Sculpture, sandstone. Said to come from the Hospice de
Salins. School of Troyes. French, about 1510-1520.

ARAB PHYSICIAN PREPARING COUGH MIXTURE.
Mesopotamian. XIII Century

Leaf from an Arab Translation of the Materia Medica of
Dioscorides, dated A.D. 1222 and signed by Abdallah Ibn
al Fadl.

    The Arab script beneath reads: "Preparation of Medicine
(Wine) for Cold or Coughs; Ease the throat by taking 1/4
oke of bitter root, 1/8 oke of liquorice root, 1/4 or 1/8 oke
of white pepper. Pulverize them together and put the re-
sulting powder into a cloth, tie it up, and immerse it in
sweet wine for three days. Strain the liquor into a clean
vessel. Drink after dinner."

GOTHIC SCRIPT. XIII Century

A Page from a Psalter and Hours of the Virgin. For
Amiens Use. French. Written and illuminated for Yolande,
Vicomtesse de Soissons.

MAPS AND PLANS

PART I

THE EARLY MIDDLE AGES

CHAPTER I

THE FOUNDATIONS OF THE MIDDLE AGES

IN A.D. 476 Rome fell, the western empire came to an end, and never again was there an Emperor in Rome, never again was Rome the seat of the government of the Roman Empire. But what was it that had come to an end? Rome had given to the world justice, peace and an ordered government that deeply impressed itself upon the imagination not only of those who dwelt within the Empire and who were subject to it, not only of those who lived upon its borders and who came from the uncivilized land that lay beyond it, but also upon those who were to live centuries later.

Since the beginning of recorded history empires and civilizations have risen and fallen; sometimes they would seem to have completely disappeared. It would probably be truer to say that the races who have developed the varying civilizations have disappeared, but that their gifts to the world have survived, not always in the form in which they gave them, but in the form in which the world has needed them.

Rome herself owed to Greece all that was most worth while in the things of the higher intellectual life, and Greece had learned much from the earlier civilizations that had preceded her. And so when the western Roman

Empire came to an end, it was the outward organization, the material things that gave way. The principles of honour and loyalty, of justice and order that had made Rome great were to endure.

The immediate cause of the downfall of Rome was the invasion of the empire by the Germanic tribes from the north. Though these invaders were not as uncivilized as they have sometimes been painted, and though at the time of their invasions they were already learning much from the Romans, they were, nevertheless, not civilized as the Greeks and Romans understood civilization. But they were to play an important part in the making of the new world that was to grow out of the break-up of the Roman Empire.

There was one other powerful influence at work in the Europe of the fifth century. Christianity had brought new ideals to the spirit of man. It had an influence and a power that transformed the lives of those who believed in it, and as will be seen later, it was the Christian Church that kept alive much of the priceless legacy of the ancient world, and that in a time of disorder preserved the Roman ideals of law and discipline.

1. *The Heritage from the Past*

ROME had been profoundly influenced by Greece, but Greek civilization was first known in western Europe in its Latin dress, and it was not until after a thousand years from the fall of Rome that the springs of Greek thought and poetry, philosophy and science were opened in any wide measure to the west. The immediate heritage of Europe came from Rome. She had ruled and civilized the lands that were to make part of the new Europe, and when the days of her might had passed, her imperishable gifts to the world were preserved.

One of the most important factors in preserving Roman civilization was the Latin language. Latin had been common to all parts of the western empire, and throughout the period known as the Middle Ages, it was the language most widely used in Europe. It was the language of the Church, of the universities, of all who were educated, and when out of what had once been the Roman Empire, new nations arose, the peoples of those nations developed languages directly descended from Latin. Because Rome had once ruled in Italy, Gaul and Spain, the Italian, French and Spanish languages came into being.

Rome had civilized the lands she had conquered and the whole Empire, north and south, east and west, was connected by great roads which served as channels along which her civilization passed. These roads are still some of the best in Europe and in most cases modern railways follow the same route.

Rome also left the tradition of law and order and of a well governed dominion. After the break-up of the Empire, the Church in her organization preserved this tradition, and Roman ideas of justice and order profoundly influenced the law of the growing states of Europe and have never been lost to the world. In whatever direction we turn today, we find ourselves on a path made possible to us by Rome.

2. *The Germanic Invaders of the Roman Empire*[1]

FOR nearly five hundred years Rome had kept her frontiers safe and the barbarian tribes who lived beyond them

[1] The greater part of this section is taken from Chapter XXIV of my *Book of the Ancient Romans*.

had been unable seriously to threaten the Roman boundaries. But towards the end of the fourth century these tribes began to push into the Empire. Many reasons brought them. Their own lands, lying outside the Empire, were poor, the forests were not cleared, the swamps were not drained, they were subject to floods and to drought, to famine and to scarcity, and so the well cultivated lands attracted them. They came first for food and then for other plunder. Then they began to value the order kept by the Roman government and they made settlements and homes just within the Roman frontiers. As time went on Germans began taking an active part in the life of the Empire, they began to serve in the Roman armies and in some cases even acted as officers. The latter were often men of great ability and from serving in Roman armies they had learnt Roman habits of military discipline and obedience.

The Roman historian Tacitus has left an account of some of these German tribes. He says:

They take pleasure in the size of their herds: these are their sole form of wealth, and they are very proud of them. Whether it is in mercy or in anger that the gods have denied them silver and gold, I do not know: nor could I definitely assert that Germany produces no vein of gold or silver: for no one has explored. But they are not affected in the same way that we are by its possession and use.

The Germans fight with spears which have a short narrow head, but are so sharp and handy that they use the same weapon, as circumstances demand, for close and open fighting. The cavalry are content with shield and spear: the infantry also shower javelins: each man carries several, and they can throw them a very long way. They fight naked or in a very light plaid. They have no elaborate apparel, and merely paint their shields with distinctive colours of the brightest hue.

Their number is fixed: a hundred come from each village, and they are known to their people as "the hundred." Thus what was at first a mere number has come to be an honourable name. The line is drawn up in wedge battalions. To retire from your post, provided you charge again, is thought to show prudence not fear. They carry away their dead, even after a doubtful battle. To lose your shield is the worst dishonour of all: one thus disgraced may not be present at a sacrifice or enter a council. After a defeat many survivors have been known to hang themselves to end their infamy.

When the fighting begins, it is shameful for a chief to be outdone in bravery, and equally shameful for the followers not to match the bravery of their chief: to survive one's chief and to return from battle is a foul disgrace which lasts as long as life.

When they are not fighting, they spend little time in hunting, much more in doing nothing. They devote themselves to sleeping and eating. Even the bravest and most warlike are quite idle, for they give over the care of house and fields to the women and the old men, and to all the weaklings of the household. They themselves merely lounge, for from a strange contradiction of character they love idleness yet hate peace. It is usual for the tribe, man by man, to contribute a voluntary gift of cattle or corn for the chiefs. They accept this as an honour, and it meets their needs.

It is well known that none of the German tribes live in cities. They cannot endure undetached houses. Their houses are separate and scattered, pitched at the call of river, plain or wood. They build villages, but not as we do with the buildings all adjoining and connected. Each man has an open space round his homestead, either as a protection against risk of fire, or because they do not know how to build otherwise.

The husband brings a dowry to his wife, not the wife to the husband. The parents come to the wedding and inspect the presents. These are not designed to please a woman's taste, nor can a young bride wear them in her hair: they are oxen, a bridled horse or a shield with spear and sword. This is the dowry which wins a wife, and she in her turn brings her husband some gift of arms. A woman must not think herself exempt from thoughts of bravery or the chances of war. By the ceremony which begins her married life she is warned that she comes to be her husband's partner in toil and in danger, to suffer and to dare with him alike in peace and war. This is plainly shown by the yoked oxen, the bridled horse, and the gift of arms. Thus she must live, and thus she must die. She is receiving a trust which she must keep worthily and hand on to her children, a trust which her sons' wives must receive in turn and pass on to their children.[1]

The earliest Germanic settlers in the Roman Empire had been the Goths. These were tribes who lived originally on the shores of the Baltic, but who had wandered south, the Visigoths settling on the shores of the Black Sea, and the East or Ostrogoths on the Danube. The Emperor Aurelian, towards the end of the third century, gave Dacia to the Visigoths, on the understanding that they would not cross the Danube or enter Roman territory. For nearly a century they lived there as friendly allies of Rome and were influenced by the habits and customs of their Roman neighbours.

In the middle of the fourth century the Visigoths in Dacia were so seriously threatened by a savage enemy coming from the East that they appealed to Rome for help. This enemy was a tribe of Asiatic people known as Huns. They were so fierce and savage that it was thought they were hardly human, and the very name of Hun terrified all who heard it. These Huns invaded Dacia and defeated the king of the Visigoths, who immediately sent an imploring message to the Roman Emperor asking that the survivors with the women and children should be allowed to cross the Danube and come into the Roman Empire, where they hoped for protection. Valens, the Emperor at the time, consented, and Roman officers were sent to see that proper protection was given to them. But the Romans plundered, robbed and ill-treated the unfortunate Goths, so that those who might have become firm

[1] Tacitus: *Germania*.

friends and allies of the Romans became their deadly enemies and in 378, rebelling against the cruel and unjust treatment they had received, the Goths rose up in arms and in a battle fought at Adrianople, not only defeated the Roman army, but also slew the Roman Emperor.

Valens was succeeded by Theodosius, who wisely made peace with the Goths. He was known as "Lover of peace and of the Goths," and as long as he lived, they gave Rome no trouble. Theodosius was the last emperor to rule over both the East and the West. From the time of his death in 395 the East and the West, though nominally still one Empire, each went its own way, along a different path which led to a different future.

Theodosius had kept peace with the Goths, but his successor was weak and hardly interested himself at all in the affairs of the Empire. It was then that the Goths grew very powerful and under a strong leader, Alaric, they ravaged the lands of the East and then entered Italy. Alaric wanted land for himself and his followers, but he does not seem to have been a wilful destroyer for the sake of destroying, and he generally spared life, if he received the submission of his enemies. He advanced to the walls of Rome and besieged the city. When the inhabitants sent out a messenger asking on what terms he would raise the siege, he agreed to depart if all their gold, silver and movable property were sent out to him. "What will be left to us?" they asked. "Your lives," was the short answer. Some treasure was sent out to him, but it was not enough and the siege continued. At length in 410 Alaric entered Rome and allowed his followers to burn and pillage at will. A great deal of damage was done, though probably not as much as was supposed, and it is said that Alaric gave orders that the churches should be spared.

Although the days of her greatness had passed, the name of Rome was still one which stood to the world for all that was great and unconquerable, and when the news of the sack of Rome by Alaric spread to distant places, every one was stupefied with horror and dismay. The news reached St. Jerome, who, far off in his cell at Bethlehem, was living the life of a hermit, and he could hardly believe what he heard. In a letter written shortly afterwards, he said: "The City which had taken all the world was itself taken. ... The Roman world is falling." As people began to recover from the shock, they asked themselves why such a disaster could have fallen upon Rome. There were still large numbers of pagans in the Empire and they blamed Christianity for the catastrophe, for the Christian religion, they said, had caused the neglect of the old Roman gods who in their anger had allowed the city to fall. But St. Augustine, the Bishop of Hippo, who was himself the son of a pagan father, but of a Christian mother, Monica, wrote a book called *De Civitate Dei, The City of God*, in which he answered the pagan accusations, and in which he declared that Rome was of the world and therefore could not last, but that the Kingdom or City, as he called it, of God was to triumph over the whole world, and that this spiritual empire would endure.

After taking Rome, Alaric left the city and soon made himself the master of Italy, and then he died. His name has become well known in history, not so much because he was himself a great man, but because he, a tall, fair-haired barbarian from without the Empire, had broken the spell that had hung about the name of Rome. His followers buried him in a river turning it aside from its course in order that they might dig his grave in its bed. In it they placed the body of Alaric together with rich treasure, and then turned back the waters into their accustomed channel. And that none might ever know where his body had been laid, they put to death the men who had made the grave.

Rome had been sacked, but she had not yet ceased to be the seat of government. The Goths withdrew from Italy and overran Spain, where they set up a Visigothic kingdom which lasted until early in the sixth century. Other tribes wandered about the Western Empire, and those who were most restless and destructive were the Vandals. At one time they lived near the Danube, then through the south of Gaul they forced their way into Spain. The Goths drove them out of Spain and they crossed to Africa, pillaging, ravaging, burning, destroying wherever they went. "Where are we going next?" a Vandal once asked his chief. "Wherever there is a people with whom God is angry," was the answer. The Vandals seized the harbours of North Africa and built themselves ships, in which they sailed like pirates over the Mediterranean, until, in the middle of the sixth century, they were subdued by the Eastern Emperor.

But now the Huns again became troublesome, and under a powerful leader, Attila, they came plundering into Europe and reached Gaul. It is said that it was the boast of Attila that grass never grew again where the hoof of his horse had trod. He was known as the *Scourge of God*, and he inspired such terror, that the Romans and Goths were willing to make friends in order to drive him away. In 451 their combined armies inflicted such a tremendous defeat on him at Châlons, that all fear of Hun dominion in Europe was dispelled. Attila left Gaul, but he made one more expedition and the next year entered

Italy and actually reached the neighbourhood of Rome. The Bishop of Rome, Leo I, called the Great, went out of the city and fearlessly confronted the savage Hun. "Thus far shalt thou come, and no farther," he said to him and demanded that he should immediately leave the land. Legend says that as he spoke, a vision of St. Peter and St. Paul with their hands outstretched in blessing over the city appeared in the sky, and that, awed and terrified, Attila withdrew. He died soon after, and the Huns troubled Europe no more.

Other invading tribes were the Burgundians, who founded a kingdom in the valley of the Rhone, and the Lombards who settled in the north of Italy. The Burgundians were not important as a kingdom, but they left their mark on the legend and poetry of Germany in the story known as the *Niebelungenlied*. The Lombards settled in the valley of the Po, where they made Pavia their capital, and they also held scattered lands further south. The Lombards were less important for what they contributed to Italy than for what they hindered. They very soon broke up into a number of small states, all independent and jealous of each other, and their influence prevented Italy from becoming a united nation.

The Visigoths had set up a kingdom in Spain; the other branch of the same tribe, the East or Ostrogoths had settled north of the Danube. In 493 Theodoric became king of the Ostrogoths. As a young man he had led them in attacks on the Balkan states of the Empire, but the walls of Constantinople stopped his advance and he was taken as a hostage to the imperial court. Alert, able and ambitious, Theodoric learnt a great deal at Constantinople. When he succeeded in returning to Italy and establishing himself as king of an Ostrogothic kingdom, he proved himself the ablest and best statesman of any of the Germanic leaders. He conquered all those who opposed him in the north of Italy and then, making Ravenna his capital, ruled as a great king. He kept order in the land. He fostered the growth of cities and spent a good deal of money in beautifying them with buildings inspired by Rome. He encouraged education and invited scholars to come to his court. Theodoric was tolerant and far-sighted. His kingdom included men of different races and religions, but he did not attempt to make them all subject to a uniform system of law. The Italians gave up one-third of their land to the Goths, but each race lived according to its own law and was allowed freedom to worship in its own way. Theodoric supported the Christian Church, but he did not compel others to do so. "Religion," he said, "is a thing which the king cannot command, because no man can be compelled to believe against his will."

Theodoric was the first king of the new Europe to recognize different nations living within their own clearly marked boundaries as equals. His reign was one of the first to foreshadow the new Europe that was to come, but at the end it was marred by an act of violence. The philosopher Boethius, who was living at his court, was suspected of being involved in a conspiracy to bring Italy under the Emperor, and Theodoric had him put to death.

Theodoric had ruled well and made the kingdom of the Ostrogoths strong, but after his death in 526 the rule of the Ostrogoths in Italy came to an end. Many of them were driven out by the Emperor, and the remainder were ruled directly for him by an Exarch who lived at Ravenna.

Of all these invading tribes none survived except as a memory and a name, but the Franks who invaded Gaul and the Angles and Saxons who invaded Britain. They invaded, but unlike the other Germanic tribes, they stayed in the lands they conquered and their story belongs to that of early France and England.

Western Europe survived all these invasions. The Germanic tribes brought vigour and new blood into a civilization that was declining because the outward and material forms seemed more important than the life and ideals that had made it great. But however weak, the life and ideals were still there and the tradition of finer things was never forgotten, so that out of the seeming confusion and disorder there arose a new civilization different from but not unworthy of that from which it had sprung.

CHAPTER II

THE EARLY CHRISTIAN CHURCH

1. *The Organization of the Early Church*[1]

THE Middle Ages had for their foundation both the heritage from the past and the new life brought by the Germanic tribes. Of equal importance in the new civilization that was to grow out of these things was that of the Christian Church.

Constantine the Great had made Christianity the religion of the Empire. In his reign a controversy arose in the Church concerning what was believed about the Person of Jesus Christ. The Emperor probably understood very little about it, but he was far-seeing enough to realize that the Christian Church was destined to be one of the great powers in the world, and that for the work it had to do, it was important that it should not be divided. When an appeal was made to him to settle the controversy, he called a council of the whole Church together at Nicæa in Asia Minor. This council met in the year 325. It was the first great council of the whole Church and was attended by bishops and other clergy from all over the Roman world. The controversy was settled, and as a result of the council the Nicene Creed was drawn up, a statement in noble

[1] This section is taken from Chapter XXI of my *Book of the Ancient Romans*.

language of what the Church held to be essential in Christian belief.

The first Christians had been simple and uneducated men and women, but as the first centuries of Christianity went by and when Christianity had become the religion of the Empire, educated men and women became Christians. Amongst them were many who had been trained in the schools of Greek philosophy, men who gave to their religion all their mind as well as all their heart. To meet their difficulties Christian scholars began to write about the Christian faith. Following soon after St. Paul were such men as Tertullian, Origen, Athanasius and St. Augustine, writers who are known as the Fathers of the Christian Church.

The word *Church* means *belonging to the Lord,* and all Christians everywhere were a part of it. The only ordered government known to the men of the first century was that of the Roman Empire, and to a large extent its forms were borrowed for the early Church. The Apostles who had been the immediate followers of Christ Himself had naturally been the first leaders in the Christian communities, and their successors were men who had been solemnly set apart for the same office. They were given the title of *bishop,* a word meaning *overseer,* and their work was to have the oversight of all the Christian communities in certain districts which were called *dioceses* or *sees.* Under them were the *priests,* men also specially set apart for the work of the Church, and to help these again there were *deacons,* an order first instituted to help the priests in the practical affairs of the Church, so that the latter might have more time for the spiritual side of their work.

In the fourth century, the most important sees were

those of Rome, Constantinople, Alexandria and Antioch, and except in Rome, the Bishops of these sees were called *Patriarchs*. Tradition has always held that St. Peter was the first Bishop of Rome, and that he and St. Paul were put to death there during the persecutions under Nero. From the beginning this gave the Bishop of Rome great importance in the eyes of the Church.

During the fourth and fifth centuries, as the Empire began to fall before the Germanic invaders, the Church grew more powerful, especially in Rome, for as the civil government became more and more incapable of keeping order, the Church gradually began to take its place. The Roman rulers were weak and incompetent, but the Bishops of Rome of this period were statesmen as well as church-men. When the Emperor and his court went to Constantinople, the Bishop was the most important man left in Rome, and he gradually assumed a position of great power and responsibility. In 445 a decree was passed which declared that the Bishop of Rome had supremacy over the whole Church, and for more than a thousand years this supremacy was never seriously questioned on the continent of western Europe.

The Church had inherited two things from the Roman Empire. She had taken and adapted to her own needs the Roman form of government, and she had also made her own the old Roman ideal of unity. The Roman ideal had been that of one political empire, with its centre in Rome, the city that had been divinely founded and that was to last for ever. The ideal of the early Church was that the whole world should be united in a great spiritual kingdom of which Rome was to be the earthly centre, but of which Christ was to be the King and which was to last for ever.

2. *The Worship of the Early Church*

DURING the first three centuries of Christianity the attitude of the Roman government towards it prevented any building of churches or any development of Christian art. But after the fourth century there was no further need for secrecy and churches began to be built where Christian worship might be worthily performed.

The earliest form of the Christian church was the *basilica*. The word basilica is Greek and means *the house of the king* and the Romans used it as the name of their lawcourt. The Roman basilica was a large oblong building with a central nave, divided from two side-aisles by rows of pillars. At one end there was a semi-circular recess called the *apse*, in which trials were conducted and in which the seat of the judge was placed. After the fourth century this type of building was adapted for the worship of the Christian Church.

The early Christian basilica was approached through a porch which gave admission to an open court or *atrium*, similar to the atrium of a Roman house. The church occupied one side of the court and the three remaining sides were surrounded by a cloister. The church was usually entered by three great doors, each corresponding to one of the aisles within. The interior, like the Roman building, consisted of a long and wide nave, with one or sometimes two aisles on each side, separated from each other by marble pillars. The apse at the end of the middle aisle contained the throne of the bishop and seats for the clergy, and the semi-dome above it was decorated with mosaics, usually of Christ in glory, with saints on either hand. The altar stood in the centre, before the apse, on a raised platform approached by a flight of steps, and above it was the *ciborium,* a canopy supported by marble pillars. Beneath the altar was the *confessio,* a subterranean chapel containing the body or relics of the saint to whom the church was dedicated.

At the foot of the altar steps, occupying the upper part of the nave, was a raised platform surrounded by a low marble wall or railing, the *cancelli.* This was the choir for the singers and readers, and at the sides were two pulpit desks called *ambones,* from which the Epistle and Gospel were read. When the Eucharist was celebrated, the bishop and the clergy came from their seats in the apse and stood with the altar between them and the people, facing the congregation.

Christian churches have changed a good deal in some of their arrangements since these early times and for that reason a rather detailed description has been given. The church of San Clemente in Rome, however, has very faithfully retained the original arrangement and gives an example of what the early Christian churches were like.

There was, of course, no need now for symbols as a means of teaching, but a great many of those that had been used in the days when secrecy was necessary survived as ornament. But this art was not enough for a church that had no need for secrecy, and with the spread of Christianity there was developed a definitely Christian art. It was necessary that teaching should be given to people who could not read, and the walls of the churches gave opportunity to artists to set forth the Christian story in pictures. This was done both in painting and in mosaic work. In the early Middle Ages this art flourished most in Constantinople and the East.[1]

It was during these early centuries of Christianity that

[1] See p. 42.

the Greek and Latin liturgies grew into the stately and reverent form of worship which has always characterized the Christian Church. In the lands of the eastern Mediterranean Greek was the language most frequently used, whereas in the west the liturgies were written in Latin. In different places different Uses, as they began to be called, were found, but in the main the form of service was the same.

This was a period, however, when not only man's mind was set on interpreting his religion in his writings and in set forms of dignified worship, but his spirit was learning new emotions through Christian teaching. Men had been devout and reverent, pure and virtuous, joyous and loving before the days of Christ. But Christian teaching had put a radiance upon these virtues that was different from what had been known before, and these new emotions took form in Christian poetry, chiefly at first in the form that we know as *Hymns*.

From the earliest times the hymn was something to be taken part in by the congregation. In his famous letter to Trajan about the persecution of the Christians, Pliny says, "They had been accustomed (on a stated day) to meet before daybreak and to recite a hymn among themselves to Christ."

At first the hymn was a simple form of poetry expressing some definite teaching. As the centuries went by this form of Christian poetry, in all the varying moods that it expressed, joy and thanksgiving, penitence and humility, adoration and worship, had a very marked influence on the lyrical poetry of Europe. The earliest Christian hymns were written in Greek. They are characterized, even in the translation in which form we know them today, by great

simplicity of language and by the absence of all senti-
mentality.[1]

In the western church the liturgy was in Latin and
from the fourth century onwards, Latin hymns were sung.
One of the greatest of the early Latin hymn-writers was
St. Ambrose, Bishop of Milan. He wrote a large number,
many of which are still sung today. His chief object in
writing them was to teach unlearned people in such a way
as to capture their imagination. Of the Ambrosian hymns
one of the best known is *O lux beata trinitas*.

O Lux beata trinitas,
　　Et principalis unitas,
Jam sol recedit igneus:
　　Infunde lumen cordibus.

Te mane laudum carmine,
　　Te deprecemur vesperi,
Te nostra supplex gloria
　　Per cuncta laudet saecula.

O Trinity, most blessed light,
O unity of princely might,
The fiery sun now goes his way;
Shed thou within our hearts thy ray.
To Thee our morning song of praise,
To Thee our evening prayer we raise:
Thy glory suppliant we adore
For ever and for evermore.

Translated by J. M. Neale. [2]

[1] Some of the best known of the Greek hymns are: The Candle-
light Hymn, *O Brightness of the Immortal Father's Face*; a hymn
from the Liturgy of St. James, *Let all mortal flesh keep silence*;
Christian dost thou see them (St. Andrew of Crete, 8th century); the
Easter hymn, *The Day of Resurrection* (St. John of Damascus, 8th
century).

[2] *The English Hymnal*, Oxford University Press, New York and
London.

One of the great early hymns was *Vexilla regis pro-deunt*, generally known today as *The royal banners forward go*. This was written by Venantius Fortunatus, Bishop of Poitiers in the year 569. The Emperor had sent a relic of the True Cross as a gift to Poitiers. It was received in a great procession and this hymn was written for the occasion. Venantius Fortunatus also wrote the Easter hymn, *Welcome happy morning*.

One last early Latin hymn may be mentioned, *All glory laud and honour*. This was written by Theodulf of Orleans early in the ninth century. In the library at Orleans there is an old manuscript which gives an account of how Palm Sunday was kept there. After the people had been blessed in the cathedral and the palms distributed, a procession was formed representing the entry of Jesus into Jerusalem. The people carried palm branches and sang the Hosanna. At the gates of the city they halted, the Gospel was sung and a prayer offered. Then from the city walls came a burst of song, children singing *Gloria, laus et honor,* (Theodulf's hymn) the refrain of which was caught up by the crowd, and at the end the procession wound its way back to the cathedral.

These hymns are part of the Christian heritage that has come down to us. The common possession of Christendom, they link together the centuries and all parts of the Church.

3. *Early Missionary Work*

a. Irish Missionaries

As the Germanic tribes from the north came into contact with the civilization of ancient Rome, so in time did they come into contact with the Christian faith. Roman legionaries had counted Christians among them, and here and there even before the fall of Rome little Christian communities had been founded. But when the full force of the Germanic invasions broke upon the weakened empire, these Christian communities were almost entirely wiped out.

But there was one land that had never formed part of the Roman Empire. It lay outside it, separated from other lands by a stormy sea, and the Christian Church which had been founded there was unharmed by the fierceness of the heathen tribes from the north of Europe. This land was Ireland, to which Christianity had been brought by St. Patrick in the fifth century.

St. Patrick was born in Scotland towards the end of the fourth century. When he was about sixteen he was carried off as a slave to Ireland where he lived for six years. Then he escaped and for many years he was away from Ireland. All kinds of tales are told of what he did during this time, but nothing of certainty is known. He probably travelled about, to Gaul certainly, perhaps to Italy. Whilst abroad he was ordained priest, and many years later we hear of him as a bishop. We are told that in his dreams Patrick had heard the Irish calling to him: "We pray thee to come and henceforth walk among us," and so, well on in years, he returned to Ireland where he preached and taught the people. He lived to be very old and when he died he was given a great funeral. It was said that "a great host of heaven's angels came with a great light to attend him. And Ireland's elders heard the quiring of the angels on that night."

For about two hundred years, from about 500 to 700, the Church in Ireland grew and flourished and Ireland gained for itself the name of the "Island of Saints." It was a land full of monasteries, in which the monks were renowned for their sanctity of life, for their learning and for their hospitality to the stranger. To these monasteries came men from afar to study not only from books, but the art of illumination for which the Irish monks were famous. In these early days the Christian life of the Irish was a very real thing. Impetuous and tender, quick-witted and warm-hearted, these men and women lived what they believed. Not content with believing themselves they became the earliest missionaries, sending out men first to Scotland and the north of England and then later to northern Europe.

First the Irish monks went to Scotland, where St. Columba made the island of Iona the centre from which missionaries went forth. Early in the seventh century Christianity had been preached in Northumbria by Paulinus, but the champions of the old pagan gods forced him to leave and it seemed as if his mission had been unsuccessful. When, however, a few years later, Oswald became king of Northumbria, he sent to Iona for some one to come and preach the Christian faith in his land. About 635 a man was sent who, Bede tells us, was very austere and met with no success.

He returned home, and in an assembly of the elders reported that he had not been able to do any good to the nation he had been sent to preach to, because they were uncivilized men, and of a stubborn and barbarous disposition. They, as is testified, in a great council seriously debated what was to be done, being desirous that the nation should receive the salvation it demanded, and grieving that they had not received the preacher sent to them. Then said Aidan, who was present in the council, to the priest then spoken of, "I am of opinion, brother, that you were more severe to your unlearned hearers than you ought to have been, and did not at first give them the milk of more easy doctrine, till being by degrees nourished with the work of God, they should be capable of greater perfection." [1]

It was suggested that Aidan was the man to be sent to those rough Northumbrians. He went and Bede tells us of the success of his mission and of how he lived himself as he taught others they should live.

He taught no otherwise than he and his followers had lived; for he neither sought nor loved anything of this world, but delighted in distributing immediately among the poor whatsoever was given him by the kings or rich men of the world. He was wont to traverse both town and country on foot, never on horseback, unless compelled by some urgent necessity. He was known for his love of peace and charity; his mind superior to anger and avarice, and despising pride and vainglory; his industry in keeping the heavenly commandments; his diligence in reading and watching; his authority becoming a priest in reproving the haughty and powerful, and at the same time his tenderness in comforting the afflicted, and relieving or defending the poor.[2]

Lindisfarne became one of the most important centres from which Christian teachers went out to the north of England, and by the middle of the seventh century monasteries had been founded in many parts of Northumbria. Of these Wearmouth and Jarrow became the most important, not only as centres of Christian teaching but as homes of learning and of art. The monastery at Wearmouth was built in 674 by Benedict Biscop, a monk who had made four journeys to Rome. He had seen the great stone churches on the continent and he sent for masons to come to Northumbria and show the people how to build in stone. From Rome he brought back "an innumerable quantity of books and relics" and a number of pictures which he put into the church in order that

[1] Bede: *The Ecclesiastical History of the English Nation.*
[2] *Ibid.*

all who entered the church, even if ignorant of letters, which-ever way they turned, might either contemplate the ever-lovely aspect of Christ and His saints, though only in a picture, or with watchful mind revere the grace of the Lord's incarnation, or else, having as it were the trial of the last judgment before their eyes, they might remember to examine themselves more strictly.

The Irish missionaries went further afield than to Scot-land and England. They went to France and Switzerland and Italy, where they founded monasteries and left Chris-tian communities behind them. All these were distinctively Irish. They were independent of the Pope, they kept Easter at a different time from the Roman date, and their churches were organized in a different way.

The influence of these Christian missionaries in the north was very great. The pagan people to whom they went thought of happiness and joy as coming from the rage of battle and the slaughter of their enemies. They knew little of tenderness, their friendships were fierce as were their hatreds. The misty lands of the north were full of supernatural terrors to them. Into all this came the teaching of Christ, bringing with it a joy and tenderness unknown before, teaching of compassion and pity, filling the world of spirits with angels, giving a new source for the hope and gladness of life.

b. St. Augustine in England
A.D. 597

In the meantime Rome had also begun to send out mis-sionaries. One of the greatest of the early popes was Gregory the Great (590-604). He was born in Rome of a wealthy family. By the time he was thirty he had been made a prefect, but when his father died and he inherited a large fortune, he used the money to found a number of monasteries and to support various charities. Then he entered a monastery and became a monk himself. His ability was well known, he had acted as papal legate in Constantinople, and he was not allowed to remain long in his monastery. In 590 he was elected pope, and for fourteen years he ruled the Church.

In the summer of 590 Rome was smitten by a plague. Gregory arranged a procession of the people to the church of Santa Maria Maggiore, one of the great "seven churches of Rome," that they might pray for deliverance. A legend says that as they crossed the bridge over the Tiber leading to the tomb of Hadrian, the archangel Michael appeared in the sky sheathing the sword of pestilence which he held in his hand, and that from that hour the plague was stayed. From thenceforth the tomb of Hadrian became known as the castle of Sant' Angelo.

Gregory I was one of the great rulers of the early Middle Ages and under him the papacy grew in power and importance in Europe. He made every endeavour to suppress heresy, he carried on an amazing correspondence on every conceivable subject connected with the Church, he understood music and introduced into the services of the Church the type of chanting known as plainsong, he wrote hymns. He was an able administrator, sometimes harsh, often autocratic, determined to be obeyed, yet he believed that an ideal ruler was one who served those whom he ruled, and it was Gregory the Great who first used the title adopted by succeeding popes, *Servus servorum Dei*, Servant of the servants of God. Besides the care of the Church in lands already Christian, the rule of Gregory was characterized by his missionary work in the northern parts of Europe, and especially by the mission he sent to England.

The story is told that once, before he was pope, Gregory was walking in the slave market at Rome, and his attention was caught by some tall, fair-haired, blue-eyed slave boys. He asked who they were and whence they came, and was told that they were Angles. *"Non angli, sed angeli,* Not Angles, but Angels,"* was his answer. He made further inquiries, and was told that they came from the distant land of England, across the sea, and that they were heathen. Gregory determined then, that if it were ever in his power, he would send missionaries to the Angles and make them Christian. The opportunity came when he was made pope. He commissioned Augustine, with a band of Benedictine monks, to set out for England. They did so, but on the way were seized with fears of the unknown dangers that lay ahead of them.

They having, in obedience to the pope's commands, undertaken that work, were, on their journey, seized with a sudden fear, and began to think of returning home, rather than proceed to a barbarous, fierce, and unbelieving nation, to whose very language they were strangers; and this they unanimously agreed was the safest course. In short, they sent back Augustine, who had been appointed to be consecrated bishop in case they were received by the English, that he might, by humble entreaty, obtain of the holy Gregory, that they should not be compelled to undertake so dangerous, toilsome, and uncertain a journey.[1]

The Pope sent Augustine back with an encouraging letter, and they set forward once more on their journey.

Augustine, thus strengthened by the confirmation of the blessed Father Gregory, returned to the work of the word of God, with the servants of Christ, and arrived in Britain. The powerful

[1] Bede: *The Ecclesiastical History of the English Nation.*

Ethelbert was at that time king of Kent; he had extended his dominions as far as the great river Humber, by which the Southern Saxons are divided from the Northern. On the east of Kent is the large Isle of Thanet containing according to the English way of reckoning, 600 families, divided from the other land by the river Wantsum, which is about three furlongs over, and fordable only in two places, for both ends of it run into the sea. In this island landed the servant of our Lord, Augustine, and his companions, being, as is reported, nearly forty men. They had, by order of the blessed Pope Gregory, taken interpreters of the nation of the Franks, and sending to Ethelbert, signified that they were come from Rome, and brought a joyful message, which most undoubtedly assured to all that took advantage of it everlasting joys in heaven, and a kingdom that would never end, with the living and true God. The king having heard this, ordered them to stay in that island where they had landed, and that they should be furnished with all necessaries, till he should consider what to do with them. For he had before heard of the Christian religion, having a Christian wife of the royal family of the Franks, called Bertha; whom he had received from her parents, upon condition that she should be permitted to practise her religion with the Bishop Luidhard, who was sent with her to preserve her faith. Some days after, the king came into the island, and sitting in the open air, ordered Augustine and his companions to be brought into his presence. For he had taken precaution that they should not come to him in any house, lest, according to an ancient superstition, if they practised any magical arts, they might impose upon him, and so get the better of him. But they came furnished with Divine, not with magic virtue, bearing a silver cross for their banner, and the image of our Lord and Saviour painted on a board; and, singing the litany, they offered up their prayers to the Lord for the eternal salvation both of themselves and of those to whom they were come. When he had sat down, pursuant to the king's commands, and preached to him and his attendants there present, the word of life, the king answered thus:—"Your words and promises are very fair, but as they are new to us, and of uncertain import, I cannot approve of them so far as to forsake that which I have so long followed with the whole English nation. But because you are come from far into my kingdom, and, as I conceive, are desirous to im-

part to us those things which you believe to be true, and most bene-
ficial, we will not molest you, but give you favourable entertainment, and take care to supply you with your necessary sustenance;
nor do we forbid you to preach and gain as many as you can to
your religion." Accordingly he permitted them to reside in the city
of Canterbury, which was the metropolis of all his dominions,
and, pursuant to his promise, besides allowing them sustenance, did
not refuse them liberty to preach. It is reported that, as they drew
near to the city, after their manner, with the holy cross, and the
image of our sovereign Lord and King, Jesus Christ, they, in con-
cert, sung this litany: "We beseech Thee, O Lord, in all Thy
mercy, that Thy anger and wrath be turned away from this city,
and from the holy house, because we have sinned. Hallelujah."

As soon as they entered the dwelling-place assigned them, they
began to imitate the course of life practised in the primitive
church; applying themselves to frequent prayer, watching and
fasting; preaching the word of life to as many as they could;
despising all worldly things, as not belonging to them; receiving
only their necessary food from those they taught; living themselves in all respects conformably to what they prescribed to
others, and being always disposed to suffer any adversity, and even
to die for that truth which they preached. In short, several believed and were baptized, admiring the simplicity of their innocent life, and the sweetness of their heavenly doctrine. There was
on the east side of the city a church dedicated to the honour of St.
Martin, built whilst the Romans were still in the island, wherein
the queen, who, as has been said before, was a Christian, used to
pray. In this they first began to meet, to sing, to pray, to say mass,
to preach, and to baptize, till the king, being converted to the faith,
allowed them to preach openly, and build or repair churches in all
places.

When he, among the rest, induced by the unspotted life of
these holy men, and their delightful promises, which, by many
miracles, they proved to be most certain, believed and was baptized, greater numbers began daily to flock together to hear the
word, and, forsaking their heathen rites, to associate themselves,
by believing, to the unity of the church of Christ. Their conversion the king so far encouraged, as that he compelled none to
embrace Christianity, but only showed more affection to the be-

lievers, as to his fellow-citizens in the heavenly kingdom. For he had learned from his instructors and leaders to salvation, that the service of Christ ought to be voluntary, not by compulsion. Nor was it long before he gave his teachers a settled residence in the metropolis of Canterbury, with such possessions of different kinds as were necessary for their subsistence.[1]

In Canterbury St. Augustine founded a Benedictine monastery and began the building of the first church on the site of what is now the cathedral. He became the first Archbishop of Canterbury, and Bede calls him the "archbishop of the English nation." Soon after his consecration he sent an account of his work to Gregory and asked various questions as to how he should deal with difficult matters. He found that the Christian churches in different places were not all following the same rule, and to his request for advice Gregory answered:

You know, my brother, the custom of the Roman Church in which you may remember you were bred up. But it pleases me, that if you have found anything, either in the Roman, or the Gallican, or any other church, which may be more acceptable to Almighty God, you carefully make choice of the same, and sedulously teach the church of the English, which as yet is new in the faith, whatsoever you can gather from the several churches. For things are not to be loved for the sake of places, but places for the sake of good things. Choose, therefore, from every church those things that are pious, religious, and upright, and when you have, as it were, made them up into one body, let the minds of the English be accustomed thereto.[2]

Ethelberga, the daughter of Ethelbert of Kent and Queen Bertha, was given by her parents in marriage to the king of Northumbria. It was a pagan land to which the Christian maiden went, but the Northumbrian king

[1] Bede: *The Ecclesiastical History of the English Nation.*
[2] *Ibid.*

welcomed with her Paulinus, who had been consecrated bishop in order to go on this mission to the north.

Through the teaching of Paulinus many Northumbrians became Christian. The wise men who advised the king were much interested in the new faith, which seemed to offer to them the certainties that their pagan beliefs denied them. After listening to Paulinus and discussing it amongst themselves, one of them said:

"The present life of man, O king, seems to me, in comparison of that time which is unknown to us, like to the swift flight of a sparrow through the room wherein you sit at supper in winter, with your commanders and ministers, and a good fire in the midst, whilst the storms of rain and snow prevail abroad; the sparrow, I say, flying in at one door, and immediately out at another, whilst he is within, is safe from the wintry storm; but after a short space of fair weather, he immediately vanishes out of your sight, into the dark winter from which he had emerged. So this life of man appears for a short space, but of what went before, or what is to follow, we are utterly ignorant. If, therefore, this new doctrine contains something more certain, it seems justly to deserve to be followed." The other elders and king's councillors, by Divine inspiration, spoke to the same effect.[1]

The later work of St. Aidan and the influence of Lindisfarne established the church in the north of England, but the northern church was independent of Rome, and in the middle of the seventh century a controversy broke out between it and the church in the south which owed allegiance to the Pope. The two churches disagreed about various customs and usages, one of which was the date of the keeping of Easter. In 664 Oswy, King of Northumbria, called a synod at Whitby in order to discuss the differences and to strive to come to some agreement. Colman from Lindisfarne pleaded for agreement with the church in Ireland,

[1] Bede: *The Ecclesiastical History of the English Nation.*

Wilfred of York for Rome. Summing up the argument, Wilfred declared that the Bishops of Rome were the successors of St. Peter, and it was to him that Christ had said: Thou art Peter, and upon this rock I will build my church; and the gates of hell shall not prevail against it, and I will give unto thee the keys of the kingdom of heaven.[1]

When Wilfred had spoken thus, the king said, "Is it true, Colman, that these words were spoken to Peter by our Lord?" He answered, "It is true, O king!" Then says he, "Can you show any such power given to your Columba?" Colman answered "None." Then added the king, "Do you both agree that these words were principally directed to Peter, and that the keys of heaven were given to him by our Lord?" They both answered, "We do." Then the king concluded, "And I also say unto you, that he is the doorkeeper, whom I will not contradict, but will, as far as I know and am able, in all things obey his decrees, lest, when I come to the gates of the kingdom of heaven, there should be none to open them, he being my adversary who is proved to have the keys." The king having said this, all present, both great and small, gave assent, and renouncing the more imperfect institution, resolved to conform to that which they found to be better.[2]

This decision at Whitby was of great importance in English history. It meant that England was no longer to be isolated, that all through the Middle Ages she was to share in the unity, order and discipline, in the art and the learning of the Church. It meant that though separated by the sea from the continent of Europe, she had become part of the civilization of western Christendom.

c. St. Martin of Tours

ABOUT the time when St. Patrick was returning to Ireland as a missionary, there died in France an old man, St.

[1] St. Matthew XVI, 18, 19.
[2] Bede: *The Ecclesiastical History of the English Nation.*

Martin of Tours. As a youth he had been enrolled in the Roman army and was stationed near Amiens. Martin was not then a Christian, though he had long desired to be baptized, and was learning all that he could of the Christian faith. He was much beloved by his companions, for he was a youth of great sweetness of temper, of modesty and of endless charity. The winter of 332 was a bitterly cold one in Amiens, so cold that men died in the streets. One day Martin was out riding when he met a beggar, shivering by the city gate, who asked him for alms. He took his sword and cut his cloak in two and gave half to the beggar. His friends laughed at him, but that night in a dream he saw the Lord surrounded by His angels and wearing the piece of cloak Martin had given the beggar. And in his dream he heard how the Lord said to the angels, "See, this is the cloak given me by my servant Martin, though he is as yet unbaptized."

After this Martin delayed no longer. He was baptized, and when he had finished his term of service in the army he devoted all the rest of his life to teaching the Christian faith. He founded a monastery at Poitiers, and his unfailing serenity, his kindness and his saintliness made him beloved in all the country round. When the diocese of Tours wanted a bishop, the people came to the monastery and begged Martin to come to them. He was consecrated, and spent the rest of his life labouring to convert the people of the country to Christianity. As he grew old he was weary and ready to die, but his friends begged him to pray that he might live yet longer. So he said, "Lord, if I am still necessary to Thy people, I do not refuse the toil." But to his great content he did not live much longer and in 401 he died. He was buried at Tours and the legend was told that heavenly music was heard as his body was

taken to the city for burial. The echoes reached Cologne
where men cried out: "It is St. Martin who is departed out
of the world, and the angels are bearing him now into
heaven."

d. St. Boniface in Germany

DURING these early centuries other missionaries went out
from Rome to teach in the lands overrun by the barbarians.
One of the most important of these was St. Boniface. He
was born in England in the eighth century. As a child he
had heard some monks describing their missionary work
on the continent, and from then onwards he was determined to devote his life to the same purpose. His father
objected at first, telling him that he would be happier
living an active life in the world than in submitting to
the discipline of a monastery. But as the boy never wavered in his desire, his father took him to a monastery in
Exeter where he was educated, and in due time he became
a monk and later was ordained priest. In 717 Boniface
went to Rome where the Pope gave him his blessing and
commissioned him to preach to "any peoples that are held
in the error of unbelief." For several years he worked in
Germany and then went again to Rome where he was consecrated bishop. This time he was commissioned to preach
to "the races in the parts of Germany and on the east side
of the Rhine who live in error and the shadow of death."

Boniface found the Germans much given to a superstitious worship of nature and of the spirits who dwelt in
trees and rivers.

Many of the people of Hesse were converted (by Boniface) to
the Catholic faith and confirmed by the grace of the spirit: and
they received the laying on of hands. But some there were, not

yet strong of soul, who refused to accept wholly the teachings of
the true faith. Some men sacrificed secretly, some even openly,
to trees and springs. Some secretly practised divining, soothsaying,
and incantations, and some openly. But others, who were of
sounder mind, cast aside all heathen profanation and did none of
these things; and it was with the advice and consent of these men
that Boniface sought to fell a certain tree of great size, at Geis-
mar, and called, in the ancient speech of the region, the oak of
Jove. (*i.e.*, Thor).

The man of God was surrounded by the servants of God.
When he would cut down the tree, behold a great throng of
pagans who were there cursed him bitterly among themselves because he was the enemy of their gods. And when he had cut into
the trunk a little way, a breeze sent by God stirred overhead, and
suddenly the branching top of the tree was broken off, and the
oak in all its huge bulk fell to the ground. And it was broken into
four parts, as if by the divine will, so that the trunk was divided
into four huge sections without any effort of the brethren who
stood by. When the pagans who had cursed did see this, they left
off cursing and, believing, blessed God. Then the most holy priest
took counsel with the brethren: and he built from the wood of
the tree an oratory, and dedicated it to the holy apostle Peter.[1]

For more than thirty years Boniface worked amongst
the Germans. He taught the people, founded monasteries
and through him the Christian teaching was spread in
Germany. His influence extended to the lands of the
Franks where he strengthened the organization of the
Church and firmly established the papal authority. As a
young man Boniface had begun his missionary work in
Friesland. In 751 he returned, and there, two years later,
whilst attempting to convert the Frisian people, a tumult
arose and he with a small band of Christians was killed.

[1] From Willibald's *Life of Boniface*, written before 786. James
Harvey Robinson, *Readings in European History*, Vol. I., Ginn and
Company, Boston.

The civilization of the early Middle Ages owed much to the Church, and the Church owed much of its position and influence to the work of Gregory the Great. Not only had he sent out missionaries who had converted pagan lands that were in time to come under the influence of Rome, but by his organization and administration of the Church, of its property and money as well as of its dioceses and parishes, in things secular as well as spiritual, he had made Rome recognized as "the chief of all the churches, whose bishop was responsible for the government of the whole church." Not for nine hundred years after the death of Gregory was this primacy of Rome seriously questioned.

CHAPTER III

THE BYZANTINE EMPIRE

1. *The Empire*

IN 330 Constantine founded a new city on the site of the old Greek colony of Byzantium. At that time the Balkan peninsula was covered with flourishing and wealthy cities and Asia Minor was one of the most fertile and populous districts in the world.

Constantinople stands in Europe, but it looks upon Asia. It has a deep and spacious harbour, and it was practically impregnable against foes whether they came by land or sea. After the fall of Rome the western empire broke up, but the eastern empire, with Constantinople as its capital, lasted for almost a thousand years longer. It only disappeared when the Turks captured Constantinople in 1453.

This Eastern or Byzantine Empire had a long and varied history. In the sixth century it had in Justinian (527-565) a ruler of great administrative ability. Unlike many of the eastern emperors he worked incessantly and tirelessly and under him the empire prospered. Practical reminders of his rule in the form of aqueducts, bridges, monasteries and churches were left in many other cities as well as in Constantinople. But the most important and most far-reaching part of his work was the great codification of law that he made. In the *Code* itself were collected all the Roman laws from the great imperial constitutions; in the *Digest* or

Pandects were found the decisions of ancient lawyers, decisions which were important because they had created precedents; and in the *Institutes* was found a commentary on Roman law written especially for the use of students.

Justinian was ably helped by his empress, Theodora. She had been a dancer and the emperor had shocked his court by marrying her instead of some great princess. She was beautiful, ambitious and proud, pleasure-loving and sometimes cruel, but she was also kind-hearted and gave active support to numerous charitable institutions of the Empire. Theodora was possessed of great courage and ably supported Justinian at several times of crisis. In 532 there was a revolution in Constantinople. It bade fair to succeed, parts of the city were in flames, the rebels had chosen a new emperor, and his advisers were begging Justinian to flee. Theodora alone held out: "It has been said," she declared, "that the voice of a woman should not be heard among the councils of men. But those whose interests are concerned have a right to speak. Death is inevitable and will come to us all, but no one is compelled to submit to the shame of surviving dignity and honour, of leaving empire for exile. If you wish to lengthen your life, O Emperor, flight is easy. You have ships and there is the sea. But think well, whether after you have escaped safely into exile, you will not wish every day that you were dead!" Theodora's counsel prevailed. Justinian put down the rebellion and for as long as he lived, his authority was unquestioned.

The successful eastern emperor was treated as ruler by divine right, he was absolutely supreme and all power was centralized in him, but the weak and unsuccessful emperor was in danger not only of seeing another usurp his place but of assassination. The later emperors were often despotic and sometimes weak. There were many conflicts over the succession, there were attacks from the Turks, at first repulsed, but later the city was neither strong enough, nor well governed enough to hold out against them. The empire was hardly ever free from fear of invasion, it was beset with dangers from within and without. Yet, weak and misruled as it often was, it held out for a thousand years.

2. *Byzantine Civilization*

THE centre of the Eastern Empire was Constantinople and within its walls was to be found the wealth of the world. It was brought there by merchants in caravans and by ships from all the seas known to the people of the eastern Mediterranean. Traders came from Persia and India and even China; from Samarcand and Bokhara, from Abyssinia and the Red Sea; they came, too, from the west by way of the Adriatic and from Hungary and Central Europe. Russians and Hungarians, Italians and Spaniards, Persians and Egyptians, Armenians and Turks, Christians and Mohammedans jostled each other in the streets and market places.

Trade in Constantinople was strictly regulated. It was in the hands of the various gilds and these were controlled by the state. No foreign merchant was allowed to carry on business until he had first reported himself to the state authorities, and only by special arrangements could he stay more than three months. One of the most carefully and jealously supervised industries was that of silk-weaving. Before the sixth century the raw silk was imported from China, but the tale is told that shortly before the end of the century some silkworms' eggs were smuggled across the Chinese border and brought to Constantinople. A flourishing silk industry soon sprang up, and silk became so common that in the twelfth century a traveller to Constantinople remarked that every one in that city went about clothed like a prince.

The prosperity of the Eastern Empire depended almost entirely on its commerce, and in spite of wars and revolutions, weak emperors and despotic government, as long as Constantinople retained her supremacy as the great trading mart of the Mediterranean world, the prosperity of the empire was not seriously threatened. No Roman really liked the sea and the Eastern Empire inherited that tradition. The Roman preferred to invest his money in land enterprises. He regarded the sea as a dangerous investment, for ships were in danger from storm and fire, from pirates and robbers of all kinds. Under the Roman maritime law, if a vessel on which money had been lent was lost at sea, the money could not be recovered. As long, however, as no rival sea power arose, these conditions did not seriously affect Constantinople, but when, at the head of the Adriatic, there arose a city which derived its wealth from the sea, the power of Constantinople began to decline. The rivalry between Constantinople and Venice became the struggle between a land power and a sea power, and the victory lay with the sea.

Constantinople was called the "Queen of Cities," and in the centuries from the sixth to the eleventh, so often called the Dark Ages in Europe, it presented a brilliant appearance. There were magnificent buildings: churches, palaces, the Hippodrome where the circuses and chariot-races took place, public baths built on the Roman plan, and triumphal arches. In the Middle Ages Constantinople was the only city that was lighted at night, and more provision was made there for the poor than in most western lands. The people were partly fed by the government, many of them did no work and none of them paid taxes. They frequented the great shows given in the Hippodrome, where the rival factions of Blues and Greens fought for victory in the chariot races. The rivalry did not end, however, in the Hippodrome. Blues and Greens came to stand not only for favourite charioteers, but for rival political factions in the city. It was said of Constantinople that "for God there was the grand church of Sancta Sophia, for the Emperor the Sacred Palace, and for the people the Hippodrome."

Byzantine scholarship was not very original, but Byzantine art was alive and creative. The architecture owed a great deal to the Roman type of building, but the walls were generally thinner, the columns were more slender, they were decorated with elaborately carved capitals and the buildings were characterized by the development of the dome. The interior of the churches built during this period are rich in colour, and in many of them the walls are covered with frescoes and mosaics. The Byzantine artist needed the coöperation of the architect, for his art needed the spaciousness and dignity that only the architect could give him.

The greatest of all the Byzantine churches was Sancta Sophia, the Church of the Holy Wisdom, built by Justinian in the sixth century. The centre of the building is a great square surmounted by a dome, and placed between two semicircular domed apses. Round these apses cluster chapels with smaller domes and the gracefully curving lines, sweeping up to the great central dome, give to the whole building a sense of proportion and of spaciousness. The richest kinds of materials were used in decorating the interior: gold and silver, ivory and rare marbles, and the walls were covered with glittering mosaics.

"Who shall describe," wrote a chronicler, "the fields of marble gathered on the pavement and lofty walls of the church? Fresh green from Carystus, and many-coloured Phrygian stone of rose and white, deep red and silver; porphyry powdered with bright spots, green of emerald from Sparta, and Iassian marble with waving veins of blood-red on white; streaked red stone from Lydia, and crocus-coloured marble from the hills of the Moors; Celtic stone like milk poured out on glittering black, the precious onyx with gold shining through it, and fresh green from the land of Atrax."

Sancta Sophia was the joy and pride of all who lived in Constantinople.

"Words worthy of it are not to be found: after we have spoken of it we cannot speak of anything else," said a contemporary writer, and another declared that God must surely forgive Justinian much if only because he had built Sancta Sophia.

Byzantine craftsmen were skilled in many of the decorative arts: carved ivories, enamel work, goldsmiths' and silversmiths' work, jewellery and all kinds of woven materials shot with gold and silver thread. The impression given by this art is of brilliance and splendour and colour, but the workmanship is of delicacy and finish, perfect in every detail, the work of patient, exquisite care.

The learning of the Eastern Empire was not very original. It consisted largely of copying and imitating the great classical writings. For the first time the manuscripts took the form of books instead of scrolls. There were some original studies made in science, and the mysterious Greek fire used in naval warfare to burn the ships of the enemy came from the East. But if the scholars of the Eastern Empire lacked originality or new ideas, they rendered a great service, for by their patient collecting and copying they preserved what might otherwise have perished.

Constantine had made Christianity the religion of the empire, but the churches of the east and the west had tended to develop differently. In the west the Bishop of Rome became supreme over all other bishops, but in the east the Patriarchs of the great cities, Constantinople, Alexandria, Antioch and Jerusalem, were of equal authority in the councils of the Church, though the Patriarch of Constantinople was regarded as the most important. The Patriarch was supported by the Eastern Emperor and as time went on, rivalry and controversies were constantly developing between the Patriarch and the Pope. The Patriarch tended more and more to be under the domination of the Emperor, whereas the Pope was independent, and as the west of Europe became Christian his power increased. For several centuries the divisions between the east and west grew more marked, until in the eighth a controversy broke out that was so sharp that it threatened the unity of the two churches. The quarrel came about over the use of pictures. There was at this time a great increase in the belief in magic and witchcraft. The churches were full not only of pictures, but of statues and images (called *ikons*) of Christ and of the saints, and the superstitious were attributing all kinds of miraculous powers, not only to the saint the picture or image represented, but to the image itself. The result was that these pictures and images were regarded as wonder-working and were worshipped.

The Emperor was opposed to the use of these images on several grounds. The Greek monasteries were very strong at this time and threatened to be serious rivals to the imperial power over the Church, and the monks were in favour of what had become known as *image-worship*. Not all the races living in the Empire were Christian. The Emperor ruled also over large numbers of Jews and

Mohammedans. Both these religions forbade the use of images, and both Jews and Mohammedans regarded the Christian use of them as materialistic. The Emperor believed that these races would be assimilated more easily to the Empire if the Christian use of images were done away with, and so for these reasons he supported the *Iconoclasts*, as the image-breakers were called. In 726 he issued an edict forbidding the worship of images and ordering all statues to be removed from the churches and the walls to be whitewashed. The Emperor was supported by a great many people, by most educated laymen, and by a great part of the army, but the monks and clergy and the illiterate peasantry who regarded their images as sacred and in many cases as wonder-working, opposed him. But the Emperor only triumphed for a short time, for by the end of the century image-worship had been restored.

This controversy added to the growing antagonism between the east and the west. Other differences began to develop over rites and ceremonies and some of the doctrines, until in 1054 the final rupture came and the Eastern Church separated definitely from the western. The latter was the Catholic Church of western Europe, owing allegiance to the Pope, western in civilization and tradition and using Latin as its official language; the former was the Eastern or Orthodox Church, owing no allegiance to the Pope, dependent in many ways on the Eastern Emperor, and Greek in its civilization, tradition and language.

The western Church became the great civilizing power of medieval Europe. Though it was separated from the Eastern Church it owes the latter a great debt, for as the Eastern Empire preserved Europe from attack by uncivilized invaders from Asia, thereby giving her time to develop a civilization on the foundations laid by Rome, so did the Eastern Church preserve Europe from a Moslem civilization that at times threatened to overwhelm her.

Byzantine Emperors and the Byzantine Empire, the controversies and antagonisms of the early Middle Ages may seem very far away from the modern world. But the Eastern Empire played an important part in the development of Europe. It was a refuge from the barbarian invaders for the ancient civilization which was preserved and cherished there. It kept alive the Roman legal system. It preserved the learning and the language of Greece and of the Hellenistic Age. Because it was the gateway between east and west, it kept out invaders who might have destroyed this civilization it had inherited, but it also made it possible for much that was of value in the east to pass into Europe.

The Byzantine Empire came to an end in 1453, but many of its traditions survived. The Balkan states, in particular Bulgaria and Serbia, inherited much from it. Their courts were fashioned on the principles of the imperial court at Constantinople, their architecture was influenced by Byzantine models to a much greater degree than on those of the west, and their early trade bound them closely to the east.

Long before 1453 the young Russian state was dependent on Constantinople for economic life. In many ways more akin to the east than to the west, Russia was drawn into relations with the Eastern Empire, and when Russia became Christian, it was from the Eastern Empire that her missionaries came. The result was that she became part of the Orthodox Church, accepting its doctrine, its ritual, its discipline and its administration. As the Emperor had controlled and regulated the affairs of the Church in the Empire, so did the Russian Emperors in Russia. The organization of Peter the Great in the seventeenth century made the Czar more like the medieval Byzantine Emperor than like the rulers of the west. The modern Slav world can trace much of its history back to the Byzantine Empire, and down to the revolution of 1917, Russian history is more clearly understood if seen with the understanding of the ancient Byzantine tradition she had inherited.

CHAPTER IV

ISLAM AND THE ARAB CONQUESTS

1. *Mohammed and His Teaching*

ARABIA is a land of desert with strips of fertile land along the sea coast. Most of the Arab people were nomads, wandering from place to place, hunting and raiding, but in the fertile stretches of country near the sea there lived more settled communities, agricultural people and traders with nearby places. Across the desert went caravans, merchants with their wares bound for the east or for Egypt and these caravans were always in danger from roving bands of Bedouin Arabs who waylaid and robbed them.

The Arab had a strong sense of his independence and he was an enemy very difficult to meet, for both horses and camels would disappear into the boundless desert, and no foe could successfully pursue them. Arab horses were famous for the purity of their breed, they were swift as the wind and so sensitive that they seldom needed either whip or spur. The Arabs had all the virtues of a nomad people, they were generous, hospitable to the stranger who came within their tents, and faithful to the ties of the tribe or clan. They had, too, their vices, they loved fighting and plundering, they were impatient at any restraint and they could be both fierce and revengeful.

Before the seventh century the Arabs were broken up into tribes, each of which had its own tribal gods, though they all recognized Allah as the chief, and they were constantly fighting with each other. Mecca was, however, a sacred city to them all. It contained the *Kaaba*, a black stone, which tradition said had come down from heaven. Every year a truce was proclaimed for four months during which every Arab who could do so visited Mecca and worshipped before the Kaaba.

At the beginning of the seventh century a young camel driver was earning his living by conducting caravans across the desert. He was an orphan, a lonely childhood had thrown him upon his own resources, and like many dwellers in wide spaces he had thought much of religion. This boy was Mohammed, whose teaching was to have a profound influence on the east. When he was about twenty-five years old, Mohammed married Kadijah, a wealthy widow, and for some years he was able to live the life of a well-to-do merchant. But Mohammed was not satisfied with the religion of those about him and he became convinced that the many gods worshipped by the Arabs were false and that there was only one God. He believed that the angel Gabriel appeared to him in a vision and told him that he had been chosen to preach the religion of God to the Arabs. He was to teach that "There is no god but Allah and Mohammed is his Prophet."

His wife, his children and a few friends were Mohammed's first converts, but except for these he had few followers. His fellow-townsmen treated him as if he were mad and at first they paid no heed to his teaching. But when he began to preach against idolatry, they feared the effect such teaching might have on the people and they began to oppose him. His fiercest enemies were those who guarded the Kaaba, for they were afraid that their privileges and honours might be taken from them if the people began to regard the sacred stone as an idol.

The enemies of Mohammed plotted to kill him, but he escaped from them and fled from Mecca to Medina. This flight was known as the *Hejira*. It took place in 622 and the Mohammedans date their calendar from this year. A number of Arabs joined Mohammed in Medina and for eight years there was constant fighting between them and the people of Mecca. At length Mohammed was strong enough to return to Mecca and to capture it. By this time most of the Arab chiefs had accepted his religion and had come to regard him as a prophet. In Mecca he destroyed the idols, except the Kaaba, and his religion was accepted.

Mohammed died in 632 and was buried in Medina. He had not only established a religion, but had set up a strong government. As the prophet of Allah he had issued decrees, made laws, and administered justice in such a way as allowed of no dissent, and he had collected and trained an army that maintained order and defeated all foes.

The religion established by Mohammed was *Islam*, a word meaning *surrender*, and those who follow it are often called Moslems. The teaching of Islam is contained in the *Koran*. Mohammed himself could only write a very little, but he dictated his teachings to his followers who copied them out and made them into a book to which, after his death, they added all that they could remember of what he had taught.

"In the Name of God, the Compassionate, the Merciful.

Praise be to God, Lord of the Worlds!
The Compassionate, the Merciful.
King on the day of reckoning.
Thee only do we worship, and to Thee do we cry for help.
Guide Thou us on the straight path,

The path of those to whom Thou hast been gracious; with whom Thou art not angry, and who go not astray."

Following this prayer comes the teaching of Islam. The first and most important thing was the insistence on one God. Mohammed recognized the great prophets, he looked to Abraham, to Moses and to Jesus as to great teachers, but he taught that the last and highest revelation of religion had come through him. He believed in a future life, but it was a life of material pleasures and ease, and was attained in its finest form by those who had died on the field of battle. The Koran gives definite teaching as to the moral obligations laid on Moslems. They were to honour their parents, to give alms to the poor, neither to make nor worship images, and to drink no wine. It was the duty of Moslems to spread their religion by the sword, they were allowed to keep slaves, to have more than one wife, and women were not held in high esteem as they were in both Jewish and Christian teaching.

The public worship of Islam is very simple and takes place in a mosque; in his private worship certain obligations are laid on the believer. He must recite the creed: "There is no god but Allah, and Mohammed is his prophet," every day; five times a day at the call of the muezzin he must kneel on his prayer-rug and with his face turned towards Mecca offer a prayer; during the sacred month of Ramadan (from about December 18 to January 18) he must fast from sunrise to sunset; and once in his life he must, if possible, make a pilgrimage to Mecca.

2. Arab Conquests

ONE of the duties of the Moslem was to spread the religion of Islam by force. During his life Mohammed had been recognized as the ruler of all Moslem people who had accepted his religion, he was to them the Commander of the Faithful. After his death the title of *Caliph* was given to the rulers who succeeded him. These Caliphs lived in Medina and were at the head of both the religious and political organizations of the Moslem people. At first they contented themselves with bringing under their sway the Bedouin tribes in Arabia, but soon they became ambitious for more lands and greater power and they began to push out into the neighbouring regions. Within ten years of Mohammed's death they had invaded Syria, Mesopotamia and Egypt and brought these lands under their rule. Possessed of Egypt the Moslems controlled one of the most important lands in the eastern Mediterranean. It secured to them their hold on the coasts of Syria, and above all, Egypt supplied what it had always supplied to the ancient world—wheat.

From these lands the Caliphs advanced further north and south, east and west. From Egypt they spread over the north of Africa, conquering Tripoli, Tunis, Algeria and Morocco; from Morocco they crossed the straits of Gibraltar and advanced north into Spain, driving out the Visigoths who had settled there and establishing a Moorish kingdom which extended to the Pyrenees. Eastward they advanced into Persia and across Asia to the boundaries of India. At the end of the seventh century the Caliphs who were the descendants of Mohammed had found their power threatened by other leaders and the Moslem Empire divided into a number of Caliphates. Of these Caliphates Medina, Damascus, Cairo and Cordova became the chief cities.

Not until the middle of the eighth century did the Moslem power receive any real check, but in 732 the

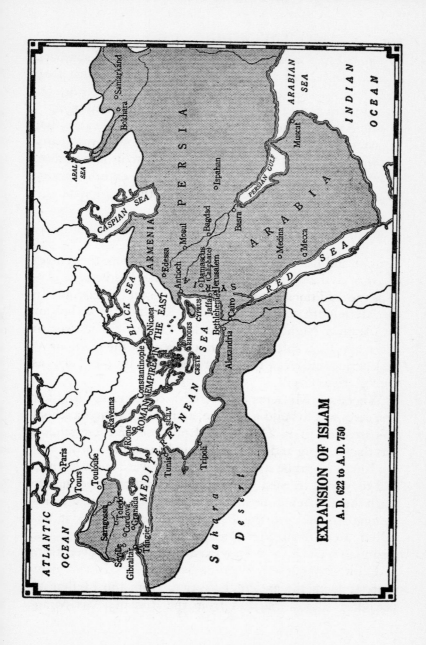

EXPANSION OF ISLAM
A.D. 622 to A.D. 750

Moors in Spain crossed the Pyrenees and invaded southern France. They had advanced as far as Tours when they were met by Charles Martel, the Frankish king, who defeated them and drove them back across the mountains.

The Arab advance had received a check in France, but in Spain, North Africa and Asia, Arabian power was firmly established. The great Moslem cities grew in importance, in wealth and in magnificence and in the eighth century Bagdad was added as the centre of another Caliphate.

3. *Arab Civilization*

BAGDAD and Damascus, Cairo and Cordova were the centres of Arab civilization, and of these Bagdad has become perhaps the traditional Arab city for wealth and splendour. In the later eighth century Haroun-al-Raschid, the Caliph of the Arabian Nights, made Bagdad famous for its wealth and marvellous splendour. It has never lost the glamour of that period and even today is referred to by the Turks as the "glorious city."

Whenever Moslems conquered a country one of their first cares was to build a mosque, and nearly always a school was attached to it. The original purpose of these schools was that reading and writing should be taught in order that the Koran might be studied. The Arabs were quick learners and they soon learned what the conquered countries had to teach them. They came in contact with many ancient civilizations. In the east the Persian (or Sassanian as it was called then from the dynasty which was ruling) had assimilated much from Babylon and Assyria and even from India; in Egypt, the civilization had developed from many sources, from the ancient Egyptian, from the Hellenistic period in Alexandria, and from the Roman; Asia Minor was influenced by the Byzantine civilization of Constantinople. From all these the Arabs learned much, but they never remained imitators, and as the centuries went by, they created a civilization of marked characteristics which was their own.

The most important Moslem contributions to architecture were the development of the dome and the use of arches. These were used in mosques, as in Cordova and Cairo, and in palaces of which the most famous was the Alhambra at Granada in Spain. Because of the prohibition against making images, there is less Moslem sculpture than architecture, but the Arabs excelled in ornament and in manuscript painting. During the seventh, eighth and ninth centuries Europe was recovering from the shock of the breaking-up of the Roman Empire. The great medieval civilization had not yet developed but the Arabs during these centuries were developing many arts and sciences. They excelled in metal-work, pottery, the making of glass, and in weaving. From Damascus came rich woven materials and the finest swords of the time; armour was made in Toledo; Cordova was famous for rich leather work.

In the sciences the Arabs were far ahead of any other scholars of the time. They contributed to the knowledge of geography and introduced the use of globes. They were mathematicians. Arabic figures took the place of the old Roman numerals and they developed the study of algebra. They knew a great deal about medicine and wrote a number of treatises on various diseases. Hospitals were founded, the first was in Cairo about 872, and a good many details of their administration have survived: lectures were given regularly to students, who were also required to give some of their time to practical work in the wards; there were examinations and inspections.

Under the Moors Spain was one of the most civilized of European countries. It was irrigated, agriculture was developed, plants suitable to the soil were introduced from other countries and Spain became a garden. In all the great Moslem cities there were schools, universities and great libraries to which came students and scholars, not only from the Moslem world, but from the Christian countries of Europe.

This great civilization was at its height in the seventh, eighth and ninth centuries. It lasted for some centuries later, but gradually the power of the Arabs began to decline. The lands ruled by them in Asia weakened as other peoples pressed upon them, and they finally gave way before the advancing Turk. In Spain the power of the Moors lasted till 1492 when Ferdinand and Isabella drove them from Granada and established the Christian kingdom of Spain.

CHAPTER V

CHARLEMAGNE

1. *Germanic Law*

THE political history of the Middle Ages is in part the history of the fusion of the old Roman ideals of the state and the administration of justice with those of the Germanic tribes. In the early centuries of their history the Germans had no organization in the least resembling the Roman state. They lived as tribal followers of a chief, but they were not bound to him because the law required their loyalty, but because they had faith in him as their leader. They followed him and fought with him and if need were, died with him.

The Germanic tribes had a system of law that was peculiarly their own, and for some centuries after the fall of Rome it was this law that prevailed in most parts of northern Europe. It was written down in Latin and is known to us as the *Laws of the Barbarians*, a document which forms a valuable source for our knowledge of the Germanic tribes.

These laws differed from both Roman law and the law of today in the matter of trials. There was no trial in the modern sense of the word, and no collecting of evidence either for or against the accused. All that was necessary was that the accused should prove his innocence by certain recognized methods. The chief of these methods were

Compurgation, the *Ordeal* and the *Wager of Battle.*

Compurgation consisted in the swearing by the accused and a certain number of other persons that he (the accused) was innocent. The value of a man's word depended partly upon his value to the community, and partly on that of the man to whom he was opposed. A noble for the murder of a noble required eleven compurgators of his own rank, for the murder of a freeman only seven, for the murder of a serf only five. A serf for the murder of a noble required thirty-five compurgators, for the murder of a freeman twenty-three, and for the murder of another serf twelve.

The Ordeal consisted in submitting to some kind of physical ordeal. The accused would be required to carry a piece of red-hot iron a certain distance, or to plunge his arm into boiling water. If at the end of a given time, generally three days, he showed no ill effects, he was judged innocent, for it was believed that God would not allow an innocent man to suffer and that, if necessary, He would save him by a miracle.

By the Wager of Battle the persons involved in the trial would meet in fight. Here, too, it was believed that the victor was in the right.

One of the Frankish tribes was known as that of the Salian Franks, and their law, the Salic Law, spread widely in the Frankish kingdom, especially after the reign of Clovis. The Salic law became famous later in European history, for by it no woman might succeed to the throne as independent ruler. The Salian Franks believed that a man's life could be valued in terms of money, and fines began to take the place of other punishments. These fines were known as *wergeld,* and the law prescribed how much should be paid for every offence from that of murder to that of an insulting word. Wounds were valued according to their position, to their length and depth and to the amount of blood shed. If the blow had been struck below the waist, the culprit had to pay ten times as much.

The laws varied in form and substance in different tribes. The following is taken from the Frisian law and gives the three occasions when a mother could take the heritage of her child:

When the child is captive and in chains in the north over the sea, or in the south over the mountains; when years of scarcity come and fierce hunger stalks over the land that the child would die of starvation; when (finally) the child is stark naked or homeless, and the misty dark night and the icy cold winter rides over the palings, and all men hasten to house and home, and the wild beast seeks the hollows of the trees and the caves of the mountains, there to eke out his existence; when the child (under age) weeps and bemoans its bare limbs, and bewails that it has no roof, and that its father, who should protect it against the cold winter and fierce hunger, is lying so deep down in the darkness under earth and oaken planks, covered and held fast by four nails: then the mother may alienate and sell her child's inheritance.

2. *The Franks and the Conquest of Gaul: Clovis*

THE Franks were the most important of the Germanic tribes who settled on the continent of Europe. They differed from the other tribes in several ways: they did not wander over Europe in search of new homes, they kept what they had and constantly enlarged their territories, and their rule was easier as they ruled chiefly over people of the same race as themselves. The history of the Franks is more closely bound up with the history of the continent of Europe than that of any other Germanic tribe. As the Roman slowly declined in power, his place began to be taken by the Frank, and the first revival of the ancient empire was made by the greatest ruler of the early Frankish kingdom.

The Frank was not rich like the Goth, nor did he plunder for the sake of plunder like the Vandal. He came to the woods and forests of Gaul, to the lands watered by the great French rivers, and he settled there, cultivating the land, making it his own, defending it against enemies and gradually extending it until it had become an important power. The Frankish kingdom of the earlier period was largely the work of Clovis (481-511).

Legend has woven many tales round the name of Clovis. Years after his death the history of the Franks was written by Bishop Gregory of Tours, who describes Clovis as a great hero, miraculously helped. We are told that

God did daily deliver the enemies of Clovis into his hand, and increased his kingdom, because he walked before his face with an upright heart and did that which was pleasing in his sight.

But historical facts do not bear out this description. Clovis was a man of great force and energy, but he was unscrupulous and cruel, and he hesitated at nothing that would in any way help to accomplish his purpose. This purpose was to make a kingdom out of the Frankish tribes, and he succeeded, but his success was brought about by treason and murder.

In one battle and campaign after another Clovis defeated the enemies of the Franks: the Romans, the Alemanni, the Visigoths, the Burgundians, the Bavarians. When Clovis began his career of conquest, neither he nor the Franks were Christian. But he had married a Christian princess from Burgundy, and the tale is told that in the midst of the battle against the Alemanni Clovis was very hard pressed.

His army was near to utter destruction. He saw the danger . . . and he raised his eyes to heaven, saying, "Jesus Christ, whom Clotilde declares to be the Son of God, who it is said givest aid to the oppressed, and victory to those who put their trust in thee, I beseech the glory of thy aid. If thou shalt grant me victory over these enemies . . . I will believe in thee and be baptized in thy name. For I have called upon my gods, but, as I have proved, they are far removed from my aid. So I believe that they have no power, for they do not succour those who serve them. Now I call upon thee, and I long to believe in thee—all the more that I may escape my enemies." [1]

Clovis was victorious and he kept his word. He and three thousand of his army were baptized.

Clovis seems something of a legendary figure far off in those early centuries of the beginning of France, but out of the tradition and legend stand definite achievements of this fierce half-civilized ruler. He established a political power in France that ended the period of the invasions, and he definitely allied himself with the Christian Church at Rome. The two great powers of medieval Europe were to be France and the Papacy, and it was the work of Clovis that first brought them into an alliance.

3. *The Mayors of the Palace*

CLOVIS was succeeded by a number of rulers, very few of whom were strong. Some of the most important ministers of the king at this time were called Mayors of the Palace, and at one period these made themselves kings. At another time the kings were so weak that they were called the *Rois Fainéants* (the Do-Nothings). But in 732 Charles Martel (Charles the Hammer) was king, and it was he who de-

[1] Gregory of Tours. James Harvey Robinson, *Readings in European History*, Vol. I. Ginn and Company, Boston.

feated the Moors at the battle of Tours and drove them back across the Pyrenees to Spain.

Charles Martel was succeeded by his son, Pepin the Short. He was determined that the position of king should be made more important. Hitherto it had depended on the will of the people, but by gaining the approval of the Pope he brought it about that the king was regarded as king by the will of God. Pepin, chosen by the Frankish chieftains, was lifted by them in the presence of the assembly, on their shields, an old Frankish custom when a man was proclaimed king, and then he was anointed with oil, first by the bishops and then by the Pope. This meant that it was not only a patriotic, but also a religious duty to obey the king, for he was the Lord's Anointed. This was to have a profound influence on the future of Europe.

4. *Charlemagne*
A.D. 768-814

THERE were great personalities in the early Middle Ages: great popes like Leo I and Gregory the Great, and stalwart warriors like Clovis and Charles Martel, but overshadowing them all is the heroic figure of Charlemagne: heroic because of his personality and achievements, because of his influence, and because of the legends and traditions that have clustered round his name.

Charlemagne, the son of Pepin the Short, was born in 742. His life was written by Eginhard, his secretary and trusted friend. Eginhard was a hero-worshipper of the great king, and all that he relates may not be historically accurate, but he gives a picture of Charlemagne that is vivid and unequalled in any medieval chronicle. There is first of all a description of his personal appearance.

His body was large and strong; his stature tall but not ungainly, for the measure of his height was seven times the length of his own feet. The top of his head was round; his eyes were very large and piercing. His nose was rather larger than usual; he had beautiful white hair; and his expression was brisk and cheerful; so that, whether sitting or standing, his appearance was dignified and impressive. Although his neck was rather thick and short and he was somewhat corpulent, this was not noticed owing to the good proportions of the rest of his body. His step was firm and the whole carriage of his body manly; his voice was clear, but hardly so strong as you would have expected. He had good health, but for four years before his death was frequently attacked by fevers, and at last was lame of one foot. Even then he followed his own opinion rather than the advice of his doctors, whom he almost hated, because they advised him to give up the roast meat to which he was accustomed and eat boiled instead.[1]

Eginhard then gives us a description of his habits, of his piety and his generosity, of his family affection and his care for the education of his children.

He constantly took exercise both by riding and hunting. This was a national habit; for there is hardly any race on the earth that can be placed on an equality with the Franks in this respect.

He wore the national, that is to say, the Frankish dress. His shirts and drawers were of linen, then came a tunic with a silken fringe, and hose. His legs were cross-gartered, and his feet enclosed in shoes. In winter-time he defended his shoulders and chest with a jerkin made of the skins of otters and ermine. He was clad in a blue cloak, and always wore a sword, with the hilt and belt of either gold or silver. Occasionally, too, he used a jewelled sword, but this was only on the great festivals or when he received ambassadors from foreign nations. He disliked foreign garments, however beautiful, and would never consent to wear them, except once at Rome on the request of Pope Hadrian, and once again upon the entreaty of his successor Pope Leo, when he wore a long tunic and cloak, and put on shoes after the Roman fashion. On

[1] Eginhard.

festal days he walked in procession in a garment of gold cloth, with jewelled boots and a golden girdle to his cloak, and distinguished further by a diadem of gold and precious stones. But on other days his dress differed little from that of the common people.

He was temperate in eating and drinking, but especially so in drinking; for he had a fierce hatred of drunkenness in any man, and especially in himself or in his friends. . . . He rarely gave large banquets, and only on the high festivals, but then he invited a large number of guests. His daily meal was served in four courses only, exclusive of the roast, which the hunters used to bring in on spits, and which he ate with more pleasure than any other food. During the meal there was either singing or a reader for him to listen to. Histories and the great deeds of old were read to him. He took delight also in the books of St. Augustine, and especially in those entitled the City of God.

In summer after his midday meal, he took some fruit and a single draught and then, taking off his clothes and boots, just as he was accustomed to do at night, he would rest for two or three hours.

·   ·   ·   ·   ·   ·   ·   ·

In speech he was fluent and ready, and could express with the greatest clearness whatever he wished. He was not merely content with his native tongue but took the trouble to learn foreign languages. He learned Latin so well that he could speak it as well as his native tongue; but he could understand Greek better than he could speak it. His fluency of speech was so great that he even sometimes seemed a little garrulous.

He paid the greatest attention to the liberal arts, and showed the greatest respect and bestowed high honours upon those who taught them. . . . He learned the art of reckoning, and with close application scrutinized most carefully the course of the stars. He tried also to learn to write, and for this purpose used to carry with him and keep under the pillow of his couch tablets and writing-sheets that he might in his spare moments accustom himself to the formation of letters. But he made little advance in this strange task, which was begun too late in life.

He paid the most devout and pious regard to the Christian religion, in which he had been brought up from infancy. And, therefore, he built the great and most beautiful church at Aix, and decorated it with gold and silver candelabras and with wicket-gates and doors of solid brass. . . . As long as his health permitted it he used diligently to attend the church both in the morning and evening, and during the night, and at the time of the Sacrifice. He took the greatest care to have all the services of the church performed with the utmost dignity. . . . He carefully reformed the manner of reading and singing; for he was thoroughly instructed in both, though he never read publicly himself, nor sang except in a low voice, and with the rest of the congregation.

He was most devout in relieving the poor and in those free gifts which the Greeks call alms. For he gave it his attention not only in his own country and his own kingdom, but he also used to send money across the sea to Syria, to Egypt, to Africa in compassion for the poverty of any Christians whose miserable condition in those countries came to his ears.

In educating his children he determined to train them, both sons and daughters, in those liberal studies to which he himself paid great attention. Further, he made his sons, as soon as their age permitted it, learn to ride like true Franks, and practise the use of arms and hunting. He ordered his daughters to learn wool work and devote attention to the spindle and distaff, for the avoidance of idleness and lethargy, and to be trained to the adoption of high principles.

He had such care of the upbringing of his sons and daughters that he never dined without them when he was at home, and never travelled without them. His sons rode along with him, and his daughters followed in the rear. . . . His daughters were very beautiful, and much beloved by their father, and, therefore, it is strange that he would give them in marriage to no one, either among his own people or of a foreign state. But up to his death he kept them all at home, saying that he could not forego their society.[1]

It was the ideal of Charlemagne to bring together all the Germanic peoples and to unite them into a great Christian empire. To this end he waged wars against

[1] Eginhard.

Saxons and Avars, Bavarians and Danes, Moors and Italians. Charlemagne was not himself a great military commander, but he understood how to plan campaigns and to inspire his captains with confidence. He made one great change in the Frankish army, a change which was to influence the later history of western Europe, not only from the military but also from the social standpoint: he made use of cavalry as well as of foot-soldiers.

The three most important of Charlemagne's campaigns were those in Lombardy, against the Saxons and in Spain.

For a long time there had been controversies between the Pope, the Lombards and the Franks. In 756 Pepin the Short had invaded Italy, conquered Lombardy, and in what was called the Donation of Pepin made a gift of Ravenna and twenty-one other cities to the Pope. In 773 the Lombard king was trying to regain these lands. Charlemagne took the side of the Pope, invaded Lombardy and besieged Pavia which surrendered to him in January 744. Charlemagne was then recognized as king of Lombardy and was crowned with the famous "iron crown." By this conquest Lombardy gained a wise and statesman-like ruler, but the negotiations between Charlemagne and the Papacy were vague, and the later results were endless controversies between popes and emperors over the rights to these north Italian lands.

The wars of Charlemagne against the Saxons lasted for thirty years. The Saxons lived on the northern borders of the Frankish kingdom. They were heathen and they disturbed the order of the frontier by plundering raids and violence. The Saxons were very formidable foes, they moved with extraordinary rapidity, their faith in themselves and their superiority to all other tribes never wavered, defeat never broke their spirit. In 772, however,

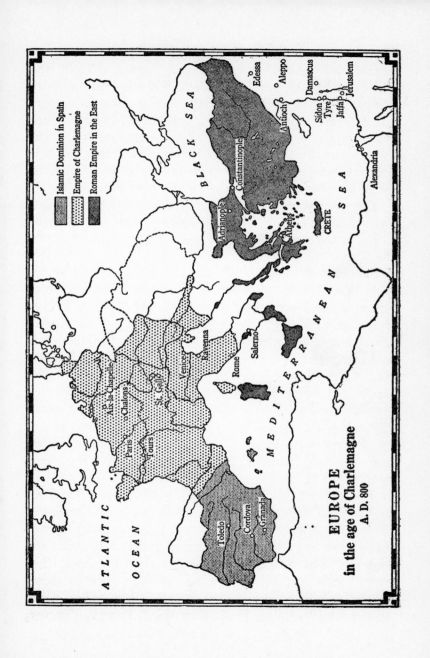

EUROPE
in the age of Charlemagne
A.D. 800

Islamic Dominion in Spain
Empire of Charlemagne
Roman Empire in the East

ATLANTIC OCEAN

BLACK SEA

MEDITERRANEAN SEA

Edessa
Aleppo
Damascus
Jerusalem
Antioch
Sidon
Tyre
Jaffa
Alexandria
Constantinople
Adrianople
Athens
CRETE
Ravenna
Venice
Rome
Salerno
St. Gall
Chalons
Aix-la-Chapelle
Paris
Tours
Toledo
Cordova
Granada

Charlemagne defeated them. He cut down and utterly destroyed their sacred tree, the Irminsul, and then made terms with them. They promised to preserve order on the frontiers and gave hostages as pledges of their good faith. But as soon as Charlemagne had left Saxony and set out for Italy, promises were forgotten, treaties ignored and war blazed out again. Charlemagne returned and again defeated them. A second time treaties were made and pledges given. The Saxons promised to become Christian and thousands of them were baptized. But as soon as Charlemagne had turned his back, war and violence broke out once more. The last rebellions were led by a Saxon hero, Wittekind, and not until 804 was peace finally made. The wars had been carried on with great brutality and cruelty, and the Saxons were forced to become Christian at the point of the sword, but once their resistance was finally overcome Charlemagne showed his statesmanship in the wisdom of his treatment of them. Saxon rulers were put over them, and as far as possible the lands devastated by the wars were rehabilitated.

The history of the Spanish wars of Charlemagne is of less importance than the legend which arose from them, for the *Song of Roland* which tells the tale is the greatest poem of the early Middle Ages. The invasion came about as the result of an appeal from Christian Spain against the Moslems. Charlemagne went, was successful and then began to organize the land as part of the Frankish kingdom. This was not what the Christian states in Spain desired and they appealed to the Moors for help in driving out Charlemagne.

The Song of Roland tells the tale of the traitor Ganelon and of the disaster at Roncesvalles, a pass at the summit of the Pyrenees. Charlemagne himself was not there. He and the greater part of his army had gone on ahead, leaving the Frankish rearguard to be led by his nephew Roland, the Warden of the Breton Marches, and his friend Oliver. They were preparing to descend into their own land when they were unexpectedly attacked by the enemy.

Oliver has mounted on a hillock and he can clearly see the kingdom of Spain and the Saracens who are assembled in such numbers. Their helmets, which are set with gold, glisten, their shields too and their hauberks, their lances and their folded pennons. He cannot even count their formations, for there are so many that one cannot number them. He is much disturbed in mind as he looks at them; as quickly as possible he descends the hill and comes to the Frenchmen and tells them all.

Said Oliver: "I have seen the heathen; never has any man on earth seen a greater number of them. There are a hundred thousand of them in front of us, with shields and laced helmets, and clad in shining hauberks; their polished lances glitter as they hold the hafts erect. You will have a battle such as there never was before. Sir Frenchmen, may you have strength from God! Stand firm, that we be not vanquished!" The Frenchmen say: "Cursed be he who flees! Never will one of us fail you for fear of death."

Said Oliver: "The heathen are in great force, and it seems to me there are very few of our Frenchmen! Comrade Roland, sound your horn; Charles will hear it and the army will return." Roland replies: "I should act like a madman! I should lose my renown in sweet France. I will strike hard blows with Durendal without delay; the blade will be stained with blood right up to the golden hilt. To their misfortune the felon heathen came to the passes; I warrant you that they are all appointed to death."

"Comrade Roland, sound your horn; Charles will hear it and will turn the army back. The king with all his barons will come to our aid." Roland replies: "May it not please God that my kinsfolk be blamed on my account, nor that sweet France fall into disrepute! Rather will I strike vigorously with Durendal, the good sword which I have girded to my side. You will see the blade all covered with blood. The treacherous heathen have come together to their hurt; I warrant you, they are all delivered up to death."

"Comrade Roland, sound your horn; Charles will hear it as he crosses the passes and I warrant you the French will turn back." "May it not please God," replies Roland, "that it should be said by any living man that I ever sounded my horn on account of the heathen. Never shall my kinsfolk be reproached on this account. When I am in the thick of the battle, I shall strike a thousand and seven hundred blows and you will see the steel of Durendal stained with blood. The French are strong and they will strike valiantly; the men of Spain will have no protection from death."

Said Oliver: "I know of no reproach in this. I myself have seen the Saracens of Spain: the valleys and the mountains are covered with them, the open country and all the plains. Great are the armies of this foreign people and we have but a very small company." Roland replies: "My desire grows greater on that account. May it not please God nor his angels that France ever lose her worth on my account! I would rather die than be overtaken by dishonour. The better we strike the more the emperor will love us."

Roland is valiant and Oliver is wise. Both of them have marvellous courage. When once they are mounted and armed they will never avoid the battle for fear of death. They are noble counts and their words are bold. The felon heathen are riding fiercely. Said Oliver: "Roland, look in front of you now. The heathen are close to us, but Charles is far away. You did not deign to sound your horn; if the king were here we should take no harm. Look up towards the Spanish passses; you can see, the rearguard is in a sad plight. He who fights in the rearguard today will never fight in another one." Roland replies: "Speak not so rashly! Cursed be the heart which quakes within the breast! We will make a firm stand on the spot, and we shall be the ones to strike and to attack."

When Roland sees that the battle will take place he becomes fiercer than a lion or a leopard. He calls aloud to the French, and he summons Oliver: "Sir comrade, friend, say no such thing! The emperor who left the French with us put ten thousand men on one side amongst whom he knew there was not a single coward. For one's lord one ought to suffer great hardships and be able to endure excessive cold or heat—yea, one ought to be ready to lose one's blood and one's flesh. Strike with thy lance and I will strike with Durendal, my good sword that the king gave me. If I die on the battlefield, he who has it after me will be able to say that it belonged to a noble vassal."

The battle began and it raged furiously. Great deeds of valour were performed by the Frenchmen, but they were outnumbered, the slaughter was great and the tide of battle turned against them. Then, knowing that the end was near, Roland sounded his horn, so that Charlemagne might come and avenge them.

Roland has put the horn to his mouth; he grasps it firmly and sounds it with all his might. High are the hills, and the voice carries a long way—a good thirty leagues away the echo was heard. Charles heard it and all his companies. And the king said: "Our men are fighting!"

Far off Oliver was wounded to death.

He feels that death is pressing hard upon him. He dismounts and lays himself on the ground and resolutely he confesses his sins aloud, his two hands joined and stretched upwards towards the sky. He prays God that he will grant him paradise, that he will bless Charles and sweet France, and his companion Roland above all other men. His heart stops beating, his helmet falls forward and his body falls at full length upon the earth. Dead is the count and his sojourn on earth ended. Roland, the baron, weeps for him and laments; never on earth will you hear a man grieving so sorely.[1]

Then Roland went back to the battle, but the odds against him were too great, and he, with all the remaining Frenchmen, were slaughtered. As he felt that death was near, he took his sword and tried to break it on the hard

[1] *Song of Roland.*

stone. But the finely-tempered steel was neither broken nor splintered.

When he sees that he cannot break it, Roland begins to lament over it to himself: "Ah! Durendal, how beautiful thou art, how clear and bright! How dost thou shine and sparkle in the sunlight! ... Ah! Durendal, how beautiful and holy thou art! In thy gilded pommel are many relics. ... It is not right that thou shouldst be in the possession of the heathen; you should ever be in the guardianship of Christians. May no man who commits a cowardice possess you!"

In the meantime Charlemagne was hurrying back to Roncesvalles. But he arrived too late. Roland was dead and all his army.

Charles has come to Roncesvalles. He begins to weep for the dead he finds there. To the Frenchmen he says: "Lords, ride slowly, for I myself must go on ahead for the sake of my nephew whom I would find. I was once at Aix on a festive occasion, and my valiant knights were boasting of great battles and furious attacks. I heard Roland speak in this wise: Never would he die in a foreign land unless he had outstripped his men and his peers; his face would be turned towards the enemy's country and he would die victoriously, like the baron that he is."

Charles went on ahead and he found the body of Roland lying on the grass, and when he saw him, he lamented:

"Friend Roland, may God have mercy upon thee! No man ever saw such a knight for joining battles and winning them. My honour has begun to decline. ... May God put thy soul among the flowers in paradise with the angels! To thy misfortune hast thou followed thy lord to Spain! Never will a day pass but I feel the pangs of sorrow for thee. ... Ah! France, how art thou bereft! I am so sad that I would that I were dead!" [1]

[1] *Song of Roland.*

Charlemagne had gathered round him a group of knights whom he called his *paladins*. They represented traditions of courage and adventure, of high-mindedness and devotion, of heroism and loyalty. The tragedy at Roncesvalles caught up these qualities and embodied them in a single figure, that of Roland, who became the symbol of all knightly virtue and gallant deeds. The ideals of chivalry which developed later owed their beginnings to Charlemagne, for whatever may have been some of his deeds, he handed down traditions of both knighthood and kingship which were touched with romance and splendour, and which in the legend of Roland became one of the great medieval epics.

Out of many different Germanic tribes, Charlemagne had succeeded in creating a kingdom, Christian, and owing allegiance to the Frankish ruler. In 800 there were difficulties and controversies about the papal power in Italy. Charlemagne went there to support the Pope and peace was restored. The Frankish king might be a danger to papal power in Lombardy, but the Pope doubtless felt that by recognizing him, his own position was made more secure. It was Christmas Day in the year 800 and Charlemagne was in Rome. Dressed as on festal days in a garment of gold cloth, with jewelled boots and a golden girdle to his cloak, he went to St. Peter's. As he knelt in prayer before the altar, the Pope approached him and placed on his head a crown of gold, saying, "To Charles the Augustus, crowned of God, the great and pacific Emperor, long life and victory." Charles, King of the Franks, had become Charles, Emperor of the West.

In 768 Charles, King of the Franks, had found a kingdom not very united and surrounded by pagan tribes who caused ceaseless warfare on the frontiers. The lords who owned the land had supreme power over all who lived in their domains. Agriculture was crude and primitive, and except in a few monasteries, education hardly existed. Very few persons could read or write. In 814, when Charlemagne died, he left a very different land.

His first care had been to establish an ordered government and to this end he issued a series of edicts called *Capitularies*. These laws show us what ideas Charlemagne had about government and what his ideals were. They deal with every conceivable topic. Over and over again he repeats that the tillers of the soil were to be free from oppression; all taxes were to be levied justly, there was to be no extortion; travellers were not to be robbed or in any way molested; agriculture was to be improved and encouraged; the clergy were to be diligent in performing their duties. For special offences the penalty was very severe, and the same for each offence. It was against the law in any way to do dishonour to the Church, to be cruel or unjust towards orphans, to oppress widows, to be unjust to the poor who had no means to defend themselves, to carry off a free born woman without the consent of her parents, to refuse military service against an enemy, to commit arson and burglary. These Capitularies not only show the character of Charlemagne as a ruler, but they are valuable sources for our knowledge of the state of society in the eighth century.

In order to enforce his laws Charlemagne created administrative positions to which he appointed men whom he could trust. He was a good judge of character and chose able and fit men wherever he found them, whether they were nobles or freemen or serfs. On the whole he was successful, though the constant repetition of certain instructions in the Capitularies would seem to indicate that the law was not always well kept. The land was divided into counties, each under a count. The districts on the frontiers were called *Marches* and were protected by strong fortresses controlled by margraves. In order to keep watch over the counts and margraves, Charlemagne instituted the *Missi Dominici*, men whose business it was to redress any injustice they found, to collect the revenues for the king, and to keep him in touch with all that went on in his vast empire.

Charlemagne was a warrior and a great administrator, but he knew that for a land to be civilized men must be trained for more than fighting. The story is told that one day Charlemagne heard that two strangers had arrived in the town where he was and that they were calling out, saying: "If any one desires wisdom, let him come to us that we may give it to him, for we have it for sale." Charlemagne was interested and sent for them and asked them whether it were true that they had knowledge to sell? "We both possess it," they answered, "and are ready to give it, in the name of God, to all who seek it worthily." The king asked them at what price they would sell their knowledge and they answered: "We ask no price; we ask only for a fit place for teaching and quick minds to teach; and besides food to eat and raiment to put on, for without these we cannot accomplish our pilgrimage."[1] Charlemagne gave the strangers what they asked, and to the end of his life he encouraged education and learning. He founded schools in various places, the best known of which was the Palace School at Aix. Unlike the monastery schools, the schools of Charlemagne were for every one, the rich and the poor, the well-born and the lowly, irrespective of what their future life was to be. He desired

[1] Monk of St. Gall.

that "all that felt the desire of learning should come freely." The Monk of St. Gall who has left us many tales of Charlemagne, tells the story of how the Emperor once went to inspect a school and he found the poorer boys were far ahead of the sons of nobles whose compositions were described as "silly and tasteless." Charlemagne assembled the young nobles and stormed at them. "If you think," he said, "that you can trust to your birth and possessions to procure advancement, you have made a mistake. I take no account of your noble birth and your fine looks though others may admire you for them. Know this for certain, that unless you make up for your former sloth by vigorous study you will never get any favour from Charles." [1]

At Aix Charlemagne gathered a group of the most scholarly men whom he could find: Alcuin from England, Peter of Tuscany, Paul the Lombard, Theodulph of the Visigoths and Eginhard from the Rhineland. These men were not original thinkers, but they represented the best learning of the day, they were good teachers and they handed on the tradition of sound scholarship they had inherited. Charlemagne was very anxious that the clergy should be better educated. He complained that the letters that came to him from bishops and abbots were "very correct in sentiment, but incorrect in grammar," and so he saw to it that the monastic schools were improved in order that "men of God should not only live by the rule and dwell in holy conversation, but should devote themselves to literary meditations, each according to his ability, that they may be able to give themselves to the duty of teaching others." In all these schools, both in the monasteries and at Aix, great emphasis was put on the copying of man-

[1] Monk of St. Gall.

uscripts, especially of the books of the Bible. Care was taken to obtain the most correct readings of these manuscripts and they were copied in a very exquisite writing.[1]

Charlemagne himself was not a scholar and he could write little more than his name, but he was possessed of a vast fund of information which his inquiring mind had stored up, for he was interested in everything, interested in a keen, lively and practical way. He had learnt from observation and experience, from travel and from incessant questioning. He was a huntsman and had probably hunted in every part of his empire, with the result that he had an unrivalled knowledge of the country, a knowledge that was invaluable to him in his military campaigns.

Charlemagne ruled for fourteen years as emperor, and then in 814 he died. He was buried at Aix in the great cathedral he had built, and on his tomb there was inscribed the simple epitaph:

SUB HOC CONDITORIO SITUM EST CORPUS KAROLI MAGNI ET ORTHODOXI IMPERATORIS, QUI REGNUM FRANCORUM NOBILITER AMPLIAVIT, ET PER ANNOS XLVII FELICITER REXIT.

It was soon found that the empire of Charlemagne was too large for any one man to rule again and it was divided several times amongst his sons and successors. In 843 the Treaty of Verdun definitely divided the empire into three parts: the Kingdom of the West, the Kingdom of the East, and Lotharingia, divisions of land that were to appear later as France, Germany and Lorraine. Charlemagne's empire as he left it did not survive, but his influence on the political future of Europe was greater than that of

[1] See p. 274.

any other single influence since that of Rome. In some form or other the Roman Empire left its mark on every state that was included within its borders, and the same thing is true of those parts of Europe which were once part of the empire of Charlemagne. Russia, Hungary and Poland were never parts of the empires of either Rome or Charlemagne, and their political and social development followed a different road from that of France, Germany, Italy and Spain.

Charlemagne had dreamed of an empire uniting people of different races and tongues. Such an empire had succeeded for a time under the Pax Romana, it had succeeded for a time under Charlemagne. The history of the world would have been different had such an empire endured. But with the break-up of both, the peoples of Europe began to develop their own racial characteristics and slowly the nations of today arose. There have been great gains in this, for the diversity of nations has added to civilization, but there have also been losses both in political and social experiments, for interests have clashed and antagonisms have developed. But in spite of all differences the nations of western Europe are bound together by certain common traditions and principles which all have inherited because they were once ruled by Rome or by Charlemagne.

CHAPTER VI
THE NORSEMEN

1. *The Vikings and Their Adventures*

FROM very ancient times there had dwelt in the far north of Europe a hardy, sea-faring race of people. In early medieval history they were all known by the same name: Norsemen, men of the north; or Vikings, men of the creek or bay; or sometimes they were all called Danes. Until the eighth century they had lived apart from the rest of Europe. They were known to the Romans as hardy seamen, sailing in strange ships that had a high prow at each end, but the Norsemen seem to have had little or no contact with Rome. The Scandinavian lands of the north were only habitable along the coasts, and those of Norway were deeply indented by fjords at the head of which were the Norse settlements.

Until the nineteenth century our knowledge of the Norsemen was very scanty and what was known of them came chiefly from the medieval monastic chronicles. But since then a great deal more has been learned about them, for their literature has been found and studied, and archæological discoveries have added very materially to our knowledge.

The Norsemen were of various kinds. Some were warlike raiders and plunderers, some were traders, some were settlers, but all were fearless seamen and all were full of a spirit of adventure.

The fighting Norsemen are most often called Vikings. They sailed in long, narrow, open boats, with one large square sail used only when the wind was in the right direction, for the rest of the time they relied entirely on the oars. The prow was high and usually ornamented with a great dragon. All round the ship hung shields, yellow and black. The largest of these ships held not more than about one hundred and twenty men; many of them were smaller. These Viking ships would set out in the summer, sail swiftly over the sea to the coasts of England and France, of Frisia and the Baltic lands. They attacked the coasts, sailed up the rivers, burned the homesteads, slaughtered men and women, and plundered the monasteries, taking the gold and silver, the jewels and ornaments that they loved. The Vikings were heathen. They worshipped Odin, the father of the gods, the giver of courage and wisdom, the lord of Valhalla, the paradise to which all gallant Vikings would go after death; and Thor, god of thunder, the guardian of warriors and the protector of the farmers. They were fierce and ruthless and so dreaded that the dwellers on the coasts and along the rivers added to their litany: "From the fury of the Norsemen, good Lord, deliver us." Yet they were not without a civilization, primitive and barbaric as it was. Their houses were crude, but in personal adornment they were splendid barbarians. Their brooches of silver and bronze, their rings and beads and various kinds of ornaments made of silver show that they possessed great artistic skill both in design and workmanship.

These were the people who at the end of the eighth century flashed into the bewildered sight of the people of Europe. Nothing quite like it had ever been known before and for the first time the Scandinavian lands of the north became known to Europe, for the Norse peoples sailed everywhere. They were known in England and in France, in Spain, Southern Italy and Sicily; they sailed to the islands of the north, to the Orkneys and the Shetlands, to Iceland and to Ireland, where they established a dominion which lasted till 1014. They went to Russia and to Constantinople; they crossed the Atlantic to Greenland and the coast of North America.

The Norse people sailed out on these voyages for many and varied reasons. Some of them went for sheer love of adventure and the lure of plunder and wealth. Some went because their own settlements were becoming overcrowded and they hoped to find lands in which to expand. Some went because the three Norse peoples, Danes, Swedes and Norwegians were gradually developing into unified kingdoms, each under a king. This irked many of the freedom-loving, roving Norsemen who sailed away intending to recognize no man as master.

In the eighth century these Norsemen were still heathen, but in the ninth and tenth centuries they gradually became Christian. Wherever they sailed they found Christians and they soon adopted Christianity. It was very difficult at first to make good Christians of them, for it was hard for them to curb their unchristian love of fighting or to give up their belief that it was the good fighters who found happiness in Valhalla. But in the tenth century their leaders had become Christian, and wherever there were real Norse settlements they began to develop as Christian communities.

Some of the Norsemen became traders. Legend says that in the middle of the ninth century Swedish merchants went to Russia and that one of their number, Rurik, became ruler of the greater part of northwest Russia. The word *Rus* was originally a Finnish word meaning *rower* and seems to have been the word used by the Slavic people near the Baltic for these invading Swedes. It is known that by 882 Norsemen had gone as far south in Russia as Kieff, and from that time on they traded in Constantinople, selling the products of the north, furs, tar, wax, hemp, amber and slaves in return for the metal-work and glass, bright stones and jewellery for which there was a ready market in the north. The Russians called these Swedes *Varangians*. The tall, healthy, fair-haired men from the north made a great impression upon the emperor and he appointed some of them as his body-guard. For two hundred years men from the north lived in Constantinople serving the emperor in this way. They were known far and wide as the Varangian Guard.

The Norsemen were sea-robbers, and they were traders. They were also explorers and settlers. The longest voyage of discovery made by Norsemen across the open sea was that of Eric the Red, who about the year 985 reached Greenland. He made a settlement there, calling it Greenland, hoping that if he gave the new land a pleasant name, settlers would be attracted to it. The following year a Norse sailor, looking for the newly-discovered land, was driven out of his course by the winds and then, overtaken by fog, he drifted, not knowing where he was until he came to a land that was probably part of Nova Scotia. Hearing of this discovery the two sons of Eric the Red, first Leif Ericsson and then Thorwald, went out in turn, and reached land still further south. They called it *Wineland*, because of the grapes that grew there. It is uncertain how far south they went, it may have been as far as Maryland, but in any case the climate of the place they reached was mild enough to grow grapes and where the cattle they had taken with them could remain out of doors all night. Thorwald liked the place so much that he seems to have planned to make it his home. But he and his men were attacked by Indians and he was seriously wounded. He told his men to make ready to depart as soon as possible, "but first," he said, "you must carry me to that headland where I wanted so much to make my home, for it seems it was the truth I spoke, when I said that I should stay there awhile. Bury me there with a cross at my head and at my feet." His men did as he asked and in the spring they sailed back to Greenland.

2. *The Norsemen in Iceland*

In three places did the Norsemen make settlements which were of lasting importance in later history: in Iceland, in France, and in England.

The first Norse settlement in Iceland was made at the end of the ninth century. The men who went there found a country where they could acquire land easily and rule it free from any obligations to an overlord. In Iceland the Norsemen found no existing civilization and so they were able to develop one that was their own. At first they seem to have lived in small independent settlements, but as these increased some kind of law between them became necessary. In 930 they established a parliament and through the thousand years of Icelandic history that parliament has survived. The Norse word for a court was *Thing* and the parliament was called the *Althing*. The Althing passed a great many laws, though the freedom-loving, independent Norsemen did not trouble to keep many of them.

The debt of the Norse people to Iceland is a great one, for it was in Iceland that certain of the Norse sagas developed, and it is from these sagas that much of the early history of the Vikings is known. This history was preserved in the tales of the *scalds*, men whose business it was to learn by heart the old legends and traditions, the hero-deeds and adventures of the Vikings of old, and then to recite them at festivals, or round the blazing fire on winter nights. The saga was not at first written down. It was a tale told to listeners. The tale was learnt by heart, told and retold, handed down word for word, keeping always to the traditional form. A good saga was vivid, the speech and deeds of the hero were reproduced in such fashion as to make the listener see them in imagination as he listened. Not until writing had become more common were the sagas written down, and by that time generations of scalds had made them well-nigh perfect. Iceland, isolated from the mainland, was in danger of losing the old traditions, but the sagas preserved them, kept alive the old traditions and hero-deeds, and maintained the continuity of history.

3. *The Norsemen in Normandy*

YEAR after year during the latter part of the ninth century the Norsemen invaded France, plundering and pillaging, burning and destroying. They sailed up the rivers, the Seine, the Loire, the Garonne. They attacked town after town, Paris and Nantes, Poitiers and Tours, Chartres and Bayeux. But with the tenth century there began a new phase of Norse history in France. In 911 Rollo, a Norwegian but at the head of an army that was largely Danish in character, attacked Chartres. Rollo and his army were driven back, but they settled themselves on the Seine where they evidently intended to stay. The king of the West Franks, realizing that it would be impossible to drive the Norsemen out of France back to their northern home, rather than risk an attack on his own capital, made a treaty with Rollo. The Norseman was to promise to become a Christian, to recognize the Frankish king as his overlord and to do homage to him. In return he should receive the land on which he had settled. Rollo accepted the terms and became Duke of Normandy.

DUKES OF THE NORMANS. 911–1087

Rollo, first Duke
911–927

|

William Longsword
927–943

|

Richard the Fearless
943–996

Richard the Good
996–1026

Emma
m. 1. Aethelred II of England
2. Canute, King of Eng-
land and Denmark

Richard III
1026–1028

Robert the Magnificent
1028–1035

William the Conqueror
1035–1087

The new duke set himself seriously to the work of ruling his territory. He restored and reëndowed many of the churches and monasteries which had been plundered by Norse raids; he divided up the land amongst his followers; he built defences for the towns and protected his land from invasion. Gradually the Norsemen adopted the language and many of the customs of the Frankish people amongst whom they had settled, but if they adapted themselves they also gave much that was of value. The hardy, vigorous, sea-faring Norman owed much to his Danish ancestors.

The dukes of Normandy who succeeded Rollo made the duchy into one of the great feudal fiefs of medieval France. In 1066 it was a duke of Normandy, a man with the blood of the Norse peoples in him, who conquered England, a land that had already known Danish invasions and that for twenty-five years had been ruled by Danish kings.

4. *The Danes in England*

THE first Danish invasion of England was in 793 when the monastery of Lindisfarne was attacked and plundered. This was followed by a century of invasion. The Danes swept round the coasts from East Anglia to Kent and Hampshire, to Dorset and Cornwall. They attacked York and London and Canterbury. In 869 they captured Edmund, king of East Anglia; they tied him to a tree and shot him to death with arrows. Not only East Anglia, but Mercia and the northern kingdom of Northumbria were now subject to the Danes.

In the south the most important Saxon kingdom was that of Wessex. In 871 a young king came to the throne,

Alfred, known to history as Alfred the Great.[1] The first thing he had to do was to face an invasion of Wessex by the Danes. Alfred had no well-trained army, he had his personal followers and the farmers and peasants who were called on to defend their land when war threatened, but who were inexperienced in warfare and knew little or nothing about military discipline. Yet for seven years Alfred resisted the Danes, not always successfully, but in 878 he defeated them at Ethandun and in the same year peace was made at Wedmore. Guthrum, the Danish king, became a Christian, Wessex was free from further attack, and Alfred recognized the rule of the Danes in the *Danelaw*, land separated from Wessex by a boundary line to be drawn through Mercia to the east coast.

The peace made between Alfred and the Danes lasted for about fifty years. Then the invasions began again. In 937 Athelstan defeated the Danes at Brunanburgh in the north of England. The Danes were joined by the Scotch, but the victory of Athelstan was complete, and for long years afterwards the story of the fight was sung by minstrels until it became almost legendary. The Anglo-Saxon Chronicle gives a vivid account of what took place:

> Here
> Athelstan king,
> of earls the lord,
> rewarder of heroes,
> and his brother eke,
> Edmund Atheling,
> elder of ancient race,
> slew in the fight,
> with edge of their swords,
> the foe at Brumby!
>
> .　　.　　.　　.　　.

[1] See p. 97.

Since the sun was up
in morning-tide,
gigantic light!
glad over grounds,
God's candle bright,
eternal Lord!—
'til the noble creature
sat in the western main:
there lay many
of the Northern heroes
under a shower of arrows,
shot over shields;
and Scotland's boast,
a Scythian race,
the mighty seed of Mars.
With chosen troops,
throughout the day,
the West Saxons fierce
press'd on the loathed bands;
hew'd down the fugitives,
and scatter'd the rear,
with strong mill-sharpen'd blades.

．　　．　　．　　．

The northmen sail'd
in their nailed ships,
a dreary remnant,
on the roaring sea;
over deep water
Dublin they sought,
and Ireland's shores,
in great disgrace.

．　　．　　．　　。

No slaughter yet
was greater made
e'er in this island,
of people slain,
before this same,
with the edge of the sword;

as the books inform us
of the old historians;
since hither came
from the eastern shores
the Angles and Saxons,
over the broad sea,
and Britain sought,—
fierce battle-smiths,
o'ercame the Welsh,
most valiant earls,
and gained the land.[1]

Under Athelstan England suffered no more from the Danes and the king called himself, "Rex totius Britannica."

At the end of the century the raids began again. Ethelred the Redeless, the man of no wisdom or counsel, irresolute and weak, was king. He began trying to buy off the Danes. To raise the money, he levied the *Danegeld*, the first general tax levied on all the people of England. The Danes took the money and sailed away, but they soon came back for more. The king of the Danes at this time was Sweyn, an able, vigorous ruler. Like most weak people, Ethelred thought that a show of force would prove his strength, and on St. Brice's Day 1002 he suddenly gave orders for a general massacre of all Danes settled in England. Swift was the vengeance of Sweyn. He descended on the coast of England, ravaged the land, and with slaughter and burning avenged the massacre of his people. In 1014 he died and was succeeded by his son Canute. Two years later Ethelred died and his son Edmund Ironside became king of England. For a brief period Edmund kept off the Danes, then he made an agreement with Canute who was to rule in Mercia, while

[1] *Anglo-Saxon Chronicle.*

Edmund kept Wessex. Wessex was saved, but only for a short time. Before the year was out Edmund Ironside was dead and Canute became king of England.

The Danes ruled England from 1016 to 1042, when a king of the Anglo-Saxon race was restored to the throne. Once again was there an invasion from the north. In 1066 Harold Hardrada of Norway invaded England. He was defeated at the battle of Stamford Bridge by Harold, the last of the Saxon kings of England. Three days after the battle, William of Normandy landed at Pevensey in the south of England. Harold hurried south, but on the field of Hastings, the last of the Saxon kings who had just defeated the last of the Norse invaders of England, was himself defeated and slain by William of Normandy, the descendant of those same Norsemen.

In a little under three hundred years the Vikings of the north had done much that was to endure in European history. It is true that they plundered and pillaged and burnt, and that they were the terror of the peaceable villages and of the monasteries who were unable to defend themselves from the fury of the Norsemen. But they did other things, too. They did much to further the art of navigation and were amongst the first seafarers to sail out into the ocean, far from the known and navigable waters. Not since the voyages of the ancient Phœnicians had there been such fearless adventurers on the high seas. Wherever Norsemen settled, a greater strength and vigour and sturdiness became characteristics of the people who were descended from them, and to the Norsemen the three great Scandinavian countries, Norway, Sweden and Denmark, owe the beginnings of their history.

CHAPTER VII
THE BEGINNING OF NATIONAL STATES

1. *England*

a. Anglo-Saxon England

EARLY Britain was inhabited by a number of tribes belonging to the Celtic race. These Britons were a primitive people and their civilization was crude, but they had gold and silver coins, they traded with each other, and they raised cattle. They lived in villages in wooden huts. The Britons were a heathen people and it is believed that they worshipped the sun. Their priests were called *Druids* and they built temples in the form of great stone circles, of which the most famous is Stonehenge.

In very early days Britain was known to the Phœnician traders who went there for the tin that they took back to the Mediterranean, but Britain was far away across the sea, in the misty north, and only the adventurous sea-traders seem to have known of it. In B.C. 55 and again in B.C. 54 during his campaigns in Gaul, Julius Cæsar crossed the narrow sea and invaded Britain, but it was not until A.D. 43 that the Romans really conquered the land. It was then organized as a Roman province and ruled by the Romans for nearly four hundred years. When in the fifth century the Germanic invaders of the empire threatened Rome itself, the legions were withdrawn from Britain, and after about 410 the Britons were left to protect themselves as best they could.

The Romans had brought peace and order to Britain. They had built roads, established towns, done much for education, developed trade between Britain and other parts of the empire, and in some places small Christian communities had grown up. But they had not taught the Britons to rule themselves, and when the latter were no longer protected by the Pax Romana, they fell an easy prey to the Picts, invaders who came from the north. In despair they sent a petition, which was called the *Groans of the Britons*, to Rome, begging for help. "The barbarians drive us to the sea," they said; "the sea drives us back to the barbarians: between them we are exposed to two sorts of death; we are either slain or drowned." But no help came from Rome.

In 449 Angles and Saxons, under two leaders whom tradition has called Hengist and Horsa, came over to Britain to help a British chieftain drive out the Picts. They drove the invaders back but then, instead of leaving, they stayed in Britain and turned against the people whom they had come to help. The *Anglo-Saxon Chronicle* tells us that they summoned other tribes to help them.

They sent to the Angles and desired them to send more assistance. They described the worthlessness of the Britons and the richness of the land. They then sent them their support.[1]

The men came from three tribes: the Angles from Schleswig, the Saxons from the region near the Elbe, and the Jutes from Jutland. They were heathen, they knew nothing of an ordered civilization, in their own land they had known famine and they were eager for new homes.

[1] *Anglo-Saxon Chronicle.*

The Britons attempted to drive them away, but they were not strong enough. The invaders captured their towns and villages, put many of the inhabitants to death, drove others westward into the mountainous districts of Wales, and then settled down and occupied the land, to which the Angles gave their name, England. In the course of time the Anglo-Saxon tribes developed into kingdoms, of which there were first seven, then three, Northumbria, Mercia and Wessex, until finally the kings of Wessex became stronger than the other kings and in the ninth century England was united under one king.

In the fifth century the Anglo-Saxon tribes who came to England were still heathen and not civilized, but they had certain characteristics and certain ways of ordering their tribal life that were to be of great importance in the history of England and of the English people. They loved freedom and independence, and though they had some slaves, their civilization never rested on slavery as did that of Greece and Rome. They spoke a language that was later to develop into the English language. Each tribe governed itself by an assembly of the freemen, the *Folk Moot* or meeting of the people. When the tribes became united as a kingdom, these smaller folk moots developed into the *Witan* or assembly of wise men. These assemblies were not always very powerful and under strong kings they did little more than give him advice, which he did not always feel bound to take, but it was from these early assemblies that representative government developed.

The story of the conversion of England to Christianity has already been told. By the eighth century there were monasteries up and down the land, places where men could pursue a tranquil life, where there was education, where scholars were to be found. In the seventh century a monastery had been founded at Whitby by St. Hilda, a woman of the race of kings, whose "prudence was so great that even kings and princes as occasion offered, asked and received her advice." In this monastery there dwelt a man named Cædmon. He had never taken the monastic habit, but had lived and worked for many years in the monastery. It was the custom at feasts in Northumbria that those present should play upon the harp and sing in turn. But Cædmon could neither sing nor play, and at entertainments when his turn came, it was his custom to rise from the table and leave the hall.

Having done so at a certain time, and gone out of the house where the entertainment was, to the stable, where he had to take care of the horses that night, he there composed himself to rest at the proper time; a person appeared to him in his sleep, and saluting him by his name, said, "Cædmon, sing some song to me." He answered, "I cannot sing; for that was the reason why I left the entertainment, and retired to this place because I could not sing." The other who talked to him, replied, "However, you shall sing."—"What shall I sing?" rejoined he. "Sing the beginning of created beings," said the other. Hereupon he presently began to sing verses to the praise of God, which he had never heard, the purport whereof was thus:—We are now to praise the Maker of the heavenly kingdom, the power of the Creator and his counsel, the deeds of the Father of glory. How He, being the eternal God, became the author of all miracles, who first, as almighty preserver of the human race, created heaven for the sons of men as the roof of the house, and next the earth. This is the sense, but not the words in order as he sang them in his sleep; for verses, though never so well composed, cannot be literally translated out of one language into another, without losing much of their beauty and loftiness. Awaking from his sleep, he remembered all that he had sung in his dream, and soon added much more to the same effect in verse worthy of the Deity.

In the morning he came to the steward, his superior, and

having acquainted him with the gift he had received, was conducted to the abbess, by whom he was ordered, in the presence
of many learned men, to tell his dream, and repeat the verses,
that they might all give their judgment what it was, and whence
his verse proceeded. They all concluded, that heavenly grace
had been conferred on him by our Lord. They expounded to him
a passage in holy writ, either historical, or doctrinal, ordering
him, if he could, to put the same into verse. Having undertaken
it, he went away, and returning the next morning, gave it to
them composed in most excellent verse; whereupon the abbess,
embracing the grace of God in the man, instructed him to quit
the secular habit, and take upon him the monastic life; which
being accordingly done, she associated him to the rest of the
brethren in her monastery, and ordered that he should be taught
the whole series of sacred history. Thus Caedmon, keeping in
mind all he heard, and as it were chewing the cud, converted
the same into most harmonious verse; and sweetly repeating the
same, made his masters in their turn his hearers. He sang the
creation of the world, the origin of man, and all the history of
Genesis; and made many verses on the departure of the children
of Israel out of Egypt, and their entering into the land of
promise, with many other histories from holy writ; the incarnation, passion, resurrection of our Lord, and his ascension
into heaven; the coming of the Holy Ghost, and the preaching
of the apostles; also the terror of future judgment, the horror
of the pains of hell, and the delights of heaven; besides many
more about the Divine benefits and judgments, by which he
endeavoured to turn away all men from the love of vice, and to
excite in them the love of, and application to, good actions; for
he was a very religious man, humbly submissive to regular discipline, but full of zeal against those who behaved themselves
otherwise; for which reason he ended his life happily.[1]

Another monastery in Northumbria was at Jarrow.
Here there lived from the time when he was a youth to
the day of his death in 735 the man who was probably
the greatest English scholar of the eighth century, Bede

[1] Bede: *The Ecclesiastical History of the English Nation.*

or the Venerable Bede, as he was called later. "I spent my whole life in the same monastery," he said, "and while attentive to the rule of my order and the service of the Church, my constant pleasure lay in learning or teaching, or writing."

To the school at Jarrow came not only the six hundred monks of the monastery, but young men from all parts of England, attracted by the fame of Bede, not only as scholar but as teacher. Bede knew something of all the knowledge of his time: history and grammar, physics and astronomy, medicine and music, and he wrote books about them all for his pupils. He knew Greek, a rare accomplishment in the eighth century. Very rightly has Bede been called the Father of English Learning. The books he wrote for his pupils are probably seldom read today, with the exception of one. He wrote in Latin the *Ecclesiastical History of the English Nation,* a book that is one of our chief sources of knowledge of early Anglo-Saxon England. He excelled as a story-teller, and in that book we read of the deeds of the men and women who made early Anglo-Saxon England, of Augustine and Aidan, of Hilda and Cædmon and Cuthbert, and the history and tradition, the life and civilization of those centuries come to life in his pages.

The last work of Bede was to translate the Gospel of St. John into English. Surrounded by some of his scholars who were helping him, he worked on this translation even to the day of his death. "It is finished," said the scribe as the last sentence was written down. "You are right," said Bede, "all is finished now," and quietly and in peace, the scholar died.

In the seventh century Theodore, a Greek monk from Tarsus, had been sent by the Pope to organize the Church in England. He divided England into bishoprics and parishes, arranged for councils of the Church, and encouraged learning and the singing of sacred music in churches. He brought order and discipline into the Church and Bede tells us that he was "the first archbishop whom all the English Church obeyed."

The work of Theodore of Tarsus is of importance not only in the history of the English Church, but in that of the English state. At the beginning of the seventh century England was still divided into independent kingdoms, but these divisions were beginning to break down and there was a growing consciousness of England as a nation. The Church was organized as the whole Church of England before the state became politically united. When England became one kingdom, it was the organization of the Church which gave a pattern for the administration of the state.

b. Alfred the Great
871-901

IN the ninth century England became united under one king. At first the kings were little more than overlords, but their power gradually increased until they were recognized as kings of all England. The most famous Anglo-Saxon king was Alfred, the only king of England to whom the title the Great has ever been given. He became king in 871 when he was just twenty-two years old. The England he was to rule had been ravaged by the Danes for nearly a century, and much of the civilization that had grown up had disappeared. It was in the monasteries of Northumbria that schools had flourished, in which the poets and scholars had lived, and it was Northumbria and other parts of the north of England that had suffered most from the Danes. The story of how Alfred fought the Danes and brought peace to England has already been told.[1] He had made peace in 878, and from then until the time of his death he devoted himself to ruling England. Until the reign of Alfred the Anglo-Saxon kings who had been most successful had been vigorous warriors and rough administrators of justice, but they had known little of the arts of peace, and they knew little or nothing of countries beyond their own. Alfred brought new ideals to kingship. In spite of a frail body, he was no mean warrior, but when he had delivered his country from the invader, his only thought was for the welfare of his people.

Alfred had been educated in a different way from that of most young Anglo-Saxon princes. Before he was ten he had made three visits to Rome. In crossing the sea to France he had found himself on a continent much larger than anything he had thought of at home; his journeys brought him to men of many different races and of many different tongues. He saw the Pope, he saw Rome and a civilization more advanced than anything he had seen in Wessex. Unconcerned with matters of state, the boy, alert and keen and observant, had time and opportunity to learn, and what he learnt he remembered.

At home he was taught the things a young prince usually learned. He could ride and hunt and he understood the use of weapons, but he was not taught to read until he was twelve years old.

Now it chanced on a certain day that his mother showed to him and his brothers a book of Saxon poetry, which she had in her hand, and said, "I will give this book to that one among you who shall the most quickly learn it." Then, moved at these words, or rather by the inspiration of God, and being carried

[1] See p. 87.

away by the initial letter in that book, anticipating his brothers who surpassed him in years but not in grace, he answered his mother, and said, "Will you of a truth give that book to one of us? To him who shall soonest understand it and repeat it to you?" And at this she smiled and was pleased, and affirmed it, saying, "I will give it to him." Then forthwith he took the book from her hand and went to his master, and read it; and when he had read it he brought it back to his mother and repeated it to her.

After this he learnt the Daily Course, that is, the services for each hour, and then some psalms and many prayers. These were collected in one book, which, as we ourselves have seen, he constantly carried about with him everywhere in the fold of his cloak, for the sake of prayer amid all the passing events of this present life.[1]

In 878 the first thing Alfred had to do was to establish order and good government, and to restore the devastation caused by the long period of Danish invasions. He collected and revised the ancient laws; he did all that was possible for a fair administration of justice. He was determined that "such as are in need and necessity should have right." Like many early kings, he was easily accessible to his people, and constantly acted himself as judge.

He heard the divine offices daily, the Mass, and certain psalms and prayers. He observed the services of the hours by day and by night, and oftentimes was he wont, without the knowledge of his men, to go in the night-time to the churches for the sake of prayer. He was zealous in the giving of alms, and generous towards his own people and to those who came from all nations. He was especially and wonderfully kindly towards all men, and merry. And to the searching out of things not known did he apply himself with all his heart.[2]

[1] Asser's *Life of Alfred.*
[2] *Ibid.*

To defend the coasts Alfred built ships and he sent for sailors from Frisia to teach the English all that they knew about sailing. He reorganized the army in such a way that the peasants took it in turns to serve, so that the farms were never left uncared for.

Alfred then set himself to restore education to England. He was disturbed at the general ignorance he found among the clergy, and said that there was hardly any one in the north of England who could understand the Latin service or translate a letter from Latin into English, and that when he came to the throne he could not remember even one south of the Thames who knew enough to translate the service into English. In order to remedy this, he encouraged the restoration of schools, and established one at his court in order, he said

that all the freeborn youth of England who have sufficient means to devote themselves thereto, be set to learning so long as they are not strong enough for any other occupation, until such time as they can well read English writing. Let those be taught Latin whom it is proposed to educate further, and to promote to higher office.[1]

Alfred had ideals not only for himself, but for those who shared with him in any way the work of government.

My task was, he said, that I should virtuously and fittingly administer the authority committed to me. Now no man... can ... administer government, unless he have fit tools and the raw material to work upon.... And a king's raw material and instruments of rule are a well-peopled land, and he must have men of prayer, men of war, and men of work.... Without these tools he cannot perform any of the tasks entrusted to him.[2]

[1] From Alfred's Preface to the *Pastoral Care* of Gregory the Great.
[2] From Alfred's translation of the *Consolation* of Boethius.

In order to help him in this task, Alfred sent far and wide for the best teachers he could find.

He would obtain whencesoever he could, those who might assist his righteous intention and who might be able to aid him in acquiring the wisdom for which he longed, whereby he should gain his passionate desire. . . . He sent messengers beyond the sea into Gaul to fetch masters, and summoned thence Grimbald, a priest and monk, a reverend man, an excellent singer, and very learned in every kind of ecclesiastical discipline and in the Holy Scriptures, and adorned with every good quality. And he summoned John, who was also a priest and a monk, a man of very cunning mind, and very learned in all the rules of the art of letters, and skilled in many other arts. By their teaching the mind of the king was much enlarged, and he enriched them with great power, and honoured them.[1]

It was not enough for Alfred that a few should understand Latin; he wanted all who could read able to know great literature, and so he began the translation of Latin books. All through his life Alfred had found time to read and to study, and many of these translations he did himself. *The Consolation of Philosophy* by Boethius, Bede's *Ecclesiastical History of the English Nation,* parts of the Book of Psalms, and many other books were thus put into English. He also continued the *Anglo-Saxon Chronicle,* a history of England. Before the time of Alfred this Chronicle had consisted of little more than a bare record of events or of lists of kings. In his reign it became a fuller narrative, full of life and interest, and after his death it was continued until the end of the eleventh century.

The personality of Alfred impressed itself deeply on all who came in contact with him. When he died the chronicler wrote of him:

[1] From Asser's *Life of Alfred.*

There passed away Alfred the king of the Anglo-Saxons, the son of the most pious king Aethelwulf, the famous, the warlike, the victorious, the careful provider for the widow, the helpless, the orphan and the poor; the most skilled of Saxon poets, most dear to his own nation, courteous to all, most liberal; endowed with prudence, fortitude, justice and temperance . . . most watchful and devout in the service of God.[1]

Anglo-Saxon England owed more to Alfred than to anyone else. In an age of violence he strove for peace and an ordered government. He valued learning and scholarship and the things of the spirit. He cared neither for renown as a warrior, nor for the glory of the world. "I desire," he said, "to leave to them that come after me a remembrance of me in good works. So long as I have lived, I have striven to live worthily."

c. End of Anglo-Saxon England

THE story of England for a hundred years after the death of Alfred in 901 is the story of how the Danes once more began their invasions, until in 1016 Canute, a Dane, became king. In 1042, a few years after the death of Canute, the Witan chose another Saxon as king, Edward called the Confessor. He had been brought up in Normandy, and when he came to England he brought with him Norman friends and counsellors and Norman ways of living. In those rough days Edward the Confessor was more fitted to be a monk than a king. When he died in 1066, a strong English party which had been opposing the Norman influence made Harold, an English earl, king. But William, Duke of Normandy, had determined on an invasion of England. He declared that both Edward and

[1] From Florence of Worcester.

Harold had promised him the throne, so when Harold was made king, he collected an army, crossed the narrow sea, and in the battle of Hastings defeated and killed Harold. He marched on London, where the Witan surrendered to him, and on Christmas Day 1066 he was crowned king of England as William I.

For England, the early Middle Ages ended in 1066. Through six hundred years of history, through periods of war with each other and wars against the Danes, through periods of peace and periods of violence, the Anglo-Saxons had become welded into a nation. England, cut off from her neighbours by the sea, had developed a civilization somewhat different from that of the continent of Europe, but with the coming of the Normans she was to become part of the great medieval civilization of western Christendom.

2. *France*

CHARLEMAGNE had united the Frankish lands into an empire, but it has already been seen that after his death no one man was able to rule so vast a dominion. By the middle of the ninth century it had been divided into three parts, one of which, the Kingdom of the West, was to develop into France. The kings of this land were weak, and in order to obtain military aid they granted large tracts of land, known as fiefs, to the great nobles. These nobles, the dukes and counts of Normandy and Brittany, of Flanders and Burgundy, of Anjou and Aquitaine and Gascony, gradually became independent, and in most cases more powerful than the king himself. For a hundred years the crown passed back and forth between the descendants of Charlemagne and some of these great lords.

In 987 the last of the Carolingians died. A great funeral

was held, after which the lords who were present considered what should be done. It was proposed to call together a meeting of all the great barons in order to choose a new king, but Charles of Lorraine, the uncle of the late king, wanted to force the barons who were present to elect him. The Archbishop of Reims knew Charles to be a bad ruler, and in order to save the country from him, he proposed that they should elect Hugh Capet, Count of Paris and Duke of France as King.

Make a choice, he said, that shall insure the welfare of the state instead of being its ruin. If you wish ill to your country, choose Charles; if you wish to see it prosperous, make Hugh, the glorious duke, king. Do not let yourselves be misled by your sympathy for Charles, nor blinded to the common good by hatred of the duke. . . . Choose the duke; he is the most illustrious among us all by reason of his exploits, his nobility, and his military following. Not only the state, but every individual interest, will find in him a protector. His great-heartedness will render him a father to you all. Who has ever fled to him for aid and been disappointed? Who that has been left in the lurch by his friends has he ever failed to restore to his rights?

This discourse was received with universal applause, and by unanimous consent the duke was raised to the throne. He was crowned at Noyon on the first of June, by the archbishop and the other bishops, as king of the Gauls, the Bretons, the Danes, the Aquitanians, the Goths, the Spaniards and the Gascons. Surrounded by the nobles of the kingdom, he issued decrees and made laws according to royal custom, judging and disposing of all matters with success.[1]

Hugh Capet was the first of a long line of kings who were to rule France for eight hundred years, but Hugh himself was not very powerful. He had no national government, no royal authority for raising money, no royal

[1] From Richer, 10th century. James Harvey Robinson, *Readings in European History*, Vol. I. Ginn and Company, Boston.

army, not even the tradition of belonging to an ancient race of kings. Yet if in fact he was weaker, in theory he was greater than the other great lords of France. He had succeeded to the office held by Charlemagne and his descendants, and could claim whatever powers they had inherited from the old Frankish kings; he was the overlord of the great feudal princes and barons, and there was no other man whose authority, even if it was but in name, extended over the whole of France. Above all he had been crowned and consecrated for his office by the Church.

For a hundred years the successors of Hugh Capet were kings in little more than name. At his coronation Hugh Capet was told that it was his duty to concern himself "with justice, with peace, with the condition of the kingdom, and the honour of the Church," and he had promised "to grant to the people who are entrusted to my care justice according to their rights," but it was a promise hard to fulfil for the eleventh century in France was a period of feudal rivalries and turmoil, of violence and often of cruelty. What these kings did succeed in doing was to increase and strengthen their royal domain, and by so doing to strengthen their own position, and to establish their family as the recognized dynasty of France.

The domains and court of the early French kings were administered by royal officials: chief of these were the *Seneschal*, who ruled the household, who kept the keys of the palace, who gave the daily password to the sentinels on guard, and who was responsible for the education of the king's son; the *Constable*, responsible for the stable and horses; the *Grand Chamberlain*, who kept the treasure and money, who collected the feudal dues and presented the vassals to the king when they came to do homage; the *Chancellor*, who wrote out decrees and laws and who always carried the royal seal. These officials were usually great barons, and in the eleventh century their offices had become hereditary and the holders all-powerful.

The feudal princes, who were vassals of the kings of France, had their own armies, coined their own money, and made their own laws. The kings of France never made laws for the whole kingdom, and they seldom dared to enter the domains of the greater vassals, who paid them homage or not as they chose. In 1066 the duke of Normandy became king of England, and for the space of a hundred and fifty years the kings of England were nominally vassals of the kings of France. By various titles, by inheritance, and by marriage, the kings of England gradually became the lords of more lands in France than the king of France himself. In 1154 Henry II, grandson through his mother of William the Conqueror, became king of England. As successor of the Norman kings he was ruler of Normandy and Brittany, through his father he was count of Anjou and Maine, and through his wife Eleanor, duke of Aquitaine, Poitou and Gascony. More than half of France owed allegiance to the English king.

In 1108, however, there had come to the French throne Louis VI, nicknamed Louis the Fat, and with him there had dawned a new era in the history of the kings of France. Louis VI was able and vigorous, and determined to be king in fact as well as name. With the help of his capable minister the Abbot Suger, "little in body and little in race," and of whom it was said: "What one must admire most in him is that nature should have lodged a heart so strong, so fine, so great, in a body so frail and thin," Louis succeeded in giving authority to the French monarchy. He subdued the barons in his own domain, the Ile de France, and made them subject to him. He in-

PLANTAGENET DOMINIONS
A.D. 1154

English Domain

Domain of
the French King

NORTH

SEA

Stirling
Bannockburn ○ Edinburgh

Durham

York

Dublin

Runnymede
Salisbury ○ Canterbury
Winchester ○ Hastings
Calais
Agincourt
Amiens

Irish Channel

Flanders

Crecy
Rouen
Reims

English Channel

Channel
Islands
Caen
Paris
Troyes
NORMANDY
MAINE
Chartres
BRITTANY
Le Mans
ANJOU
Blois
Tours
Chinon
Burgundy

BAY OF

BISCAY

Poitou
Poitiers

Limoges

AQUITAINE

Bordeaux
Avignon
GASCONY
LANGUEDOC
Provence
Marseilles

Scale of miles
0 50 100 150 200

creased his power over other feudal lords and he lessened the power of the great court officials by making their appointment dependent on the king instead of being hereditary. He strengthened the monarchy and the idea of kingship, making it clear that the king was greater than any feudal lord, for he did homage to no one.

Louis VI was succeeded by his son Louis VII. It was in his reign that the territory of the kings of England was so much increased, but though he supported some of the discontented barons against Henry II, he was powerless to regain any of the lands the king of England ruled. Nevertheless the French monarchy under Louis VII lost none of the position it had won for itself under his father. When he died in 1180 he was succeeded by Philip Augustus, in whose reign the kings of England lost their French dominions, and under whom France became a more unified state than she had been at any time since the death of Charlemagne.

PART II

THE UNITY OF THE MIDDLE AGES

CHAPTER VIII

THE MEDIEVAL CHURCH

THE twelfth and thirteenth centuries were the great period of the Middle Ages. In all parts of western Europe men had things in common during those centuries. They shared in the ideals of feudalism and chivalry; they went together on Crusades; they studied together in the universities of England and France and Italy; wherever there were towns, masters and apprentices worked together under the same system of craft gilds. Men had all these things in common, but that which bound them most closely together as a great society was the Church.

1. *The Place of the Church in Medieval Life*

THE ideal of the medieval Church was that of a great spiritual society that should include all Christendom, and for many centuries it seemed as if the ideal were to be realized. As the pagan peoples of Europe became converted to Christianity they took their place in the organization of the Church, an organization that represented the old civilization in its ideals of discipline and order. In 1054 the Eastern and the Western Churches had separated, and it was the latter, ruled by the Bishop of Rome, that became the great church of western Christendom.

The Church was first and foremost a spiritual society

and it set before men a definite way of life. There was only one Church in the Middle Ages, all Christians belonged to it and in all parts of it the teaching and the worship were the same. The Church influenced almost every part of the life of a medieval man. If he went to school, it educated him, for nearly all schools were connected in some way or other with the Church. If he lived in the country, once a year at Rogation-tide (the three days before Ascension Day) he marched in procession with all the people of the parish round the fields praying for a blessing on the crops. If he lived in a town and were a craftsman, the gild to which he belonged maintained a chapel in the cathedral or parish church to which the members of the gild went in procession on their annual festival. If he were of noble birth, he kept vigil in the church the night before he was made a knight, and the religious side of the ceremony was the most important. Whether he lived in castle or manor or town, he attended Mass on Sundays and Holy Days, and he observed the rule of the Church which bade him keep Fridays and vigils and the forty days of Lent as fast-days. All through the year the chief holidays were the holy days of the church, such as Christmas, Easter and Whitsuntide, Midsummer's Day (the feast of St. John the Baptist, June 24.) and Michaelmas Day (the feast of St. Michael and All Angels, September 29). The first medieval dramas were plays of the Nativity and other biblical subjects and were presented in the church itself.

The work of instructing the people in the faith of the Church and in their religious duties and obligations was done by the parish priest. He was expected not only to teach them the faith, but to explain to them the services of the Church, especially the Mass, and to instruct them how to behave. That they were not always as reverent or as well-behaved as they should can be gathered from a book written in England in the fourteenth century. In this book it was said that people must be taught to come into church quietly and to "holden no parliament" with their neighbours, to stand when the Gospel was being read even if they did not understand what it was about, and that they must not be allowed to walk about in the churchyard whilst the sermon was being preached.

It was also the duty of the parish priest to see that the poor and strangers in the parish were cared for. There was no organized system of relieving poverty in the Middle Ages and feeding the hungry, giving drink to the thirsty, shelter to the homeless, clothing to the naked, and visiting the sick were amongst the works of mercy to which the parish priest exhorted his people.

Towards the end of the Middle Ages the parish priests were often criticized for neglecting their people. Their task was often a very difficult one. They were nearly always poor, their parishes had grown large, especially as the towns increased in size and population, and visits to the people had to be made on foot. There were doubtless priests who failed in their duty, but there must also have been many like the "Poor Persoun of a Toun" who went with Chaucer on the pilgrimage to Canterbury.

> A good man was ther of religioun,
> And was a povre Persoun of a toun;
> But riche he was of holy thoght and werk.
> He was also a lerned man, a clerk,
> That Cristes gospel trewely wolde preche;
> His parisshens devoutly wolde he teche.
> Benigne he was, and wonder diligent,
> And in adversitee ful pacient;

And swich he was y-preved ofte sythes.
Ful looth were him to cursen for his tythes,
But rather wolde he yeven, out of doute,
Un-to his povre parisshens aboute
Of his offring, and eek of his substaunce.
He coude in litel thing han suffisaunce.
Wyd was his parisshe, and houses fer a-sonder,
But he ne lafte nat, for reyn ne thonder,
In siknes nor in meschief to visyte
The ferreste in his parisshe, muche and lyte,
Up-on his feet, and in his hand a staf.
This noble ensample to his sheep he yaf,
That first he wroghte, and afterward he taughte;
Out of the gospel he tho wordes caughte;
And this figure he added eek ther-to,
That if golde ruste, what shal iren do?
For if a preest be foul, on whom we truste,
No wonder is a lewed man to ruste;

.   .   .   .   .

Well oghte a preest ensample for to yive,
By his clennesse, how that his sheep shold live.

.   .   .   .   .

And though he holy were, and vertuous,
He was to sinful man nat despitous,
Ne of his speche daungerous ne digne,
But in his teching discreet and benigne.
To drawen folk to heven by fairnesse
By good ensample, was his bisinesse:
But it were any persone obstinat,
What-so he were, of heigh or lowe estat,
Him wolde he snibben sharply for the nones.
A bettre preest, I trowe that nowher noon is.
He wayted after no pompe and reverence,
Ne maked him a spyced conscience,
But Cristes lore, and his apostles twelve,
He taughte, but first he folwed it him-selve.[1]

[1] From Chaucer's *Prologue to the Canterbury Tales*. Oxford University Press, New York and London.

2. *The Growth of the Papacy as a Temporal Power*

THE medieval church influenced not only the daily life of men, it also became one of the great political powers of the time. In the first place it owned a great deal of property. From time to time kings and other rulers had bestowed land in Italy on the bishops of Rome. These lands were known at first as the Patrimony of St. Peter, later they developed into the States of the Church, ruled over by the Pope in the same way as any other ruler governed his domains. He drew a revenue from them, he administered justice in them, he had a papal army in order to defend them.

In other parts of Europe the same thing was happening. Land was given to the great bishops and abbots and as a result the Church was drawn into the feudal system. These lands were held as fiefs from the feudal lords, and the bishops and abbots became their vassals. But the bishops could in turn give out land to subtenants and there were parts of Europe where the bishops were themselves great feudal princes. In 1215 Innocent III called together a great council at the Lateran at which four hundred and twelve bishops and more than eight hundred abbots and priors were present. The council lasted for three days and it is said that the Bishop of Liège, wishing every one to know that he was a feudal prince as well as a bishop of the Church, dressed each day according to one of the positions he held. On the first day he appeared as a count, on the second as a duke, and on the third as a bishop. The fiefs held by bishops were not, however, hereditary, and the custom grew up of bishops and abbots being appointed by the feudal lords and kings. As they were often chosen for their political influence, the power of the

Church increased and by the end of the eleventh century it was recognized as one of the great powers of Europe.

Other reasons had contributed to the growth of the power of the Church. All through the early Middle Ages it was the Church that had fostered and encouraged learning, and it was in the Church that the traditions of law and order had been preserved. It was in the Church, therefore, that the best educated men and the best administrators were found, and such men became the counsellors of the medieval kings and emperors.

The Church had also established its own courts of law, the highest of which was the papal court in Rome. Controversies from all over Europe were taken to the papal court as to a final court of appeal, with the result that the papal authority was constantly strengthened at the expense of that of kings or feudal princes.

This increase in the temporal power of the Church had taken place gradually during the four and a half centuries that lay between the death of Gregory the Great in 604 and the accession of Gregory VII in 1073. There were grave dangers to the Church in this increase of temporal power and she did not escape them. But in the eleventh century a reformation took place within the Church, and when in 1073 the monk Hildebrand became pope as Gregory VII, he was able to claim for the papacy superiority over all other rulers.

Opinions have differed greatly over the character of Gregory VII. Some people have seen in him a passion for justice and righteousness and have believed him to have been inspired by a vision of the Church as a great spiritual empire that should rule the world. Others have seen in him only a passion for power and believe that he used his position in the Church as a means to further his own personal ambition. Motives are very hard to determine, and whatever those of Gregory VII may have been, there is no doubt as to the claims he made for the papacy. He laid down the principles that the pope was above all temporal rulers, whether they were princes, kings or emperors; that it was in his power to depose emperors; that he could annul decrees, no matter by whom they had been issued; that he alone could appoint bishops; that he had power to release subjects from any oath of allegiance taken to a wicked ruler; and that the Roman Church could not err.

Gregory VII also turned his attention to the further reform of certain evils in the Church. Now the position of a medieval bishop was a very difficult one. As a bishop of the Church he owed allegiance to the Pope who, upon his consecration, gave him a ring and staff, the outward symbols of his office. As a feudal holder of land he owed allegiance to the king or emperor of whom he was a vassal. Many of the eleventh century kings and emperors were in the habit of appointing the bishops, and in consequence they claimed the right not only to receive their homage, but to invest them with the symbols of their spiritual office. Gregory VII disputed this claim and it brought him into conflict with the other great medieval power that claimed to be a world state, the Holy Roman Empire.

3. *The Papacy and the Holy Roman Empire*

In the early Middle Ages Germany was broken up into a number of small independent states. They were constantly at war with each other and the land was always in a state of disorder. In the tenth century the dukes of Saxony became strong enough to unite a number of these states under their rule and to get themselves elected as kings of Germany. One of these kings, Otto I, was ambitious. He became involved not only in the conflicts and disorders of Germany and its borders, but also in those of northern Italy. He aided the Pope against his enemies and then he went to Rome, where on February 2nd, 962, he was crowned by the Pope as Holy Roman Emperor.

A hundred and sixty-two years earlier Charlemagne had also been crowned in Rome as emperor, but when he died in 814 the empire had been divided. In 962 it seemed to have been restored. But there was a difference between the two empires. Charlemagne had ruled over many people, speaking many tongues; Otto ruled chiefly over Germans. Charlemagne had attempted to create an imperial system of government; Otto left each German state with its own laws, not so much as a policy, as because he was unable to control them. Charlemagne had dreamed of a great world state, united, Christian and civilized, unattainable perhaps, but the ideal left its mark on the thought of the Middle Ages. Otto had no such vision, and was probably more concerned with extending his dominions than with lofty imperial ideas.

The emperors who after 962 ruled over this empire, were elected by German electors, and through the Middle Ages, they played an important part in the political affairs of Europe. Their close connection with Italy and the Papacy made them demand a voice in the election of the popes; the popes, on the other hand, claimed the right to have some part in the election of the emperors. It was with this empire that Gregory VII came into conflict over the question of investiture.

When Gregory VII became pope, Henry IV was emperor. He disregarded the decrees of Gregory concerning investiture and appointments, and he refused to recognize the pope as his superior. When Gregory attacked him for these things, Henry wrote him a letter in which he refused even to address him as pope, saying he was no pope, but a false monk, and demanded that he leave Rome. "I Henry, king by the grace of God, demand this of you," he wrote, "and with all my bishops I say unto you, Come down, come down."

Gregory retorted by excommunicating the emperor, and releasing his subjects from allegiance to him.[1] Henry threatened to depose him, and for two months he held out. Then, realizing that he would be ruined unless he made his peace with the pope, he set out for Italy. It was midwinter and Gregory was at Canossa, a strongly fortified castle in the Apennines. Henry was at Speyer in Germany and with a very small retinue he travelled through Burgundy, crossed the Alps and arrived in Lombardy. His Italian subjects refused to support him, and he climbed up the mountains to Canossa. On January 21st, 1077, Henry presented himself at the gate of the castle, but Gregory refused to see him unless he gave up his "crown and insignia of royalty and confessed himself unworthy of the name and honour of king." Henry was at length admitted into the courtyard of the castle, and for three days he waited there in the bitter cold, dressed as a penitent, barefoot and fasting. On the fourth day Gregory received him. "Holy Father, spare me!" cried Henry in abject submission. Gregory raised him to his feet, absolved him and on Henry's accepting certain conditions, sent him away.

[1] Excommunication meant the cutting off of a person from the services and sacraments of the Church.

In the meantime the Saxon subjects of Henry were conspiring against him and even the pope's forgiveness did not avail to restore their allegiance. Soon after his return they elected another king and civil war broke out. Henry continued to ignore Gregory's decree concerning investiture and in 1080 he was excommunicated a second time. This time Henry was supported by a number of the German bishops who resented Gregory's interference with them, and encouraged by their help, Henry in turn declared that Gregory was deposed and appointed a new pope. There were now two emperors and two popes and war broke out between them all. Henry and his allies seized Rome and Gregory was besieged in the castle of Sant'Angelo. Then Normans from Sicily came to the help of Gregory. After a four days' siege they took the city, sacked it and then went home. Gregory was free, but the city was desolate and he was old. He went to Salerno where he lived in exile. In 1085 he died.

The investiture question was not settled, and Gregory died in exile, but he had been one of the great popes of history, perhaps the greatest of the Middle Ages. Whatever some of the results of his work may have been, he made of the Papacy one of the great powers of the Middle Ages. If he claimed too much for it in temporal power, he never compromised in the ideals he put before it as a spiritual power. "I have loved righteousness and hated iniquity," he said, "therefore I die in exile."

4. *The Papacy and England*

FROM early Anglo-Saxon days the position of the Church in England had been strong. Its organization was older than that of the state and the archbishop of Canterbury was often the chief adviser of the king. The English people were loyal to the Church and all that it represented; they recognized the Pope as the head of the Church; they paid Peter's pence, money collected and sent directly to Rome; but in many ways they were more independent than the Church on the continent. In England it was always the king and the Witan who appointed the archbishops and bishops; it was the king and the Witan who called together church councils and synods. In England the bishops were all English, they were members of the Witan, and the courts in which justice was dispensed were presided over by bishops as well as by the Saxon ealdormen. English parish priests married and were subject only to the rule of their own bishops.

With the Norman Conquest this state of affairs changed. The history of the Church in England from the accession of William I in 1066 to the death of John in 1216 is an important part of medieval history, for it was during this century and a half that the issues between the church and the state were being fought out. On the one hand the papacy, strong in the position gained for it by Gregory VII, was asserting its claims over state as well as church; on the other, England was determined that there should be no interference by a foreign power in matters that concerned the state. There was also the king to be reckoned with. His power was increasing and the Church was ever on the alert to prevent it becoming tyrannical.

The controversies between England and the papacy during these years concerned four important principles: the question of jurisdiction, how far the pope might interfere in English affairs; the question of investiture, which had not been settled at Canossa; the question of church courts; and the question of the appointment of the archbishop of

Canterbury. These controversies were the result of several things that took place in England after 1066. William I had introduced a more highly developed form of feudalism into England than had been known there in Anglo-Saxon times, and as on the continent the Church was drawn into that system and the bishops became feudal vassals of the king. Under the Normans the royal power was very much strengthened and the government was centralized more and more in the hands of the king. As a result controversies were inevitable between him and the church, which in earlier days had performed many of the functions which the king now considered to be solely his. In many ways the Norman and early Plantagenet kings were more French than English, and they appointed Normans to all the more important positions in England. These Normans coming from the continent where they had been influenced by the reforms brought about in the Church by Gregory VII, introduced a discipline into the English Church which was often resented by the clergy who had been accustomed to the more lenient rule of the Anglo-Saxon bishops.

These controversies were not only important because of the principles that were at stake, but because they were carried on by some of the greatest of the medieval kings and popes and archbishops. William I and Henry II, Gregory VII and Innocent III, Lanfranc, Anselm, Becket and Stephen Langton were amongst the great personalities of the twelfth and thirteenth centuries.

The first controversy was over papal jurisdiction. William I was determined to be king in England in fact as well as in name, and to recognize no one as his superior. When the pope, Gregory VII, demanded that William pay him homage, the king of England refused. He was willing, he said, to send Peter's pence to Rome, but "to do homage, I refuse, because I never promised to do it, nor do I find that any of my predecessors have ever done it." William and his great archbishop, Lanfranc, then asserted certain principles concerning the jurisdiction of the pope in England. No pope was to be recognized without the consent of the king; no bull (a papal decree) was to be issued in England without the king's consent; and no royal minister was to be excommunicated until the king had been consulted.

This controversy was not marked by any bitterness. Gregory VII was a statesman, and he realized that England under strong Norman kings was more likely to become a real part of western Christendom than when she had been under Anglo-Saxon rule. During the century preceding the Norman Conquest the foreign relations of England had been chiefly with the turbulent Scandinavians, now she was brought into closer relations with the organization and discipline of Rome. The motive that determined William I was probably the determination to be king and to have no rival, the result was twofold. On the one hand, his policy was one that brought England into closer relations with Rome, on the other, it was the first step in making the English Church more national in character.

Henry IV had submitted to Gregory VII at Canossa, but the question of investiture had not been settled. Lanfranc died two years after William I, but for four years no new archbishop was appointed. William II, extravagant and wasteful, was indifferent to his duties and responsibilities and made no appointment, so that the crown might enjoy the revenues from the vacant see. But when in 1093 he fell dangerously ill, he seized Anselm, the Abbot of Bec, who happened to be in England, and forced him to become archbishop. Anselm was well known for his scholarship and for the saintliness of his life. He was happy at Bec and had no wish to be thrust into a position where trouble and difficulty probably awaited him. "What are you doing," he said to those who acclaimed him as archbishop, "you are yoking together an untamable bull and an old and feeble sheep." William recovered, repented of having sent for Anselm, and forced him into exile out of England.

Anselm returned in 1100 when Henry I became king, and almost at once the question of investiture came up. William I had invested bishops with their ring and staff, Lanfranc had made no objections, and Gregory VII had been forced to acquiesce. But the question had never died down, and whilst Anselm was abroad he had taken part in a council in Rome where investiture of bishops by laymen was forbidden. On his return to England he refused to consecrate bishops if the king invested them. After some controversy and discussion the matter was at length settled, and investiture ceased to be a question of any further conflict between the kings and the Church. The Church, in the person of the pope or the bishop whom he appointed to represent him, was to invest bishops with the ring and staff, the symbols of their spiritual office; the king was to receive their homage for land which they held from him as his vassals.

The victory lay with the Church, but for England it had a significance greater than was involved in a quarrel between the king and his archbishop. The Norman kings were strong rulers and under them the royal power was being strengthened and centralized. But they had not tamed the Church, and at this period in her history it was the Church that withstood the encroaching power of the king, and that by resisting him made possible the preservation of English liberties.

The most famous of all the medieval controversies between the king and the Church was that which resulted in the murder of Thomas Becket, archbishop from 1162-1170. As a young man Becket had lived in the household of Archbishop Theobald. He had studied abroad, at Bologna, the most famous school of law in the Middle Ages, and in 1155 the king, Henry II, made him his chancellor. For seven years he was Henry's closest friend and adviser, and he had every opportunity of studying the working of English law. Henry II had increased the importance and the power of the King's Court, a policy which had brought him into conflict with the Church Courts. When, in 1162, the archbishop of Canterbury died, Henry appointed Becket to succeed him, believing that in his former chancellor he would have a firm supporter, but to his surprise and anger, Becket opposed him.

There were at this time in England two courts of law, the King's Court and the Church Court, the difference between them being not the offences which each could try, but the offenders to be tried. All clerical offenders had the right to be tried by a church court, they had what was called "benefit of clergy." A clerk was any one who had received the tonsure, and this was given freely, not only to monks and priests, but to any one who could read and write, no matter what profession he intended to follow. Benefit of clergy was also claimed by anyone who worked in any capacity whatever for the Church. The punishments in church courts were milder than those in the king's court, and the result of this situation was a growing lawlessness amongst men who were not subject to the king's law and who claimed benefit of clergy whenever they were accused of an offence, even for serious offences such as murder or robbery. Henry proposed that the church courts should only have the power to convict of a crime, and that the offender after conviction should be handed over to the lay court for punishment. Becket refused to agree to this, and Henry attempted to make him swear obedience to what he called the ancient customs of England. These were written down in the Constitutions of Clarendon and at first Becket agreed to them. Then, realizing that if he did so, he was bringing the Church more under the power of the crown than he believed right, he refused and like Anselm, went into exile.

More controversy followed, but at last a reconciliation was made and Becket returned to England. In his absence the archbishop of York had crowned the young son of the king, and Becket obtained from the pope a sentence of excommunication against him and the bishops who had taken part in the ceremony, for crowning the king was the prerogative of the archbishop of Canterbury. Then Becket attempted to excommunicate all the barons who had sided with the king against him. "Is there no one who will avenge me on one upstart priest?" said Henry in anger when he heard what Becket was doing. Four knights took him at his word. On a dark December afternoon (December 29th, 1170) they rode down to Canterbury, forced themselves into the presence of the archbishop, demanded of him that he withdraw the excommunication, and on his refusal left to arm themselves.

It was the hour of vespers and Becket went as usual to the cathedral. The knights, armed, pursued him and shouted for the traitor. "No traitor, but a priest of God," answered Becket. He turned, retraced his steps, and met his enemies in the transept of the great church. They struck him down and killed him and then they fled, leaving the body of the archbishop lying in the dark to be cared for by the frightened monks.

Becket was a martyr and within fifty years of his death the magnificent shrine placed behind the high altar in Canterbury cathedral became one of the chief places of pilgrimage in medieval Europe. In the meantime Henry had been forced to do penance at Becket's tomb and practically to annul the Constitutions of Clarendon. By his death Becket gained what he had fought for more completely than he did during his life. In the controversy itself, Henry was probably more in the right than Becket, but Becket, like Anselm before him, stood as the champion of those who opposed tyranny, as the upholder of the independence of the Church, and it was for that reason that he became one of the most beloved of English martyrs, and that the shrine of St. Thomas of Canterbury was venerated by the medieval world.

In 1198 Innocent III, one of the great medieval popes, began his reign. He was only thirty-seven years old when he became pope, he had studied theology in the university of Paris and law at Bologna, he was gifted and able. Two great aims dominated his policy: one was the recovery of the Holy Land, and the other the reform of the Church. To further the first he encouraged a crusade, the fourth, doomed to be a failure, and then that undertaken by the Emperor Frederick II. In order to reform the Church he worked to stamp out all heresies; he authorized the new orders of friars, and he attempted to extend the power of the pope in making appointments. This brought him into conflict with King John of England.

In Anglo-Saxon days the king and the Witan had appointed the archbishops and bishops, but as a result of various changes and agreements, it had become the custom by the beginning of the thirteenth century for the cathedral chapter or the convent to elect its bishop. The king had the right to propose a candidate and in all cases he must approve of the appointment when made. In 1205 the archbishop of Canterbury died and the monks without consulting the king, elected their sub-prior archbishop. They sent him at once to Rome to be invested by the pope with the pallium, worn by all archbishops. John named another candidate, and he, too, was sent to Rome. But Innocent III rejected both men and not only appointed, but consecrated an archbishop of his own choice. John refused to have anything to do with him and in 1208 Innocent placed the whole of England under an interdict. Churches were closed, no Mass was celebrated, no Christian service might be held for the dead.

John was indifferent to the interdict except in so far as it gave him an opportunity to confiscate church property and enjoy some of its revenue. The following year John himself was excommunicated. He still paid no attention, but he was unpopular, rumours of plots against him were rife, and then in 1211 the Pope threatened that if he did not submit, he would issue a bull releasing all his subjects from allegiance to him. John submitted, and in 1213 he agreed to receive the archbishop, and to surrender England to the pope from whom he received it back as a fief of the papacy. It was a betrayal of his trust as king, and this act of John's involved England in later conflicts between Church and State. But though he knew it not, when John received the pope's candidate as archbishop, it was the death blow to his own despotism, for it was this archbishop who was to stand as the champion of English liberties.

The archbishop whom John was forced to recognize was

Stephen Langton. When he arrived in England he found the king hated and powerless, the barons divided, with no leader, united only in their opposition to the bad government and tyranny of the king. Stephen Langton placed himself at the head of the barons, and in 1215 they forced John to sign Magna Carta, by which the tradition of their ancient customs and liberties was secured to the English people. Once again the English Church had opposed tyranny.

CHAPTER IX

MONKS AND MONASTERIES

1. *The Monastic Ideal*

THE belief that withdrawal from the world is the surest way to attain peace and serenity is a very ancient one, and at some time or other during their lives most of the great religious teachers of the world have practised it. The monastic ideal, however, is not that of withdrawal for a space, and then a return to the work of the world, but of a life spent wholly in a place apart.

The first Christians who practised this way of living were hermits. These were men who lived quite alone, sometimes in the desert, sometimes in caves, always in lonely places. In the fourth century groups of men began living together, bound by certain rules. These communities were called monasteries and the men who lived in them monks, and one of the earliest was that founded by St. Basil in the east. All kinds of reasons took men into monasteries. Some wanted a quiet and peaceful spot where they could study undisturbed by the distractions of the troubled world outside the monastery walls; others desired to escape from the evil they saw all round them and which they seemed powerless to change; to some the life in a monastery offered wider interests than their narrow life in the world, for all kinds of occupations could be followed in a monastery; to some who were friendless, homeless and poor, the monastery offered a refuge and friends.

Underlying all these reasons was the belief that in a monastery a life wholly devoted to God could be led more easily than in the world.

The monastic rule most widely followed was that of St. Benedict. He is said to have fled from Rome because of the wickedness of the city and to have lived for a long time in a grotto in the hills near Rome. He was joined there by others who wanted to share his life of seclusion and devotion. After a time, the community having increased in numbers, Benedict decided to move to a more suitable spot, and in 529 the first Benedictine monastery was established at Monte Cassino, a lovely place in a valley amongst the hills between Rome and Naples.

The Benedictine Rule became the model for most monasteries. The monks lived together as a community under the rule of an abbot, to whom they promised absolute obedience when they were professed. The monastery was the home of the monk and unless he were sent elsewhere by his abbot, he remained in the same monastery all his life.

Before a man took the final vows of a monk, he lived in the monastery as a novice, generally for a year. The Benedictine Rule made the life of a novice very difficult, for no one was wanted who was not likely to make a good monk.

In the case of any one newly come to essay conversion of life, let not an easy entrance be accorded him; but as says the Apostle: "Prove the spirits, whether they are from God." Therefore if any one who comes shall have persevered in knocking for admission and after four or five days shall have been found patiently to bear all the injuries inflicted upon him and the difficulty of gaining entrance and shall be found to persist with his petition, let entrance be granted him and let him be in the guests' house for a few days. After that, let him be in the novices' cell where he may meditate and eat and sleep. And let there be deputed to take charge of him, a senior, such an one as is well fitted to win souls, to be solicitous for his welfare and to watch with scrupulous care, whether in very truth he seek God and be solicitous as to the Work of God, obedience and humiliations. Let there be set before him all the hard and the rough things through which lies the way to God; and if he shall have given promise of stability and perseverance let this rule be read through to him after the lapse of two months and let this be said to him: "Behold the law under which thou dost wish to serve as a faithful soldier; if thou art able to keep it, enter; but if thou art not able, depart free." If thus far he shall have stood firm, then let him be conducted to the aforenamed novices' cell and be again tested in all patience; and after the lapse of six months let the rule be re-read to him that he may know upon what he is entering; and if thus far he stand firm, after four months let this same rule again be re-read to him; and if, having deliberated of the matter with himself he shall have promised that he will keep it all and observe everything ordered him, then let him be received into the community, knowing himself to be now established by the law of the rule so that it is not lawful for him from that day onwards to go forth from the monastery, nor to shake free his neck from beneath the yoke of the rule which it was permitted him after such prolonged deliberation either to refuse or to accept.[1]

The Benedictine Rule recognized that a monk might wish to leave the monastery or that he might have to be sent away, but these occasions were very rare and were regarded as a tragedy. To break a vow is always a serious matter.

The novice who was to be received into the order and professed as a monk, took a threefold vow: of obedience, of poverty, and of chastity. He was required to give up everything he possessed, for the Rule did not allow a monk to own anything.

[1] *Rule of St. Benedict*, Chapter LVIII.

Let not any one presume to give or accept anything without the abbot's orders, nor to have anything as his own, not anything whatsoever, neither book, nor writing-tablet, nor pen; no, nothing at all, since indeed it is not allowed them to keep either body or will in their own power, but to look to receive everything necessary from their monastic father; and let not any one be allowed to have what the abbot has not either given or permitted. And let all things be common to all, as it is written: "Neither did any one of them say or presume that anything was his own." [1]

The Benedictine Order was a working order and the monks were required to work, some in the fields, some in the different workshops of the monastery, some in the scriptorium. The Rule gives definite instructions about the work of the monastery and the habits and discipline both of the body and of the spirit that a monk should practise.

The cloister of the monastery and stability in the community are the workshop wherein we may diligently effect all these works.

2. *The Daily Life of a Monk*

ON the south side of the monastic church was the cloister, four long sheltered walks forming a square and surrounding the cloister garth. All the monastic buildings were grouped round the cloister: the refectory where the monks took their meals; the chapter house in which they met for all kinds of convent business; the dormitories in which they slept; special cells for study and meditation. It was round the cloister that the daily life of most of the monks centred, but within the monastery precincts there were a number of other buildings, especially if the monastery were a large one. There would be the kitchen and the bakery, sometimes also a brewery, workshops of all kinds, storehouses and an infirmary.

[1] *Rule of St. Benedict*, Chapter XXXIII.

At the head of the monastery was the abbot or prior if the monastic church were also the seat of a bishop. The abbot was elected by the monks and the Benedictine Rule describes the kind of man who should be chosen.

Let him who is to be elected be chosen for his worthy manner of life and his fundamental wisdom, even if he be last in order of community seniority.... Let him who is elected abbot always bear in mind what manner of burden he has received, and Who it is to Whom he will have to render an account of his stewardship; and let him know that it behoves him to be of service rather than to be served. It behoves him therefore to be learned in the divine law, that he may thence bring forth things old and new; to be chaste, sober, merciful; and let him always exalt mercy above judgment, that himself may attain it. Let him hate the faults, let him love the brethren. In the matter of correction let him act prudently and not too severely, and let him always keep an eye upon his own frailty and remember that the shaken reed must not be crushed, by which we do not mean to say that he is to permit faults to be nourished, but that he cut them off prudently and with charity, as he sees to be expedient for each; and let him take pains to be loved rather than feared. Let him not be full of commotion nor anxious, jealous nor too suspicious, because such an one is never at rest. In the matter of the commands he gives let him be provident and considerate before God and man.[1]

Under the abbot were certain monks who were responsible for the order and discipline of the monastery. The precentor was in charge of the conduct of all the services and the music; the sacrist looked after the church and its furnishings, the altars and the hangings, the candles and lamps, and whatever treasures the church possessed, he saw to the ringing of the bells; the cellarer looked after the food, he went to the neighbouring fairs and markets and was responsible for whatever supplies had to be bought:

[1] *Rule of St. Benedict*, Chapter LXIV.

the chamberlain was in charge of all the clothing and everything connected with it, repairs and washing, habits and boots and shoes; the infirmarer was at the head of the monastic infirmary and cared for all who were sick; the almoner distributed the gifts, generally food, to the poor of the neighbourhood; the guest master received the guests and made provision for whatever hospitality was to be given them; the porter guarded the gate.

A monastery was said to be a house that was always "watchinge unto God" and the plan of the day centred round the recitation of the Hours, short services or offices in which psalms were said, a hymn sung, and short prayers offered. Just before midnight a bell rang and the monks rose, dressed and passed in silence to the choir of the church for *Matins* the first of the offices of the day. After a short interval *Lauds* was said and then the monks returned to bed. At six in summer and sometimes seven in winter they rose again for *Prime*. This was followed by an early Mass, then a very light breakfast, and the morning meeting in the chapter house. At this meeting the business of the day was discussed, special announcements made, discipline administered if necessary and letters read out. At nine o' clock *Tierce* was said, the High Mass followed soon after and from then until five in the afternoon the monks dispersed to their different occupations. The offices of *Sext* at noon, *Nones* at three and *Vespers* at four were attended by those monks whose work did not take them far beyond the walls. At five the single real meal of the day was eaten. During this meal one of the monks read aloud, either from the Bible or from a writing of one of the Fathers of the Church. A brief space of leisure and recreation followed, during which the monks could talk, play games if they wished, and then the last office, *Com-*

pline, was said. The day was over and silently the monks went in procession to the dormitory. By nine o'clock, sometimes even earlier, they were in bed, and the "time of the Great Silence" was observed until the ringing of the bell for Matins.

3. *The Monastic Orders*

After St. Benedict had founded his monastery at Monte Cassino, daughter-houses were established first in many parts of Italy, then over all parts of Europe. By the tenth century some of these houses had grown lax concerning the strict observance of the Rule and at Cluny in Burgundy a number of reforms were introduced and the discipline made stricter. It was not intended that the monastery at Cluny should withdraw from Benedictine control, but in time the Cluniac Order was recognized as independent.

In 1098 a Benedictine monastery was founded at Citeaux in Burgundy and like Cluny, a century earlier, it became the centre of reform and of a stricter observance of the Rule. In 1113 there was admitted to this monastery a young Burgundian noble called Bernard. He had long been attracted by the monastic ideal but had not taken any definite steps towards entering a monastery. One day when he was returning from an expedition with the duke of Burgundy, he left his companions and entered a church where he prayed, he tells us

with a great storm of tears, stretching out his hands to heaven, and pouring forth his heart like water in the presence of God his Lord: and from that day the intention of his heart remained firm.

For a year Bernard underwent such severe discipline in the monastery, "beyond what was human," that his health suffered. In 1115 he was sent by his abbot to be head of the monastery that had just been founded at Clairvaux, and this daughter-house of Citeaux, under the rule of him who is known today as St. Bernard, was soon the chief monastery of the Cistercian Order.

St. Bernard became very well known. As abbot of Clairvaux he was strict, but of such sympathy and understanding that his monks were inspired to work with enthusiasm for all that the Order represented. The numbers of monks increased to such an extent that before his death sixty-five bands of monks had left Clairvaux to found new houses. St. Bernard was a man of great personal charm, and it was said that "mothers hid their sons from him, wives their husbands and companions their friends" lest he should persuade them to follow him into the cloister. The influence of St. Bernard spread far beyond his own monastery. Pope and emperor, kings and nobles sought his counsel. He feared no one and denounced evil wherever he saw it, but above all, at all times and in all places he taught that the greatest thing in the world was the love of God. From Clairvaux the Church has inherited some of the loveliest of the medieval hymns, tradition says written by St. Bernard himself.

Another important monastic order of the Middle Ages was that of the Carthusians. This was founded in 1084 by St. Bruno who left the cathedral at Reims where he was working and went to a wild and lonely spot at Cartusia near Grenoble. He lived there at first as a hermit, but when a number of other men joined him, he founded a monastery where they lived under a very strict rule. The monastery, high up in the mountains, was called the Grande Chartreuse, and it was said to be "built almost above the clouds and very near to God." The monks called themselves Carthusians and they lived a life of austere discipline and loneliness. Each monk had his own garden and prepared his own food, he only went into the church for Mass and the night offices, the others he said alone in his cell.

These men, it was said, who live on the rocks are harder than the rocks themselves: they have no pity on themselves, or on those who dwell with them. Their site is fearful, but their order is yet more fearful.

The severity of the Rule did not prevent Carthusian houses being founded in many parts of Europe. In England the Charterhouse was one of the great medieval monastic houses.

The austere life of these Carthusian monks impressed itself on the imagination of the Middle Ages. The vision of the Carthusian, austere and lonely, lifting up his hands in prayer for his fellow men filled them at times with a sense of awe. Henry II of England was returning once from a journey to France and he was nearly shipwrecked. There may have been superstition mingled with what he felt, but there was also the belief that the monk in his cell was playing a part in the life of the time.

O, cried Henry, if that little Carthusian of mine, Hugo, were now pouring forth his private prayers, or if he were standing with his brethren, newly risen from their beds, and saying the night office, surely God would not have forgotten me for so long.

The work of the monks was one of the civilizing influences in the Middle Ages. At a time when society was crude and warlike, they gave an example of a disciplined and peaceful life. The Benedictine principle of work was that it was good for the body not only because what such work produced was useful, but because by means of work both body and mind are engaged in a wholesome, self-respecting manner. The monks developed large tracts of land that would otherwise have been left uncultivated, and monastic estates were among the best cultivated of any medieval domains. A large part of the burden of caring for the sick and poor was undertaken by the monks, and no one in need of any kind was ever turned away from a monastery gate. The extent of the contribution of the monks to learning and to art would be impossible to estimate. By their schools, their libraries, their work in copying manuscripts they preserved the tradition of scholarship, a tradition which might otherwise easily have been lost, and it was the great monastic orders that inspired the building of the churches and cathedrals that were the glory of the Middle Ages.

All monks did not always live up to the high traditions of their order, and medieval literature, especially towards the end of the Middle Ages has many criticisms of them. A monk could own nothing as an individual, but by holding possessions in common, a monastic order could possess a good deal. In this way the orders became wealthy, and though the world has benefited by their wealth because of the buildings on which they lavished it, the orders themselves suffered.

4. *The Architecture of the Church*

FROM the sixth to the eleventh centuries the greatest builders in western Europe were the monastic orders. They were wealthy and they spent money generously on their abbeys and churches. The architecture of these centuries is known on the continent as Romanesque, in England as Norman.

All Romanesque architecture is not alike, different countries developed different types, but there are certain characteristics that are common to them all. The walls and pillars were very thick, the windows narrow, and the arches were round. This architecture had inherited much from the older Roman tradition, but it developed characteristics of its own, especially in its ornament and sculpture. The doorways were often elaborately decorated and the carving on the capitals of the pillars was done with originality and beauty.

Towards the end of the twelfth century architecture began to change. The thirteenth century, one of the great centuries in the history of Europe, was perhaps the greatest of the Middle Ages. In architecture it was the period when the Gothic cathedrals were built. Changes in construction and development in the use of the arch and the vault made it possible to build with thinner walls, Gothic arches were pointed, the buildings were loftier, the windows were larger and filled with stained glass.

The finest examples of Gothic architecture are the great cathedrals and churches which were built between the thirteenth and fifteenth centuries, but during this period the church was not the only builder. Towns were growing in importance and secular buildings, town halls, gild halls and belfries were built by the townspeople. The monastic orders were still building churches, but many of the cathedrals, especially in France, were built by the townspeople. Nothing quite like this enthusiasm for building had ever been known, and the chronicler has left an account of how the cathedral at Chartres was built.

In this same year (1144) at Chartres men began to harness themselves to carts laden with stones and wood, corn and other things, and drag them to the site of the church, the towers of which were then a-building. It was a spectacle the like of which he who hath not seen will never see again, not only here, but scarcely in all France or Normandy or elsewhere. Everywhere sorrow and humility prevailed, on all sides penitence, forgiveness and remorse. On every side you could see men and women dragging heavy loads through the marshy bogs, and scourging themselves with whips. Miracles were being done on every side, and songs and hymns of praise sung to the Lord. You might say that the prophecy was being fulfilled which says, The Spirit of Life was in the wheels of the chariots.

Another account of this same sight was written in a letter that was sent to England.

Who has ever seen or who heard in all the ages of the past that kings, princes and lords, mighty in their generation, swollen with riches and honours, that men and women, I say, of noble birth have bowed their haughty necks to the yoke and harnessed themselves to carts like beasts of burden, and drawn them, laden with wine, corn, oil, stone, wood and other things needful for the maintenance of life or the construction of the church? But what is even more astonishing is that, although sometimes a thousand or more of men and women are attached to one cart— so vast is the mass, so heavy the machine, so weighty the load— yet so deep a silence reigns that not a voice, not a whisper even can be heard. And when there is a halt called on the way there is no sound save that of the confession of sins and the suppliant prayer to God for pardon. . . . Forward they press unchecked by rivers, unhindered by mountains. You might think that they were the children of Israel crossing Jordan, and for them, as for the children of Israel, miracles are wrought. But when they come to the church, they set their waggons in a circle so as to form, as it were, a spiritual camp, and all the following night the watch is kept by the whole army with hymns and songs of praise.

Candles and lamps are lit on each waggon; the sick and the feeble are placed thereon; the relics of the saints are brought to them in the hope that they may find relief. The clergy at the head of a procession, and the people following, pass by and pray with renewed fervour that the sick may be healed.

Other arts were closely allied to Gothic architecture and many of them were developed in connection with the building of churches, especially sculpture. Sculptured figures were used as one means of giving people who could not read much of the teaching of the Christian faith. Over the doorways of the churches were the stories in sculpture of the birth of Christ, of His life and death, of His resurrection and His ascent into glory; there were stories of the Virgin and of the lives of saints; Old Testament heroes and figures symbolizing virtues were there; and always over one door there was the Last Judgment as a warning and a hope to those who passed beneath it.

The Church needed and developed other arts besides sculpture. Finely wrought metal work for doors and gates, embroidery for vestments, tapestry for hangings of all kinds, carving in ivory and the work of the goldsmith and silversmith for crucifixes and shrines, and the vessels used in the churches, all these arts were developed and encouraged by the Church. Of all the arts that which was most perfectly developed in the Middle Ages and which has never been excelled since, some people would say not even equalled, was that of stained glass.

It has been said that to explore the cathedral at Chartres is to explore the Middle Ages. As the sculpture was the Bible in stone, so are the windows at Chartres the Bible in glowing pictures. To study them is to bring the medieval world to life, for the stories they depict and the teaching they give are placed in a medieval setting. The great windows that make the glory of Chartres were given by the craft gilds, and thirty or forty of these gilds are represented in little medallions in the windows, showing them at work and commemorating their gift.

CHAPTER X

FEUDALISM

1. *The Feudal Lord*

> Labours de clerc est Dieu prïer
> Et justice de chevalier.
> Pain lor truevent li laborier.
> Chil paist, chil prie, et chil deffent.
> Au camp, a le vile, au moustier
> S'entreaïdent de lor mestier
> Chil troi par bel ordenement.

("The labour of the clerk is to pray to God, of the knight to do justice, and the labourer finds their bread. One provides food, one prays and one defends. In the field, the town and the church these three help each other with their services in a well-ordered scheme.") [1]

IN this way do these lines from a thirteenth century poem, *Miserere*, describe the threefold division of society in the Middle Ages. Another medieval writer described society as resembling the human body. The priests and clerks, he said, were the head and eyes, the spiritual guides of men; the nobles were the hands and arms, their protectors and defenders; and the peasants, the feet and legs, for it was on their labour that the whole of society was based.

Feudalism was the system in the Middle Ages by which

[1] Joan Evans, *Mediæval France*. Oxford University Press, New York and London.

the nobles and knights, the protectors and defenders of society, were bound together. It was a system which was based on the holding of land, and the feudal holding of land always carried with it the obligation of service. In the case of the lord or knight the service was military in time of war and the giving of counsel in time of peace. In the case of the peasant the service was rendered by his labour with plough and spade.

Feudalism developed differently in different countries, but there were certain principles that all forms of feudalism had in common. The king was regarded as the owner of the entire land, but in return for certain definite services he would grant portions of it to his great lords. These lords could in their turn grant portions to lesser lords, who would again sub-divide it amongst knights, and in England sometimes amongst squires. The land thus granted was called a *fief* and all men to whom it was granted were called *vassals*, each vassal owing services to the overlord from whom he had received his land. The great lords, the dukes and marquises and counts ruled the land given to them as feudal princes and as was seen in the case of France in the early Middle Ages, they were far more powerful than the king. They were practically independent, carrying on their own private warfare as they chose, holding their own courts of justice, coining their own money.

The services required of vassals varied in different places, but certain services were common to all vassals everywhere. These were known as the three feudal aids. The vassals were bound to ransom their lord from captivity if he were taken prisoner in war; to pay the expenses of making the lord's eldest son a knight; and to provide a dowry for his eldest daughter. In addition to these aids, a vassal was required to give forty days' military service a year; to attend the lord's court whenever summoned; to entertain his lord or even to place his whole castle at his disposal should he require it; and to accompany the lord on expeditions and wars. In the latter case the distance the vassal need go and the time he was to give were usually specified. The tale is told that Edward I demanded more service than one vassal, Roger Bigod, the Earl Marshal, would give:

"I will willingly go with you (to Flanders), O king, riding before you in the first rank, as is my hereditary right." And the king answered: "You will even go without me, like the rest." But Bigod said: "I am not bound, nor is it my wish, O king, to take the road without you." The king angrily broke out with the words (it is said): "By God, earl, you will either go or hang." To him replied the earl: "By the same oath, O king, I will neither go nor hang." [1]

He neither went nor was hanged and Edward had to give way.

Originally feudal fiefs were granted for life only, but by degrees it became customary on the death of a vassal to grant the same fief to his son or heir, and so the land became hereditary. Whenever a new heir succeeded, heavy fees were demanded by the overlord and homage was paid by the new vassal.

Paying homage was the ceremony in which a vassal placed himself under the protection of his overlord, took an oath of allegiance and was invested with his land. Bareheaded and unarmed the vassal knelt before his lord, placed his hands between the hands of the lord and declared that he was his man. Then the lord kissed him, raised

---

[1] Walter of Hemingburgh. R. B. Mowat, *A New History of Great Britain*. Oxford University Press, New York and London.

him to his feet and the vassal took an oath of fealty, swearing that he would be true and loyal, that he would never harm his lord, his person, his family or his honour. The act of fealty was followed by the investiture. The lord gave to his vassal a twig or a stick, sometimes a glove, as a symbol that the fief had now passed into his possession. Except in England, vassals always paid homage to the lord from whom they had directly received their land, with the result that the greatest lords, dukes and marquises and counts, were overlords through their sub-vassals of large numbers of men. In England every landowner paid homage directly to the king and great estates held by one baron were generally in different parts of the country. This form of feudalism was introduced into England by William the Conqueror, himself a vassal of the king of France. As a result the English barons were not as powerful as the feudal princes on the continent, and there was much less private war carried on.

On the continent much of the private war was between the lesser lords. In many places they were little more than robber barons whose aim was to seize a neighbour's castle, destroy his crops and orchards, and if possible take him prisoner in order to obtain a ransom. As early as the tenth century the Church made efforts to stop such fighting and plundering by placing under a curse all who in private war despoiled churches or robbed the poor. Later, the lords themselves entered into a pact to limit the extent of their warfare. In 1023 one such pact was made at Beauvais when the lords of that region made the following oath:

I will not invade in any way churches, or the crypts of churches, unless it be to seize malefactors who have broken the peace or committed homicide; I will not assault clerks or monks not bearing secular arms; I will carry off neither ox, nor cow, nor any other beast of burden. I will do nothing to cause men to lose their possessions on account of their lord's war, and I will not beat them to make them give up their property. From the first day of May until All Saints' Day I will seize neither horse, nor mare, nor foal from the pastures. I will neither destroy nor burn houses, nor root up nor cut down the vines under pretext of war.[1]

The influence of the Church had made itself felt to good purpose and by the middle of the eleventh century what became known as the Truce of God was an established custom.

From the hour of vespers on Wednesday until sunrise on Monday let there reign a settled peace and an enduring truce between all Christians, friends and enemies, neighbours and strangers, so that for these four days and five nights at all hours there may be safety for all men, so that they can devote themselves to business without fear of attack. Let those who, having pledged themselves to the truce, break it, be excommunicated, accursed, and abominated, now and forever, unless they repent and make amends. Whosoever shall kill a man on a day of truce, shall be banished and driven out of his country, and shall make his way into exile at Jerusalem.[2]

Each of these days on which the Truce of God was to be observed had Christian associations: Thursday was sacred to the memory of the Ascension, Friday to the Passion, Saturday to the vigil at the Holy Tomb, and Sunday to the Resurrection. Later, there were included the forty days of Lent, and then the weeks from Easter to Pentecost, and some Saints' Days, especially those of St. John the Baptist (June 24), the Assumption of the Virgin (August 15) and St. Martin (November 11).

[1] Joan Evans, *Mediæval France*. Oxford University Press, New York and London.

[2] Joan Evans, *Monastic Life at Cluny*. Oxford University Press, New York and London.

These seasons had a double significance in medieval life. They were days of Christian obligation, but they were also the times and seasons when the peasant was ploughing and sowing, reaping and harvesting. When fields were trampled and crops burnt, both the peasant and the lord whom he served suffered, so the protection afforded by the Truce of God was welcomed by rich and poor alike.

2. *The Castle*

THE castle was one of the outward signs of feudalism. The whole system had grown up owing to the need of every man for protection of some kind or other, and to the feudal lord the castle symbolized both his independence and his power to protect and defend all that belonged to him. In the earlier Middle Ages practically every one was attached in some way or other to a castle, for those who tilled the land outside were accustomed in time of need to take refuge within the castle walls.

A castle was protected by strong walls which surrounded the whole enclosure, with towers at the corners. Encircling the walls outside was the moat, wide but not necessarily very deep. The bottom of the moat was soft and muddy, so that in case of attack it was very difficult to place scaling-ladders against the walls. The moat was crossed by a drawbridge, which could be raised or lowered according to whether enemies or friends were approaching the castle. The castle yard was entered by a portcullis. Within the castle walls there was a large enclosure. In the middle was the *donjon* or keep, the hall where most of the public life of the inmates of the castle was spent, and the rooms in which they slept. There were inner and outer courtyards, a chapel, storehouses and stables, a garden, a well and some-times a labyrinth of underground passages, some leading to the dungeons and prisons, some leading out into the country. Castles varied, of course, in size, but the larger and more important had most of these characteristic parts.

A very busy life went on in the castle. In addition to the lord, his lady and children, there lived in the castle the various officials who were responsible for its administration and defence: the seneschal and steward, pages and squires, grooms and men-at-arms, retainers of all kinds, servants, both men and women.

The lord of the castle might be away fighting, but when he was not, there were his estates to be managed, there was hunting and fishing, he must hold his court, he must receive his guests. Indoors, his life was not so active and in the winter when the days closed in early, there must have been many a long evening when he found him-self with little to do. A favourite game of the Middle Ages was chess, a very feudal game, with its kings and queens, its bishops and knights, its castles, its pawns. Eagerly wel-comed, especially in winter, were the jongleurs and wan-dering minstrels.

The lady of the castle shared with her lord in its ad-ministration and in his absence she was responsible for its defence. The general care of the large household was in her hands. It was she who trained the pages and the maid-ens who came from other castles in their duties. She superintended all the needlework done, the spinning and weaving, the fine embroidery and the making of tapestry. As they sat and worked the ladies and their maidens used often to sing songs, *Chansons de Toile* (Sewing Songs), as they were called. Such a song was that of Fair Yolande.

Fair Yolande in a chamber still,
On her knee some stuffs unfolds,
Sews with a thread of gold and one of silk.
Her stern mother chides her;
 "I chide you for it,
  Fair Yolande."

"Fair Yolande, I chide you,
You are my daughter, do your duty."
"My lady mother, what is it for?"
"I will tell you, by my faith;
 "I chide you for it,
  Fair Yolande."

"Mother, for what do you chide me?
Is it for sewing or cutting,
Or spinning or brushing,
Or is it for sleeping too much?"
 I chide you for it,
  Fair Yolande."

"It is not for sewing nor for cutting,
Nor for spinning nor for brushing;
Nor is it for too much sleeping,
But for speaking too much to the knight.
 I chide you for it,
  Fair Yolande."

The medieval lady needed a wide knowledge of herbs and medicinal plants, for the care of the sick and of wounded knights was in her hands. Her garden was full of the herbs she needed. Amongst them there would be wormwood, good for fever and for headache; marigold and fennel, good for weak eyes; lavender, which gave sleep to the sleepless; hore-hound, used as a remedy for coughs; lad's love, which kept the moths away; thyme and borage, both good for giving courage; balm, good for the memory; and sage, full of virtue for many ills and the giver of long life if eaten in the month of May.

As long as society was feudal, and as long as a sure place of defence was needed, the castle retained its importance in medieval life. In the earlier Middle Ages a strong castle was almost impregnable. It could be starved into surrender, occasionally treachery within the walls opened the gates to the enemy, but the taking of a castle was no easy matter. When, however, in the fourteenth century gunpowder was introduced into the warfare of western Europe, castle walls were no longer an adequate defence. Many things brought the Middle Ages to an end. Gunpowder was one of them.

CHAPTER XI

THE AGE OF CHIVALRY

1. *Knighthood*

CHIVALRY was a military order in the Middle Ages, the members of which, called knights, were pledged to the protection of the Church and the succour of all who were in distress or in any way oppressed. In its early days chivalry was closely bound up with the obligations of feudalism, but whereas the feudal fief came to be hereditary, knighthood was not. No one was born a knight, though as a rule it was only men of gentle birth who were given knighthood. In the Middle Ages it was a dignity bestowed, generally after training as page and squire, or as a reward for gallant deeds; it was something that had to be merited.

The ideals of the chivalry of the Middle Ages were essentially Christian: they were ideals of service, of loyalty, of fearlessness in the cause of the right, of integrity in word and deed, of courtesy and generosity, of consideration for those in distress or need. The ideals of chivalry were not always lived up to, but in an age that was often rough and violent, they were a civilizing influence, and they set a standard that was deeply respected. *Noblesse oblige* expresses what was required of those who were bound by the obligations of chivalry.

The training of a knight began at the age of seven or

eight, when, as a small boy, he was sent away from home to the household of some great lord or knight. There, for six or seven years, he would learn all that a page should know. He would be taught to be of service, to be courteous and to have good manners. Books of etiquette were written full of instructions as to how a child should behave. He was to be up early in the morning.

Arise betimes from your bed, cross your breast and your forehead, wash your hands and face, comb your hair, and ask the grace of God to speed you in all your works; then go to Mass and ask mercy for all your trespasses. Say "Good Morning" courteously to whomsoever you meet by the way.

When ye have done, break your fast with good meat and drink, but before eating cross your mouth, your diet will be the better for it. Then say your grace—it occupies but little time—and thank the Lord Jesus for your food and drink. Say also a Pater Noster and an Ave Maria for the souls that lie in pain, and then go labour as you are bound to do. Be not idle, for Holy Scripture says to you of Christian faith that if you work, you must eat what you get with your hands.

Look you be true in word and deed, the better shall you prosper; for truth never works a man shame, but rather keeps him out of sin.

Make no promise save it be good, and then keep it with all your might, for every promise is a debt that must not be remitted through falsehood.

Love God and your neighbour, and thus may ye say without fear or dread that you keep all the law.

Uncalled go to no council, scorn not the poor, nor hurt any man, learn of him that can teach you, be no flatterer or scoffer, oppress not your servants, be not proud, but meek and gentle, and always walk behind your betters.

When your better shows his will, be silent; and in speaking to any man keep your hands and feet quiet, and look up into his face, and be always courteous.[1]

[1] From the *Young Children's Book.*

Training in good manners at table was a very important part of this early education.

Now must I tell you shortly what you shall do at noon when your lord goes to his meat. Be ready to fetch him clear water, and some of you hold the towel for him until he has done, and leave not until he be set down, and ye have heard grace said. Stand before him until he bids you sit, and be always ready to serve him with clean hands.

When ye be set, keep your own knife clean and sharp, that so ye may carve honestly (i.e., decorously) your own meat.

Let courtesy and silence dwell with you.

Cut your bread with your knife and break it not. Lay a clean trencher before you, and when your pottage is brought, take your spoon and eat quietly; and do not leave your spoon in the dish, I pray you.

Look ye be not caught leaning on the table, and keep clear of soiling the cloth.

Do not hang your head over your dish, or in any wise drink with full mouth.

When ye shall drink, wipe your mouth clean with a cloth, and your hands also, so that you shall not in any way soil the cup, for then shall none of your companions be loth to drink with you.

Do not carry your knife to your mouth with food, or hold the meat with your hands in any wise; and also if divers good meats are brought to you, look that with all courtesy ye assay of each; and if your dish be taken away with its meat and another brought, courtesy demands that ye shall let it go and not ask for it back again.

When ye have done, look then that ye rise up without laughter or joking or boisterous word, and go to your lord's table, and there stand, and pass not from him until grace be said and brought to an end.

Then some of you should go for water, some hold the cloth, some pour upon his hands.[1]

[1] From the *Babees' Book*, or *A Little Report of How Young People Should Behave.*

Above all, a child was taught to be courteous to all who were older than he.

When you enter your lord's place, say "God speed," and with humble cheer greet all who are there present. Do not rush in rudely, but enter with head up and at an easy pace, and kneel on one knee only to your lord or sovereign, whichever he be.

If any speak to you at your coming, look straight at them with a steady eye, and give good ear to their words while they are speaking . . . nor let your eyes wander about the house, but pay heed to what is said, with blithe visage and diligent spirit.

.   .   .   .

Take no seat, but be ready to stand until you are bidden to sit down. Keep your hands and feet at rest.[1]

.   .   .   .

Whenever you come unto a door, say, "God be here," ere you go further, and speak courteously, wherever you are, to sire or dame or their household.

Stand and sit not down to meat until you are told by him that rules the hall; and do not change your seat, but sit upright and mannerly where he bids, and eat and drink and be fellowly, and share with him that sits by you—thus teaches Dame Courtesy.[2]

Then there were other things the page must learn. He would be told the stories of knights of old, tales of Hector and Troy, of Arthur and Camelot. The chaplain of the castle would instruct him in religion, and would tell him about saints and heroes like St. Martin and St. George, and he would teach him to read and write. The huntsman and the falconer would teach him the beginning of the art of hunting; the squires would show him how to mount a horse and ride, and how to throw a spear. He would learn to sing and dance, perhaps to play the harp. By the time

[1] From the *Babees' Book.*
[2] From the *Young Children's Book.*

he was fifteen or sixteen a well-educated page was ready to become a squire.

There was no youth in France better brought up, nor who knew better how to speak to a gentleman. He knew enough about horses and arms, and if you like I will tell you how: for his father made him often ride through the woodland and in the meadow and learn how to trot and turn the horse, and showed him by word and deed, and Aiol remembered it well as a sensible youth. He knew all about the courses of the stars, the changes of the moon. . . . Avice the duchess had shown him; there was no wiser woman in ten cities. And Moses the hermit had taught him, and schooled him in letters and grammar. Well did Aiol know how to read and write, how to speak in Latin and French.[1]

As squire a young man learned to tilt and use a lance, sword and battle-axe. He accompanied his lord to tournaments and war, had the care of his armour and armed him, fought by his side ready to protect him, and if he were wounded it was the squire's duty to carry him away to a place of safety, no easy task when the lord was clad from head to foot in heavy armour. In a medieval book on *How to Acquire Knighthood*, it was laid down that

. . . it is fitting that the son of a knight while he is an esquire should know how to take care of a horse, and it is fitting that he should serve (at table) first, and be subject before he himself is a lord (or knight) for otherwise he will never know the nobleness of his knighthood when he comes himself to be a knight. For this reason should every knight put his son into the service of another knight so that he may learn to carve at table and to serve the rest, and to arm and robe a knight. Thus like a man who would learn to be a tailor or a carpenter it is fitting that such a one should have a master who is a tailor or a carpenter;

[1] From the *Romance of Aiol*, 13th century. Joan Evans, *Mediæval France*. Oxford University Press, London and New York.

so too, it is fitting that every nobleman who loves the order of his knighthood, should have had first a master who was a knight.

A squire did not necessarily become a knight. Many men remained squires all their lives, sometimes because they were not rich enough to meet the demands made on knights, sometimes they were not of sufficiently gentle birth, sometimes they had neither the love of adventure nor the gaiety of heart that inspired a man to knightly deeds. Such men often remained faithful, loyal squires, and in England it was not uncommon for them to be granted lands or manors. But probably the larger number of squires became knights, certainly those who served a fair lady and had had the training and experience of Chaucer's squire.

> With him ther was his sone, a yong Squyer,
> A lovyer, and a lusty bacheler,
> With lokkes crulle, as they were leyd in presse.
> Of twenty yeer of age he was, I gesse.
> Of his stature he was of evene lengthe,
> And wonderly delivere, and greet of strengthe.
> And he hadde been somtyme in chivachye,
> In Flaundres, in Artoys, and Picardye,
> And born him wel, as of so litel space,
> In hope to stonden in his lady grace.
> Embrouded was he, as it were a mede
> Al ful of fresshe floures, whyte and rede.
> Singinge he was, or floyting, al the day;
> He was as fresh as is the month of May.
> Short was his goune, with sleves longe and wyde.
> Wel coude he sitte on hors, and faire ryde.
> He coude songs make and wel endyte,
> Juste and eek daunce, and wel purtreye and wryte.
> So hote he lovede, that by nightertale
> He sleep namore than doth a nightingale.

Curteys he was, lowly, and servisable,
And carf biforn his fader at the table.[1]

The young squire who was to be knighted spent the night before the ceremony in a vigil in the church, kneeling before the altar on which his arms were laid. In the morning he bathed, was clothed in white, attended Mass and received the sacrament. Then he made his knightly vows, promising to use his sword in defence of the Church and of all who were in distress and to maintain his knightly honour and integrity. On leaving the church he was invested piece by piece with his armour, with his knightly spurs, and lastly with his belt and sword. When he was thus fully armed, he knelt before the lord who was to give him his knighthood, and he received the *accolade*, either three taps with the flat of the sword on his shoulder or a sharp blow with the fist on the back of his neck. The accolade was given him with the words: "In the Name of God, St. Michael and of St. George, I dub thee Knight; be gallant, be courteous, be loyal."

The newly made knight was next presented with a helmet, a shield and lance and a horse. He was expected to mount the horse, if possible without touching the stirrup, and to show his prowess in horsemanship by galloping round and round before the assembled company. The rest of the day was given up to feasting and rejoicing, and if the knight were rich there would be a tournament and jousting. A new knight was expected to show generosity and to give liberally of what was called *Largesse*. He made generous gifts to the Church and to the poor, to his friends, to the wandering minstrels and jongleurs, to all who had attended or in any way served him.

[1] Chaucer: Prologue to the *Canterbury Tales*. Oxford University Press, London and New York.

A knight who was the eldest son had his duties and obligations at home. For other young knights there were various opportunities of service. Accompanied by their squires they could attach themselves to a lord or older knight and follow him on his various expeditions, or they could set out in search of adventures of their own. There were forests to clear of outlaws, there were robber barons to defy on the roads, there were damsels in distress who needed help and deliverance, and there were always jousts and tournaments where a knight errant, as wandering knights were called, was welcomed, and where he could try his skill against other knights.

Knight-errantry involved many discomforts, but a true knight had been taught to face them with gaiety of heart.

Galloping, trotting, leaping, riding, vigils, privations and fatigue will henceforth in errantry be my pastime. Armed with wood, iron and steel, I shall endure heat, cold, frost; scattered meadows will be my dwelling-place. Discords and severities must serve the place of love-songs, and I shall maintain the weak against the strong.[1]

Knights were not always faithful to their vows, they did not always live up to the highest ideals of chivalry, but a false knight was always held up to contempt. In poetry and in song knightly virtues were extolled and in the Lament for Sir Launcelot in the *Morte d'Arthur* we have a picture of the characteristics of a true knight.

Ah Launcelot, thou wert head of all Christian knights, and now there thou liest, thou that were never matched of earthly knight's hand. And thou wert the courteoust knight that ever bare shield. And thou wert the truest friend to thy lover that ever bestrad horse. And thou wert the truest lover of a sinful man

[1] Raymbaud de Vagueiras.

that ever loved woman. And thou wert the kindest man that ever struck with sword. And thou wert the goodliest person that ever came among press of knights. And thou was the meekest man and the gentlest that ever ate in hall among ladies. And thou wert the sternest knight to thy mortal foe that ever put spear in the rest.[1]

2. *Tournaments*

TOURNAMENTS and jousts gave the knights training in the art of war. In jousts there were two combatants only; in tournaments groups of knights fought on each side. A joust might be an encounter merely for pleasure or exercise; in that case it was called a *Jouste à plaisance;* the lances used had blunt tips and the swords had sharp edges, but were not pointed. In the *Jouste à outrance* sharp weapons were used, and the fight was to the death.

A tournament was an occasion of great festivity. Knights from far and wide assembled to take part in this mimic warfare to show their prowess, to fight wearing the colours of the ladies they served, hoping to receive the prizes from their hands.

The holding of a tournament was announced by the heralds who went out on horseback to castles and towns accompanied by trumpeters. In castle-yards and in the market place in towns the trumpeters blew their trumpets and the heralds announced the date and place and conditions of the approaching tournament.

PROCLAMATION OF A TOURNAMENT

All stranger knights and squires
And all others who seek renown
Hark, hark to the honour and the praise

[1] From *Le Morte d'Arthur*, by Sir Thomas Malory.

And of arms the very great festival;
It is by order of the knight
Of the Golden Eagle, with him thirty on horseback
All garbed alike, tilting in his company,
And ready to run a course with any of their profession
On the morrow of the Day of Magdalene.

In the noble city, so it is understood
Which bears the name of Paris as its right;
There will be the Queen adorned like an angel,
Thirty ladies dressed after the same habit and fashion.
As for the secret isle, the herald
Will give you its name; on Sunday dancing,
And on Monday tilting for splendid prizes,
As many lances as one likes to use,
On the morrow of the Day of Magdalene.

He who jousts best of all without substitution (i.e., another taking his place)
Shall have for prize a chaplet of gold, fine and good
With a diamond set lozenge-shaped therein,
Which the Queen will present and give,
And stranger shall have
Fifteen days to come and fifteen to return
Fair-safe-conduct without villainous treason,
Thus doth the Golden Eagle make proclamation
For the morrow of Magdalene's Day.

After the day all squires may present themselves;
For on Tuesday other tilts will be arranged
By a squire and with him thirty in his array,
Equipped alike will be the comrades
So that the ranks may be formed and dressed,
And a demoiselle with fair lightsome body
Shall there be, with her thirty of the same habit and bearing,
To watch and counsel the jousters
On the morrow of Magdalene's Day.

The best jouster of all shall not have a woollen scarf
But of fine silver a chaplet for his diadem,

And within it a clasp of gold without alloy,
The demoiselle will give it them, so 'tis said,
The Golden Eagle will give a dinner
On Monday evening, and will keep festival;
The noble King of France will hold full court
On Tuesday evening; the Festival has been proclaimed
For the morrow of Magdalene's Day.

Envoy.

Prince, who wishes to exploit great deeds
To such festivities thou shouldest counsel
The knights; for it is time that then should be understood
Great deeds by those who have gone to war.
For this cause be pleased to advise these matters
For the morrow of Magdalene's Day.[1]

Tournaments took place within an enclosure known as
the lists. This space was generally oblong with rounded
corners and at each end were gates wide enough to allow
two horsemen riding abreast to enter at once. At each gate
were stationed heralds, trumpeters and men-at-arms, who
were responsible for the orderly entrance of the knights
who were to take part in the tournament. The tents of
these knights were outside the lists, and on each tent was
hung the shield of the occupant. Surrounding the lists
were galleries set up for the occasion. They were covered
with brightly coloured cushions and carpets and rich tap-
estries, and intended for the ladies and nobles who had
come to watch the tournament. Less important seats were
occupied by squires and yeomen, and all round the lists
every tree or hill that commanded even a distant view
of the tournament was full of spectators. Generally
the middle seats of one gallery were more richly adorned
than the others, and sometimes the central seat of all had

[1] From Eustache Deschamps.

the appearance of a throne, with a canopy above it. Here would sit the fairest of all the ladies known for that day as the Queen of Beauty and Love.

Though each tournament had its own rules, the general conditions were alike. To the sound of trumpets the knights who were the challengers entered at one end of the lists, and the champions who opposed them at the other. In the earlier tournaments these knights fought head on encounters, and both men and horses suffered grievous hurt, sometimes losing their lives. Later, a rope was stretched the length of the lists and hung with tapestry. This was called the *toile*, and the knights fought with it between them. Sometimes the toile was made more solid and was a firmly erected wooden screen covered with cloth or tapestry. The prize was presented to the victor by the Queen of Beauty.

Tales of tournaments and of knights and their gallant deeds of courtesy and generosity make a picturesque story of life in the Middle Ages, but there was another side to medieval life. There was the violence and disorder brought about by private warfare, there were the peasants whose toil made so much of the gaiety possible, and who suffered when their fields and crops were destroyed. It is true that knightly virtues were expected only of knights, and that knights were not always patterns of chivalry. Nevertheless it was the influence of knightly ideals that helped to make "trouthe and honour, fredom and curteisye" the ideals of all Christian manhood, so that of the man who lived up to them it might be said:

He was a verray parfit gentil knight.

3. *Troubadours and Minstrels*

In the twelfth and thirteenth centuries Provence in the south of France had developed a civilization very different from that of the north. It was a sunny land, its soil was rich and well cultivated, flowers and fruit abounded. There were castles, but though they were well defended they were less like fortresses than some of those in the north, and both the lords of the castles and the counts who ruled in the towns held courts that were unrivalled for gaiety and colour, for music and dance. Provence, Toulouse and Aquitaine were practically sovereign states, and the cities of Marseilles and Toulouse, of Nîmes and Arles were centres of a gay and pleasure-loving civilization.

Provence was the name that was often given to this whole region. The language spoken there was called the Langue d'Oc, a language that has almost disappeared now, for it was the language of the north, the Langue d'Oil spoken in the Ile de France, that was finally to prevail and become the French language as we know it today. But in the twelfth and thirteenth centuries the Langue d'Oc was rich in lyric poetry and this poetry was the work of the troubadours.

Troubadours were men of knightly rank. Provençal feudalism was less aristocratic than the feudalism of the north, and knighthood was often conferred on burghers of the towns and sometimes even on peasants if they had shown themselves worthy of it. Troubadours were usually both poets and minstrels, for the poems they made were always to be sung, not recited. Well known troubadours travelled from court to court and wherever they went, they were welcomed and fêted. They sang of courtly love, for the "gay science" as it was called, was the subject that enthralled the society of Provence. The troubadour served a lady to whom he had devoted himself, and he sang to her honour in contests of skill in poetry and music, just as the knight in arms fought for her in a tournament. These courts of love were always romantic and often absurd and extravagant, but the skill demanded of the troubadour left its mark on the forms of lyric poetry which were developed, and the poems themselves are valuable in what they tell us of Provençal life in the Middle Ages.

> Whene'er the lark's glad wings I see
>   Beat sunward 'gainst the radiant sky
> Till, lost in joy so sweet and free,
>   She drops, forgetful how to fly—
>   Ah, when I view such happiness
>   My bosom feels so deep an ache,
>   Meseems for pain and sore distress
>   My longing heart will straightway break.
>
> Alas, I thought I held the key
>   To love! How ignorant am I!
> For her that ne'er will pity me
>   I am not able to defy;
>   My loving heart, my faithfulness,
>   Myself, my world, she deigns to take,
>   Then leaves me bare and comfortless
>   To longing thoughts that ever wake.
>
> .   .   .   .
>
> But since my lady hears no plea,
>   Scorns justice, mercy will deny,
> And smiles to see me on my knee,
>   I plead no more,—I say good-bye;
>   Good-bye to all I would possess!
>   She strikes: my death shall answer make;
>   She bids: heart-sick I acquiesce,
>   And welcome exile for her sake.[1]

[1] Bernart of Ventadorn. (Troubadour.)

The troubadour sang chiefly to the aristocratic society of the south, and though he scorned neither gifts nor extended hospitality, he did not sing in order to earn his living. Minstrels and jongleurs were of humbler birth, they were versatile in their talents, especially the jongleurs, and they expected to be paid. They were very popular and were found wherever people met in large numbers. In the north minstrels were warmly welcomed in the castles, especially in the winter when the days were short and outdoor occupations were limited. These singers composed poems telling the tales of heroes and preserving early traditions, but they also made new songs which soon became popular.

On arriving in a strange place minstrels would often announce what they could do.

> I know well how to serve a knight,
> And of fine tales the whole sum;
> I know stories, I know fables,
> I can tell fine new tales.
> Songs with refrains, old and new,
> Poems satirical and pastorals.
>
> . . . .
>
> I can sing at your desire
> Of King Pepin and Saint Denis,
> Of the men of Lorraine the whole history,
> I know their meaning and have them by heart—
> Of Charlemagne and Roland
> And the fight of Oliver.
>
> I know of Ogier, I know of Aymon,
> And of Girard of Roxilion,
> And I know of King Louis
> And of Buevon de Conmarchis.
>
> . . . .

> I can give counsels of love
> And make crowns of flowerets,
> And love gifts,
> And speak well of gracious service
> To those who are in love.[1]

Minstrels travelled far and wide and from their travels they brought back both new tales, and strange and unfamiliar instruments. They played not only on the lute and harp but on the bagpipes and hurdy-gurdy, on the rebec, the psaltery and dulcimer, on the guitar and on cymbals.

The jongleur was still more versatile than the minstrel and very often he was little more than a mountebank. He was expected to sing and to play a variety of instruments, but he was also expected to do juggler's tricks, acrobatic marvels, and to imitate all kinds of animals. He was always poor and depended on the gifts made him for his livelihood and the support of his family. He did not always receive the reward he expected, but he did not hesitate to upbraid a stingy lord in whose castle he had been singing.

> Lord Count, I have fiddled
> Before you in your house,
> Yet nothing have you given me
> Nor paid my fee,
> It is shameful—
> By the faith I owe to Our Lady
> No longer will I serve you.
> My alms-purse is ill furnished,
> My pouch ill filled.
> Sir Count, pray tell me
> What you will do for me.
> Sire, if it please you,
> Grant me a good gift
>   From courtesy.

[1] Fabliau des deux bordeors.

I have great desire, do not doubt,
To return to my family.
When I go there with empty purse
My wife is not merry.
Why, she says, "Sir Needy,
In what land have you been
That you have earned nothing?
Have you disported yourself too much
About this town?"

. . . . . .

But when I come to my house
And my wife has seen
The bag well filled behind me.
And myself well garbed
In a furred robe;
Know that she throws down at once
Her needle, truthfully,
She smiles at me for kindness,
Throws two arms round my neck.

My wife goes to rifle
My bag without delay!
My serving-man to water
And care for my horse;
My servant-maid to kill
Two capons to cook
In garlic sauce;
My daughter brings me a comb
In her hand from courtesy:
Then am I king in my house,
Very joyful and without care
Beyond what I could tell you.[1]

Troubadours, minstrels and jongleurs, all these belonged to the age of feudalism and of chivalry, to the age when few men could read for themselves, and so they listened gladly to the tales told them in song. When printing had

[1] Colin Muset.

been invented and books were put into the hands of those who once had known nothing of letters, the troubadours and minstrels were no longer so necessary a part of medieval life. But the Song of Roland, the legends of King Arthur and his knights, all that was most characteristic of medieval chivalry have come down to us in the form that they were given by the poets and singers of the Middle Ages.

CHAPTER XII

THE MANOR

IN the Middle Ages land-holding was the foundation on which all social life depended. Until the towns developed, nearly all men were attached in some way or other to land; either they were the feudal overlords of great domains or they were freemen superintending the work on the domains, or they were the serfs who did the work. In medieval society the landless man was not only an exception, but he was looked upon either as some one to be pitied or as a danger to the community. An Anglo-Saxon poem describes the conditions of a man who has lost his lord:

"Thus homeless and often miserable, far from my kinsmen, I have had to bind my heart in fetters ever since the grave closed over my patron—since I wandered away destitute over the sea amid wintry gloom seeking in my grief the dwelling of some prince, if far or near I could meet with one who would have regard to me in his hall or console me in my friendlessness and treat me kindly. He who experiences it knows what a cruel companion anxiety is to one who has no kind guardians. He is confronted not with gold rings but with homeless wanderings, not with the good things of the earth but with his own chilled breast. He calls to mind the men of the court and the treasure he used to receive, and how in his youth he was continually feasted by his patron. All his happiness has passed away." [1]

The manor was the name given to the estate of a medieval lord. In their main characteristics manors were alike in

[1] From *The Wanderer*.

most parts of Europe. On the continent, however, the lords of the manors were feudal barons who usually had a number of estates in various parts of their vast domains. In England, on the contrary, the larger number of lords of the manor had only one, they lived more simply and there was less difference between them and the freemen who worked for them.

A manor was nearly always self-supporting. Grain and vegetables were grown for food, cattle were raised for the meat and milk, and sheep for wool. The men and women on the manor did all the work, built the houses, made the tools, and did the spinning and weaving. Besides the lord's house and garden the manor included a church with the priest's dwelling, a mill, pasture and woodland, fields, houses of the manor officials, and the huts of the serfs and peasants.

Medieval agriculture knew nothing of fertilizing the soil, but farmers had evolved the three field system, by which a rotation of crops was practised. Every manor had three fields that were cultivated in turn. One was used for winter planting, one for summer crops, and one always lay fallow. Each field was divided into strips and the serfs were given strips of their own in each of the different fields. In addition to these strips they had rights on the common pasture land where they were allowed to keep a certain number of cattle, sheep, pigs and poultry, and in the common woodlands where they might gather fuel.

The serf was not a freeman, he belonged to the manor and could not leave it without the consent of the lord. In theory he was secure in the possession of his hut, miserable and poor as it often was, and of his strips in the fields as long as he paid service for them, but not longer. Serfs,

PLAN OF A MANOR.

however, were seldom turned out, as the daily life and welfare of the lord and his family depended on their work. A serf had to give three days' work a week in the lord's fields, and special services and payments, generally in kind, at certain seasons. He was required to convey produce that might be sent to be sold at fairs "wherever and whenever he was bidden." He would have to use his own ox or horse to convey such produce and if he were too poor to own an animal, he would have to shoulder the load on his own back. He was obliged to have all his flour ground in the lord's mill, his bread baked in the lord's oven, and he had to pay for these services. The serf could neither marry himself, nor could his daughter be married, without the lord's consent. The serf was always poor, often he was wretched and oppressed, and at all times he had to work hard.

Now Ploughman, what work do you do?

I work very hard. I go out at dawn driving oxen a-field and yoke them to the plough. For fear of my lord I dare not stay at home even when the winter is very cold. Every day I must plough a full acre or more.

Have you any companions?

I have a boy to threaten the oxen with a goad. He is quite hoarse with the cold and shouting.

What else do you do?

I have to get hay for the oxen, water them and clean out the sheds.

Great is your labour!

Verily, it is because I am not free! [1]

[1] From Aelfric's Colloquies written about the year 1000. These were dialogues written in Anglo-Saxon and Latin in order to teach Latin to boys in the monastic schools. They describe the work not only of the ploughman, but of the shepherd, the hunter, the merchant and many other people. J. Turral, *Select Source-Book of British History*. Oxford University Press, London and New York.

Very often the serf did not have enough to eat, especially when the season was a bad one. *The Vision of Piers the Plowman* written by William Langland in the fourteenth century gives us a good deal of information about the English serf. We hear how hungry he was sometimes.

> "I've no penny," quoth Piers, "Young pullets to buy,
> Nor bacon nor geese, only two green cheeses,
> Some curds and some cream, and an oaten cake,
> Two bean-loaves with bran, just baked for my children.
> And I say, by my soul, I have no salt bacon,
> Nor eggs, by my Christendom, collops to make;
> Only onions and parsley, and cabbage-like plants;
> Eke a cow and a calf, and an old cart-mare
> To draw afield dung, while the drought shall prevail.
> By such food must we live, until Lammas-time come,
> I hope I may have then some harvest afield;
> And I'll dight thee a dinner, as dearly will please me." [1]

The conditions under which the serfs worked probably varied very little during the Middle Ages. One of the medieval Nativity Plays, the *Second Shepherd's Play* written probably very early in the fifteenth century, opens with a conversation between two shepherds who are out on a winter's night watching their sheep.

> First Shepherd:
>   Lord! what, these weathers are cold, and I am ill happed;
>   I am near hand-dold,[2] so long have I napped;
>   My legs bend and fold, my fingers are chapped,
>   It is not as I would, for I am all lapped
>   In sorrow.
>   In storms and tempest,
>   Now in the east, now in the west,
>   Woe is him that has never rest,
>   Mid day nor morrow.

[1] From the *Vision of Piers the Plowman* by William Langland.
[2] Numb of hand.

But we silly shepherds, that walk upon the moor,
In faith, we are near hands out of the door;
No wonder, as it stands, if we be poor,
For the tilth of our lands lies fallow as the floor,
We are so lamed,
So taxed and shamed,
We are made hand-tamed,
　　With these gentlery-men.
Thus they rieve us of rest, Our Lady them wary,
These men that are lord-fest; [1] they cause the plough tarry.
That men say is for the best, we find it contrary,
Thus are husbands [2] opprest, in point to miscarry,
　　In life.
Thus hold they us under,
Thus they bring us in blunder,
It were great wonder,
　　And ever should we thrive.
For may he get a paint sleeve, [3] or a brooch now on days,
Woe is he that shall grieve, or once again says,
Dare no man him reprieve, what mast'ry he has,
And yet may none believe one word that he says—
　　No letter.
He can make purveyance,
With boats and bragance, [4]
And all through maintenance,
　　Of men that are greater.
There shall come a swain, as proud as a po, [5]
He must borrow my wain, my plough also,
Then I am full fain to grant or he go.
Thus live we in pain, anger, and woe,
　　By night and day;
He must have if he longéd
If I should forgang it.
I were better be hangéd
　　Than once say him nay.

[1] Bound to a lord.
[2] Husbandmen.
[3] A painted sleeve.
[4] Bragging.
[5] Peacock.

It does me good, as I walk thus by mine own,
Of this world for to talk in manner of moan
To my sheep will I stalk and hearken anon
There abide on a balk, or sit on a stone
    Full soon.

Second Shepherd:
    "Beniste" [1] and "Dominus!" what may this bemean?
    Why fares this world thus, oft have we not seen.
    Lord, these weathers are spitous, and the weather full keen;
    And the frost so hideous they water mine een,
        No lie.
    Now in dry, now in wet,
    Now in snow, now in sleet,
    When my shoon freeze to my feet
        It is not all easy. [2]

The administration of the manor was entrusted to a
number of officials of whom the *Seneschal* and the *Bailiff*
were the most important. A thirteenth century book called
the *Seneschaucie* describes the qualifications necessary for
manor officials and gives their various duties. The Seneschal was responsible for all the manors of any one lord,
and he was required to visit them regularly; he was to be
a man of prudence and judgment, loyal to his lord whose
interests he was to protect. The Bailiff superintended the
work of the serfs, he was to "rise early every morning
and survey the woods, corn, pastures and meadows," and
the disposition of any surplus produce was in his hands.
The *Seneschaucie* describes the work of a number of other
officials including that of the ploughman and waggoner, of
whom it was to be required that they should know how to
work both oxen and horses without hurting them.

Every manor had its own court, presided over by the

---

[1] Benedicite.
[2] From the *Second Shepherd's Play*.

lord. Disputes of all kinds were settled in this court, fines and other punishments were imposed, any matters concerning the general administration of the manor could be discussed there. The well-being of a manor depended on the character of the lord, but the private wars of the feudal barons which resulted so often in pillaging and plundering, in burning houses and crops and orchards, must have brought untold misery on the serfs and peasants. But here and there one comes across a recognition that they were important and that consideration was due them. In the twelfth century we find it said:

"A lord owes greater loyalty to a tenant than to a lord or lady; very dear should we hold our men, for the villeins bear the burdens by which we live, whether we be knights, clerks, or ladies." [1]

[1] Etienne de Fougères, 1178. Joan Evans, *Mediæval France*. Oxford University Press, London and New York.

CHAPTER XIII
THE CRUSADES

1. *The Eve of the Crusades*

SYRIA has always been a land to capture the imagination. From time immemorial it has been one of the great meeting-places of the nations, and in the Middle Ages it was an important link between the east and the west. Eastward it looked towards Mesopotamia and caravan routes carried the trade of Damascus to Bagdad and from thence to Samarcand and still further east; westward it looked over the sea to Europe; to the south was the Nile and the magic and mystery that belonged to Egypt; to the north lay mountains and beyond the mountains the Black Sea and peoples little known in the early Middle Ages, but whose trade, coming down to Constantinople, was beginning to penetrate to the East.

To the south of Syria lay Palestine, the Holy Land of the Christian world, for in Palestine was Bethlehem, where Christ had been born, Nazareth where He had lived, and above all Jerusalem, where He had been crucified and buried and on the third day had risen from the dead. On the site of the Holy Sepulchre a great tomb had been built, and to go to Jerusalem was one of the great pilgrimages of the Christian world.

In the seventh century Palestine had been conquered by the Arabs. They were Mohammedans, but Jerusalem was also one of the holy places of Islam. Recognizing Jesus as one of the prophets, they reverenced the places connected with His life, and Christian pilgrims were allowed to visit them in peace. From the seventh to the ninth centuries the Mohammedans ruled Palestine well, and it seems to have been safer to travel there than in Italy. Bernard of St. Michael's Mount has given a picture of the conditions he found there:

I will tell you how Christians hold the law of God in Jerusalem and Egypt. Now the Christians and the pagans have peace one with another, in such wise that if on my journey the camel or ass that bore my little property were to die, and I were to leave all my chattels with none to guard them, while I went to another city, on my return I should find everything untouched. But if in any city or on any bridge or road (he is writing of Italy) they find a man journeying, whether by day or by night, without some charter or seal from the king or ruler of the district, he is straightway thrust into prison till he can give an account of himself whether he be a spy or not.

The people of the medieval world looked to the approach of the year 1000 with fear and trembling. The tenth century had ended in years of famine and it had been foretold that in 1000 the world would come to an end. For many people the early years of the century passed in fear and uncertainty, in 1033 a thousand years had passed since the crucifixion, and they dreaded they knew not what. But when as the years passed on, the dread grew less, Europe was swept by a wave of religious emotion, an emotion which took pilgrimages as one of its outward forms, and especially, whenever possible, a pilgrimage to Jerusalem.

At this time there began to flow towards the Holy Sepulchre so great a multitude as, ere this, no man could have hoped for.

First of all went the meaner folk, then men of middle rank, and, lastly, very many kings and counts, marquises and bishops; aye, and a thing that had never happened before, many women bent their steps in the same direction.

In the eleventh century the Seljuk Turks swept as conquerors over the east from Persia to Syria. The Eastern Emperor was afraid that Constantinople might not be strong enough to stop this victorious advance of the Mohammedan power and sent a desperate call for help to the rulers of the west.

From Jerusalem to the Aegean, he cried, the Turkish hordes have mastered all; their galleys, sweeping the Black Sea and Mediterranean, threaten the imperial city itself, which, if fall it must, had better fall into the hands of Latins than of pagans.

Added to this cry for help came the tales that the new rulers of Jerusalem were interfering with the pilgrims, treating them harshly and preventing them from reaching the Holy Sepulchre.

To meet this crisis, in a great address that he made at the Council at Clermont in 1095, the pope, Urban II, exhorted the people of western Europe to set out on a Crusade to recover the Holy Places for Christendom.

From the confines of Jerusalem and from the city of Constantinople a grievous report has gone forth and has repeatedly been brought to our ears; namely, that a race from the kingdom of the Persians, an accursed race, a race wholly alienated from God . . . has violently invaded the lands of those Christians and has depopulated them by pillage and fire. They have led away a part of the captives into their own country, and a part they have killed by cruel tortures. They have either destroyed the churches of God or appropriated them for the rites of their own religion. . . . On whom is the labour of avenging these wrongs and of recovering this territory incumbent, if not upon you,—

you, upon whom, above other nations, God has conferred remarkable glory in arms, great courage, bodily activity, and strength to humble the heads of those who resist you? Let the deeds of your ancestors encourage you and incite your minds to manly achievements;—the glory and greatness of King Charlemagne, and of his son Louis, and of your other monarchs, who have destroyed the kingdoms of the Turks and have extended the sway of the holy Church over lands previously pagan.

But if you are hindered by love of children, parents or wife, remember what the Lord says in the Gospel, "He that loveth father or mother more than me is not worthy of me." . . . Let none of your possessions retain you, nor solicitude for your family affairs. For this land which you inhabit, shut in on all sides by the seas and surrounded by the mountain peaks, is too narrow for your large population; nor does it abound in wealth; and it furnishes scarcely food enough for its cultivators. Hence it is that you murder and devour one another, that you wage war, and that very many among you perish in intestine strife.

Let hatred therefore depart from among you, let your quarrels end, let wars cease, and let all dissensions and controversies slumber. . . . Undertake this journey eagerly for the remission of your sins, with the assurance of the reward of imperishable glory in the kingdom of heaven.

When Pope Urban had said these and many similar things, all who were present cried out: It is the will of God! It is the will of God! When he heard that, with eyes uplifted to heaven, he gave thanks to God and commanding silence with his hand, said:

Let this be your war cry in combats. When an armed attack is made upon the enemy, let this one cry be raised by all the soldiers of God: It is the will of God! It is the will of God! Deus vult! Deus vult!

. . . .

Whoever shall determine upon this holy pilgrimage shall wear the sign of the cross on his breast. When, indeed, he shall return from his journey, having fulfilled his vow, let him place the cross on his back between his shoulders. Thus shall ye, indeed, fulfil the precept of the Lord, as he commands it in the Gospel,

"He that taketh not his cross, and followeth after me, is not worthy of me." [1]

There are several accounts of this great speech, and from them all we find that Urban had appealed to everybody, to the clergy and the monks, to the feudal lords, to knights and squires, to peasants. He appealed to every kind of motive that would impel men to go: to their faith and their courage, to their love of adventure and their ambition, to their love of freedom, and also to their greed and love of power and wealth. He held out promises that would induce all kinds of people to take the cross. Debts were to be cancelled, taxes were suspended whilst a man was fighting for the cross, serfs were to be set free, even prisoners might be set at liberty.

The appeal of the pope was followed by the preaching of Peter the Hermit, a native of Amiens, who in 1092 had been on a pilgrimage to Jerusalem and had himself seen the hardships of the Christians. Small and dark, full of energy, a man of intelligence, and inspiring in his appeal, Peter the Hermit travelled over the greater part of northeastern France, persuading men to fight for the holy places. The response was immediate, enthusiasm ran high, and by the spring of 1096 the First Crusade was ready.

Why were men so moved as to go on Crusades? Motives were probably very mixed. Before the first Crusade the desire to free the holy places from the infidel was a very honest and a very real one, and countless crusaders set out with no other thought in their minds. The popes probably furthered the Crusades as part of their policy of a world-wide Christian empire, and it is possible that the leaders of the Church saw in the Crusades the oppor-

[1] James Harvey Robinson, *Readings in European History*, Vol. I. Ginn and Company, Boston.

tunity to use the fighting spirit of the eleventh to the thirteenth centuries to some better account than in private warfare. They had done something to this end by the Truce of God, the Crusades gave them the opportunity to turn the fighters away from Europe. For ambitious knights and barons the Crusades offered the lure of kingdoms and lands in the east where they heard that wealth was to be had beyond anything that they knew in Europe. Italian towns, such as Venice and Genoa, seized on the Crusades as a means by which they might extend their commerce and acquire eastern products more easily and cheaply. Then there were the adventurers and the restless, those who found life dull, those who found it evil, those who at any time will seize upon anything that is new and exciting and that seems to offer them a carefree life, to such men the east spoke of wealth and luxury and endless possibilities of success. For all these different reasons, some of them good, some of them bad, some of them worldly, not a few of them single-minded, men went on Crusades. They lasted for some two hundred years, and then, the face of Europe having changed, they came to an end. The change in Europe, however, owed not a little to the Crusades themselves.

2. *The First Crusade*

IN 1096 Peter the Hermit and Walter the Penniless set out with five companies of men for the Holy Land. The enterprise was a failure. The men were neither well equipped nor well led, they were an undisciplined, disorderly host. They had enthusiasm, but little else. Three of the companies never even reached Constantinople. The other two, under Peter the Hermit and Walter the Penniless actually did arrive, and leaving Peter in Constantinople, Walter led the men across the Bosphorus into Asia Minor. But there they perished and the first expedition came to an end.

Before the year 1096 had ended another and very different expedition had started out. This Crusade was led by four great medieval knights: Godfrey de Bouillon, Raymond of Toulouse, and Bohemond and Tancred of Sicily. They went by different routes, all of them reaching Constantinople by the end of the year. The name of Godfrey de Bouillon has always stood for that of the crusader at his best. A brave and chivalrous knight, a stern and merciless warrior, he was inspired solely by the desire to fight for his faith and to free the Holy Land. Legend and song have preserved the memory of this crusader and have shown him as courteous and unselfseeking. The three other leaders were men of different character. They were jealous of each other from the beginning, and were chiefly interested in satisfying their own ambitions.

Though the emperor Alexius had implored the princes of the west to come to his aid against the approaching Turk, he was none too pleased when the crusading army, large, well led and disciplined, arrived. He suspected the good intentions of the leaders and would give them no help in furthering their march into Asia Minor until they took an oath of fealty to him, on the grounds that the lands they were setting out to conquer had once been part of his empire. There were many delays, but at length in May 1097 the crusaders arrived in Asia Minor. They besieged and captured the city of Nicæa, defeated the Turks at the battle of Dorylæum, and on October 21st, 1097, they laid siege to Antioch.

The siege lasted until June 1098, but as soon as the crusaders entered the city the Turks closed in on them and they were in turn besieged. Food was scarce, the privations were great and fear and despair took hold of the besieged. They began to see signs in the sky, superstitions were rife, and the excitement reached its height in the discovery of what was believed to be the lance that had pierced the side of the Saviour. A man named Peter Bartholomew declared that St. Andrew had appeared to him in a vision telling him where the lance was hidden and bidding him take the news to Raymond of Toulouse. He hesitated at first but finally did so. Twelve men were sent to the Church of St. Peter where the lance was said to be and began to dig. As soon as they were fatigued, others took their places until, we are told by an eye-witness

"the Lord showed us the Lance.

"And I, who have written these things, as soon as ever the blade appeared above ground, greeted it with a kiss; nor can I tell you how great joy and exultation filled the city."

The enthusiasm reinvigorated the weary men. They went out from Antioch and fought the enemy in the open.

"As we marched from the bridge towards the mountains it was a toilsome journey, for the enemy strove to hem us in. Yet though we were hard pressed, thanks to the Lord's Lance, none of us were wounded, no not so much as by an arrow. I, who speak these things, saw them for myself, since I was bearing the Lord's Lance."

Confident that they had divine help the crusaders, hungry, weakened in numbers by loss of men during the siege, gave battle to the Turks and defeated them. "These men may be slain," said the Turkish commander, "but they will not be put to flight." The enthusiasm in the Christian army was great and the men believed that heavenly help had been sent to them.

For there came out of the mountains innumerable armies on white horses, and bearing white banners. And our men seeing this host knew not who they were, till they recognized it for the promised aid of Christ. These things are worthy of belief for many of our men beheld them.

A year went by. The crusading leaders spent these months in independent expeditions, they quarrelled a good deal among themselves and sought to establish feudal principalities in the surrounding country. At length they decided to go forward to do that for which they had crossed the sea and undertaken so many hardships. They marched to Jerusalem.

It was on June 6th, 1099, that the first crusaders encamped outside the walls of the holy city and besieged it. The siege lasted a little over a month. On July 15th it surrendered and the crusaders entered triumphantly. It was a terrible sight and not a very Christian one. There was no thought of pity or compassion, no mercy for the enemy, only a ruthless hatred of the infidel and an appalling massacre.

Such a slaughter of pagan folk had never been seen or heard of; none knows their number save God alone.

Thus did the crusaders take possession of Jerusalem.

Jerusalem had been captured and it was necessary to organize some kind of government. The leaders met and decided to elect a king of Jerusalem. Their choice fell upon Godfrey de Bouillon, whose character and deeds seemed to fit him more than any one else for the honour. But Godfrey refused to be crowned as king, for he said he would not wear a crown of gold in the place where his Lord had worn a crown of thorns, and he refused, too, the title of king, preferring to be known as the "Baron of the Holy Sepulchre."

Less than a year after the capture of Jerusalem Godfrey died, and with his death the First Crusade ended. There were to be more crusades and kings were to lead them; Jerusalem was to be lost and gained and then lost once more. But never again was there a crusade quite like the first. Round no other crusade have quite so many legends gathered. In their early days all great movements inspire enthusiasm that is sometimes difficult to maintain, and the Crusades were no exception. Not even Richard Cœur de Lion or St. Louis were able to surround their crusades with the glamour that was part of the first. There were ambitions and jealousies and quarrelling during the first crusade, but these were less sordid than those of later years. There was ruthless fighting and merciless slaughter, and yet with it all there was a devotion and a unity of purpose, strange forms as these sometimes took, that did perhaps redeem the First Crusade.

3. *The Third Crusade*

GODFREY DE BOUILLON died in 1100 and was succeeded by his brother Baldwin who took the title of king of Jerusalem. This Latin kingdom of Jerusalem lasted until 1291 and in many ways its organization and power resembled the feudal domains of western Europe. Crusading lords had made Antioch, Tripoli and Edessa into feudal fiefs and had built great castles for themselves, but though the king of Jerusalem claimed the overlordship of these fiefs, their rulers were very independent and treated him more as an equal than as a superior. The kings of Jerusalem had armies, but no fleets; for sea power they depended on Venice and Genoa. These Italian cities gave their support in return for commercial concessions. They were set free from tolls in all towns captured, and they were given their own quarters where they traded and procured the many articles from the east for which there was a growing market in Europe.

In 1145 Edessa was captured by the Saracens. Preached by St. Bernard, and led by kings, Louis VII of France and Conrad III of Germany, a second Crusade set out in 1147. But it was a disaster and ended in quarrels and controversies, and for forty years no further expeditions went to Palestine. And then in 1187 a thunderbolt fell on western Europe. Jerusalem had been captured by the Saracens. For a brief space something of the spirit of the First Crusade was recaptured. The heroes of those days had passed into legend and their deeds were told again and again by poets and minstrels. The imagination was stirred, and in 1189, led by three of the greatest of the kings of Europe, the Third Crusade set out.

Jerusalem had been captured by Saladin, the Saracen ruler who had inherited Egypt from his uncle, conquered Syria and gradually extended his power until he ruled an empire that extended from Carthage to Bagdad. But Jerusalem was still in the hands of the Franks. Saladin had been well educated and had become a great warrior. He was a devout Moslem, generous and chivalrous, just and merciful. The empire he ruled was incomplete without Jerusalem, and he tried negotiating for it with the Frankish rulers. But though his terms were generous, he failed, so he besieged the city which surrendered in less than two weeks. Saladin showed the kind of conqueror he was by his treatment of Jerusalem. Order was kept throughout the city and he forbade any acts of violence or insult towards any Christian. The Christian inhabitants left the city, but were required to pay for their freedom as they left. Any who were too poor to pay were, however, allowed to go out freely.

It was against this Moslem warrior that the three great kings of Europe, Richard of England, called Cœur de Lion, Philip Augustus of France, and the Emperor Frederick Barbarossa, went forth. They were to meet at Acre.

The German crusaders marched through Hungary. The Eastern Emperor made a good many difficulties about their passage through the empire, but though reduced in numbers during their march to the east, they finally arrived in Asia Minor. Frederick was seventy years old, but forty years before he had taken part in the disastrous Second Crusade. Now it seemed almost a certainty that the Franks would win, and he hoped before he died to help in the recovery of Jerusalem. But as he was crossing a river in Asia Minor he was drowned, and only his weakened army reached Acre. Frederick Barbarossa had been a good ruler and a gallant soldier, and legends soon gathered round his name. It was said that he was not dead, but had vanished from sight for a space, and that in the hour of need he would return to save the people he had ruled.

The armies of the English and the French arrived by different routes in Sicily where they spent the winter of 1190-91. Then, again by different routes, they proceeded to Acre. Two years earlier the Frankish knights in Palestine had begun the siege of Acre, the possession of which they considered essential to the recovery of Jerusalem. Conditions in the crusaders' camp were very bad. There was sickness, fever and ague; there was a scarcity of food and men were eating horses and grass; the army of the Franks was dwindling daily, whereas that of Saladin seemed to be increasing. The leaders were quarrelling and seeking each his own interest and to fulfil his own ambitions.

Philip Augustus and the French arrived first, and as soon as they were joined by Richard and his reënforcements there was a change. The fame of Richard was known not only to the Frankish army, but to Saladin and the Saracens. A Moslem writer of the time described him as a king "of mighty strength, vast courage and firm will: great battles had he fought and daring was he in war." Richard had great military ability and was the best commander of the Third Crusade. He was gallant and fearless and had great personal strength. He could be both chivalrous and generous, savage and cruel. He was masterful and ruthless towards those who stood in his way and his very name inspired terror in the east. He was a Plantagenet, a family of whom it was said that "from the devil they came, and to the devil they would return," and he had many of the qualities that had given rise to that saying.

The fame of Saladin was equally great, in the Christian camp as well as in his own. Richard proposed a meeting, but Saladin refused, saying that kings at war with each other should not meet as friends. A treaty was made, however, and on July 12th, 1191, Acre surrendered.

The months spent by Richard and Philip Augustus in Sicily had resulted in wrangling and controversies between the two leaders and their quarrelling had spread to their followers. The hostility between them increased after their arrival at Acre, all the more so as all the military glory was given to Richard. Soon after the surrender of Acre Philip Augustus returned to France, leaving Richard to continue the Crusade. Richard remained in the Holy Land for a year after the departure of the French king, then he defeated the Saracens in a battle and began negotiations with Saladin. He wrote to Saladin:

Both Moslems and Franks are worn out; all their cities are being destroyed; lives and wealth are perishing on both sides. This matter has gone far enough. It is only a question of Jerusalem. Jerusalem we are resolved not to renounce as long as we have a single man left; and, as regards the Holy Cross, to you it is nothing but a worthless bit of wood, whereas it has great value in our eyes and the Sultan will be doing us a great favour if he restore it. Everything will then come right of itself and we shall enjoy a pleasant rest after long toils.[1]

To this appeal Saladin made answer:

To us Jerusalem is as precious, aye and more precious, than it is to you, in that it was the place whence our Prophet made his journey by night to heaven and is destined to be the gathering place of our nation at the last day. Do not dream that we shall give it up to you or that we can be so obliging in this matter. As to the land—it belonged to us originally, and it is you who are the real aggressors. When you seized it, it was only because of the suddenness of your coming and the weakness of those Moslems who then held it. So long as the war shall last God will not suffer you to raise one stone upon another. Finally as regards the Cross, its possession is very profitable to us and we should not be justified in parting with it unless to the advantage of Islam.[2]

There was more fighting and then Richard proposed peace:

My compliments to the Sultan and say that I beg him in God's name to make peace. There must be an end to all this. My coun-

[1] *The Crusade of Richard I.*
[2] *The Crusade of Richard I.*

try over the sea is in a bad way. There is no use to us or to you in going on with this.

But again the negotiations failed and a battle was fought at Jaffa. In the midst of the battle Richard's horse was killed under him, but as he fought

there came swiftly up to him a certain Turk upon a foaming steed. He had been sent by Saladin's brother, a man of a most generous character and worthy to be compared with the very best of our men, were it not that he were an unbeliever. Now this Saphadin sent two splendid Arabian steeds to the king as a token of his admiration for his valour. These steeds he earnestly prayed the king to accept and mount; for at that time he seemed to need them sorely. If (ran the message) by divine grace the king should issue from this awful peril in safety he might bear this service in mind and recompense as seemed best. These horses the king accepted and afterwards made a most splendid return for them. O virtue rare and praiseworthy though in an enemy. Thus a Turk and an enemy thought fit to honour the king because of his valour; and the king, not refusing the gift, declared that in so urgent a moment he would accept many such horses even from a fiercer foe.[1]

After the battle Richard fell ill. Messengers went back and forth between him and Saladin, and when in his fever Richard longed for fruit and cooling drink, Saladin sent him snow from the mountains and pears and peaches and other fruits.

The crusaders were now leaderless. Frederick Barbarossa was dead, Philip Augustus had returned to France, Richard of England was ill, and the Saracens still held Jerusalem. The Third Crusade which had begun with enthusiasm and high hope had been fruitless of result. The leaders had quarrelled, their own rights and privileges, their ambitions and rivalries, their national and political

[1] *The Crusade of Richard I.*

jealousies had taken the place of crusading faith and ardour. On September 2nd, 1192, Richard signed a truce with Saladin. There was to be peace for three years, Jerusalem remained in the hands of Saladin, but both Moslem and Christian pilgrims were to be allowed to visit the holy city in peace and safety.

Richard returned home. He set sail from Acre, and lamentations broke out as the royal fleet set sail.

O Jerusalem, thou art indeed helpless, now that thou art reft of such a champion. If by any chance the truce is broken, who will protect thee from thy assailants in king Richard's absence? ... Then the king, whose health was not yet fully restored, set sail with the prayers of every one. And all night long the vessel went on its course by starlight, till, as the morning broke, the king, looking back with pious eyes upon the land behind him, after long meditation broke out into prayer: "O Holy Land, to God do I entrust thee. May He, of His mercy, only grant me such space of life that, by His good will, I may bring thee aid. For it is my hope and intention to aid thee at some future time." And with this prayer, he urged his sailors to display full sail so that they might make a speedier course.[1]

On his way back to England, Richard was shipwrecked in the Adriatic and he was forced to make the rest of his way home by land. In Austria he was captured and imprisoned in a high castle. The tale is told that the place of the king's imprisonment was discovered through the singing of Blondel, his favourite minstrel. After the payment of an enormous ransom Richard was set free. In his absence his brother John had been intriguing against him and making friends with Philip Augustus. "Beware," wrote the French king to John, on hearing that Richard was free, "the devil is loose again."

[1] *The Crusade of Richard I.*

4. *The Military Orders*

In order to protect pilgrims on their way to Jerusalem, there were founded Military Orders, the members of which were bound by the obligations of both monk and knight. They took the monastic vows of poverty, chastity and obedience, but unlike monks they bore arms and were pledged to succour the pilgrim in danger or distress of any kind. The most important of these orders were those known as the Hospitallers and the Templars.

The order of the Knights Hospitaller of St. John of Jerusalem was founded in 1113. The order maintained a hospital for sick pilgrims, it was pledged to charitable works of various kinds and the members were bound to defend Jerusalem with the sword if necessary. Over their armour they wore a tunic on which was embroidered a Maltese Cross. The Knights Hospitaller kept to their vows, and though entirely re-constituted, the order is still in existence.

The order of the Templars was founded in 1118 by a young Burgundian knight. At first there were only eight knights, bound like himself, to defend pilgrims on their way to Jerusalem. They were given a house near the site of Solomon's Temple from which came their name. Ten years later the order had grown, a rule was drawn up for it and the order was authorized. The original rule was very austere. A Templar was pledged not only to the monastic vows, but to a life of warfare against the infidel till death. He might never refuse to fight, even if he were only one against several, he might never give ransom, he might never ask for quarter. Over his armour a Templar wore a white cloak on which was a red cross.

Unlike the Hospitallers the Templars failed to keep

strictly to their vows. The order acquired vast estates, and in 1162 they were freed from any kind of jurisdiction except that of the Grand Master of the Order and of the Pope. As the crusading period drew to an end and the needs for which the order had been founded were no longer there, the Templars grew lax, and they forgot the purpose for which they had taken their vows. The wealth of their estates made them luxurious, they demanded privileges and grew so insolent and arrogant that in the fourteenth century the order was dissolved.

5. *The Later Crusades*

THE Crusades did not come to an end with the truce made between Richard I and Saladin. Ten years later Innocent III encouraged a fourth expedition. Doomed like the second to be a failure, the Fourth Crusade was even a worse failure, for the Crusaders, getting as far as Constantinople, made no attempt to reach the Holy Land. The western knights had always had a grudge against Constantinople, partly because of the homage the emperors demanded of their leaders, partly because of the difficulties put in their way as they marched through the empire. There were also old trade rivalries and jealousies between Constantinople and Venice whose fleets had maintained the sea power of the crusaders. In 1204 the arrival of the Frankish armies before Constantinople resulted in an attack on the city which the Crusaders captured and sacked. Fire destroyed part of the city and from end to end the rest was plundered. The churches and palaces were robbed and stripped of everything that was of value. The Fourth Crusade had turned into a plundering raid.

In the year 1212 two strange and pathetic expeditions,

known as the Children's Crusade set out. Two boys, Stephen, a French shepherd lad, and Nicolas, a young German, gathered hosts of children bidding them follow them to the Holy Land, not to fight, but to convert the infidel. The German children perished by the way. Stephen got as far as Marseilles, where he and as many of the children as had survived the hardships of the journey were kidnapped by slave-dealers, who shipped them to Egypt and sold them into slavery. Nothing was left of the childish hosts but a pathetic memory. But Innocent III, still determined to encourage a Crusade, used these childish efforts as a spur: "The very children," he said, "put us to shame. While we sleep they go forth gladly to conquer the Holy Land." The result was a Fifth Crusade, but the emperor who had promised to take the cross in person, failed to go and an eight year treaty was made with the Saracens.

The Emperor was Frederick II, called by the chronicler the "Wonder of the world." He was a great and gifted ruler, he spoke many languages, he loved art and was himself a poet. He had promised to lead a crusade, yet he scoffed at holy things and made delays and excuses. When in 1227 he finally did set out, he fell ill and refused to go on, whereupon the Pope excommunicated him. Then the next year he started, an excommunicated king leading a crusade!

There was no fighting. In 1229 by means of skilful diplomacy Frederick made a treaty with the Sultan of Egypt by which a ten years' peace was made, and Jerusalem, Bethlehem and Nazareth were given to the Christians. Once again the Holy City was to be ruled by a Christian king. But the spirit of 1229 was as different from that of 1099 as Godfrey de Bouillon was different from

Frederick II. Godfrey had refused to wear a crown of gold in the place where his Saviour had worn a crown of thorns, Frederick II was not only king of Jerusalem, but he was an excommunicated king and he took his own crown from off the altar and crowned himself. Fifteen years later Jerusalem was lost again. Not until more than six hundred years had passed did a Christian conqueror again enter the Holy City. The last of the crusaders was General Allenby who entered Jerusalem in 1917.

Only one other important crusade took place after 1244 and that was led by St. Louis of France. He started in 1248 with a gallant company amongst whom was the Sieur de Joinville, his biographer. A voyage by sea was always an adventure in those days. Joinville tells us that when both men and horses had embarked,

the master mariner called to his seamen, who stood at the prow, and said: "Are you ready?" and they answered, "Aye, sir—let the clerks and priests come forward!" As soon as these had come forward, he called to them, "Sing, for God's sake!" and they all, with one voice, chanted: *"Veni Creator Spiritus."*

Then he cried to his seamen, "Unfurl the sails, for God's sake!" and they did so.

In a short space the wind filled our sails and had borne us out of sight of land, so that we saw naught save sky and water, and every day the wind carried us further from the land where we were born. And these things I tell you, that you may understand how foolhardy is that man who dares, having other's chattels in his possession, or being in mortal sin, to place himself in such peril, seeing that, when you lie down to sleep at night on shipboard, you lie down not knowing whether, in the morning, you may find yourself at the bottom of the sea.[1]

St. Louis made two expeditions. On the first he was taken prisoner and ransomed, then he spent four years in

[1] Joinville's *Chronicle of the Crusade of St. Louis.*

the Holy Land, but never retook Jerusalem. When his mother, who was acting as Regent in France, died, he returned home, but sixteen years later he took the cross for the second time. He went first to Tunis, but he was taken ill there and died. Prince Edward of England had followed the example of St. Louis and had gone to Acre, but there were no results and he, too, went back home. Twenty years later the last of the Franks left Syria.

For two hundred years the crusaders had come and gone; kings and princes, barons and knights had led them. They had gone forth with enthusiasm and faith, they had taken Jerusalem, they had built castles in which they had entrenched themselves and defied the infidel. Now, as the thirteenth century drew to its close all that seemed left were tales and legends of their prowess and the ruins of their castles, which showed how strong were the men who once had ruled there. Was that all?

6. *The Results of the Crusades*

THE end of the Crusades did not come with violence. No great catastrophe drove the Christians out of Syria. The Crusades ceased, that was all. And they ceased for a number of reasons. As Godfrey de Bouillon was different from Frederick II, so was the Europe of 1100 different from that of 1300. The east was less of a novelty, new interests had arisen in Europe, many of them, it is true, the result of the Crusades. The kings of England and France were more concerned with administrative affairs in their own countries than with a Holy War across the sea, especially as in the end those Holy Wars had seemed unsuccessful. But though they failed in their original purpose and Jerusalem remained in Moslem hands, the Crusades had influenced almost every aspect of medieval life.

Venice and Genoa had been the cities through which the products of the east had reached Europe. Owing to the privileges given them in Constantinople and Acre, in Jaffa and Tyre, they had extended their trade and the fruits and spices, drugs and dyes, gems and silks and brocades, all the many luxuries of the east were brought more easily into Europe. They were taken from Venice to the north, to Bruges and to Antwerp whence they were again distributed through Flanders and across the sea to England. The towns along the trade routes helped in the distribution of this commerce and grew in importance. All over Europe towns were growing more powerful during the crusading period. In return for money their overlords had given them charters which secured their independence, and the thirteenth century saw the development of town life and the growth in importance of the Third Estate.

The Crusades brought the west into contact with the east. Men saw for the first time a civilization that was in many ways new to them and a religion that was alien. They crossed the sea, the imagination was quickened by the adventures of travel, and the knowledge of geography and of Arabic science and mathematics increased and influenced the west. In these new experiences poetry found new springs and the medieval mind was broadened and quickened.

The Crusades often degenerated into sordid quarrels amongst the crusaders themselves, they served as excuses for political aims and ambitions, too often they fell far short of the purpose for which they started. But in the beginning they were wars for an idea and at some time or other every Crusader came in some way under the spell of the idea for which they were fighting. The Crusades were a united effort of western Christendom, and in spite of all their failure and weakness, the intolerance and pride of race they too often developed, at their best they inspired idealism, sacrifice and chivalry.

CHAPTER XIV

THE TOWNS

1. *The Origin of Medieval Towns*

BEFORE the eleventh century life in most parts of Europe centred round the castle and the manor and in most countries knights and serfs played a more important part in daily life than merchants or craftsmen. The manor was self-sufficing, but what it produced was limited in kind and in many parts of Europe needs were developing which the immediate neighbourhood could not satisfy. Cold winters created a demand for warmer clothing and hangings to keep out the draughts. Knights began to demand more finely wrought armour and weapons. Ships were needed for crusaders and suitable timber did not grow everywhere. The period of the Crusades made the fruits and spices, dyes and perfumes, silks and jewels of the east better known to Europe. The Italian towns through which these articles passed on their way to central and northern Europe made glass and metal-work, and the demand for these articles increased in those more northern countries in which life had been cruder and more primitive during the earlier Middle Ages.

It was to further the exchange of all this commerce that towns began to grow up. From the eleventh century onwards they began to grow both in size and importance. Sometimes they were a development from the old manorial village; sometimes a great lord, seeing the possibilities of a town, founded one on his land; sometimes they grew up on the site of an old Roman town because of its good situation either on a river, or for easy communication with the neighbouring country; sometimes they grew up round some centre, this was especially true of monasteries, churches or shrines which attracted large numbers of people. The early towns were nearly always under the control of some overlord, either of the king, or of a baron, or of the Church, and the relations between such overlords and the towns was a feudal one. Just as the lord owed military service to the king, and the serf agricultural service to the lord, so did the towns owe feudal services in the form of taxes and tolls to be paid as well as agricultural services in connection with the surrounding land outside the walls. The towns were generally under the jurisdiction of the feudal courts and their affairs were regulated by feudal officials, by sheriffs and bailiffs appointed by their overlords.

The history of the towns from the twelfth century onwards is the story of how they won their independence. Each town has its own history, but the three things for which all towns struggled and which they finally obtained were freedom from paying feudal dues whether in money or services, freedom to carry on trade without any interference from any one outside the town, and freedom to govern themselves.

By degrees the towns of the Middle Ages won exemption from all these burdens and their rights and privileges were made sure in charters, generally given under the royal seal. These charters were obtained in various ways. Kings and lords often granted them to the towns in return for money they needed for the Crusades. In times of war, especially of feudal war between barons, both sides gave privileges to towns in return for their support, not only in money but in supplies of all kinds.

Charters usually conceded to towns the right to preserve all their ancient customs. These were usages and traditions which had been handed down and which the townspeople recognized as having the force of law. A great many tolls and taxes were done away with, and those that were kept might be paid in one lump sum. Most important of all, charters gave to the townspeople the right to elect their own officials, to have their own courts where local suits and trials could be heard, and the right to control their own trade. In Germany and Flanders many of the towns were completely self-governing and independent of any royal authority. In England, where the central government was stronger, though they managed their own local affairs, the towns still owed allegiance to the king.

A medieval town was walled and entered by gates that were shut at nightfall and not opened again till sunrise. The streets were narrow and the houses high. It was not until the later Middle Ages that the great merchants began to build spacious and lordly houses for themselves, like that built by Jacques Cœur at Bourges in the fifteenth century. In the centre of the town was usually a large market square, round which were built the town buildings: the town hall, often with its tower and belfry, the halls of the various gilds, and the great church of the town. In England a large number of the cathedrals were monastic churches, but on the continent, in France especially, the cathedrals were the churches built by the townspeople.

2. *The Gild Merchant*

GILDS were associations which grew up in the towns during the Middle Ages for the protection and regulation of trade. The Gild Merchant was the association which regulated all the trade in general in any one town. It aimed at keeping a monopoly of trade and it was concerned with its own interests rather than with the development of the trade and commerce of the country as a whole.

Most gilds were organized under the rule of an alderman of the town and two stewards, assisted by a council. They drew up the regulations for the members. No townsman not a member of the Gild Merchant might buy or sell in the town except under conditions laid down by the gild. Foreigners from other countries as well as traders from other towns were forbidden to buy or sell in any way that might interfere with the interests of the townsmen, and they had to pay all the tolls and taxes from which townsmen might be exempt. By a townsman the Gild Merchant meant a man who owned a house or land within the town limits.

The general business of the gild was transacted at meetings held three or four times a year. In England the meeting was called the *"Morning Speech."* The members of the gild paid certain fees, held feasts, and observed certain festivals at which they attended Mass together at the same church. The Gild Merchant always had a special hall for its meetings and in many places the Gild Hall became later the Town Hall.

Besides the business connected with the regulation of trade, the Gild Merchant undertook certain duties and obligations towards its members. The following duties of the Gild Merchant at Southampton are typical of most gilds in the Middle Ages:

If a gildsman is ill and is in the city, wine shall be sent to him, two loaves of bread and a gallon of wine and a dish from the kitchen; and two approved men of the gild shall go to visit him and look after his condition.

And when a gildsman dies, all those who are of the gild and are in the city shall attend the service of the dead, and gildsmen shall bear the body and bring it to the place of burial.

And if a gildsman shall be imprisoned in England in time of peace, the alderman with the steward shall go at the cost of the gild, to procure the deliverance of the one who is in prison.

If any gildsman falls into poverty and has not the wherewithal to live, and is not able to work or to provide for himself, he shall have one mark from the gild to relieve his condition when the gild shall sit.

Provision was made for the election of the officers of both town and gild and for the safeguarding of all charters and treasure:

The common chest shall be in the house of the chief alderman or of the steward, and the three keys of it shall be lodged with three discreet men . . . who shall loyally take care of the common seal, and the charters and treasure of the town, and the standards and other muniments of the town; and no letter shall be sealed with the common seal, nor any charter taken out of the common chest, but in presence of six or twelve sworn men, and of the alderman or steward; and nobody shall sell by any kind of measure or weight that is not sealed, under forfeiture of two shillings.

The medieval merchant was, as a rule, a generous, practical and wealthy man. He was liberal with his money in founding institutions and in building churches. He was a good citizen with a strong feeling towards the civic duties required of him. This was especially true of the great

Flemish burghers. After the thirteenth century the burgher began to take a recognized and dignified place in the social and political life of the time, and in England after 1295, the year of the Model Parliament, representatives from the towns sat in Parliament side by side with knights from the shires.

3. *The Craft Gilds*

THE Gild Merchant was concerned with the trade of the whole town, by degrees its place in importance was taken by the Craft Gilds. These craft gilds were formed to regulate the trade of particular crafts. Spinners and weavers, tailors and furriers, bakers and brewers, silversmiths and goldsmiths, every craft represented in the town had its own gild. In the fifteenth century the city of York had as many as sixty craft gilds.

The earliest craft gilds were formed in order that there should be some control exercised over the actual work produced; it was required that before a man could engage in a trade he must prove his ability to do so. They were also concerned with both wages and prices and their effort was directed towards a system that would be fair to both the consumer and producer.

The most characteristic feature of the craft gild was its system of apprenticeship. This varied in different places, but the purpose was the same. In return for certain specified obligations a master was required to give bed and board and a training in his craft to his apprentices. Sometimes he was also required to educate them in other ways and to teach them reading and writing. Sometimes he had to provide a certain amount of clothing, in some places even a small salary. The master was responsible for the behaviour of his apprentices and he cared for them if they were ill. Above all, the apprentice was to be taught his craft. The length of apprenticeship varied; it might be anything from four to seven years, but seven years was the most common. In the sixteenth century it was stated that a craftsman could not be expected to have mastered his craft until he was at least twenty-three years old, and most apprentices reached that age before their term was over.

At the end of his apprenticeship a young man became a journeyman. On the continent he seems to have set out on a period of wandering and to have worked for masters in various places before qualifying himself as a master. In England he travelled less, but he was a wage-earner and not tied down to any one place. As a matter of fact, in many cases a journeyman served the same master under whom he had been trained as an apprentice.

The final stage in the training of a craftsman was when he was permitted to set up himself as a master of his craft. Here again, different crafts and different places and periods had different requirements, but in some form or other a journeyman had to give evidence as to his skill and ability. Sometimes he was required to produce a specimen of his work; sometimes he had to pass some kind of examination by the masters of the gild he wished to enter; sometimes he was examined as to whether he was not only a good workman, but as to whether he was likely to become a good citizen.

The craft gild touched every side of medieval life. It was first of all an organization for the regulation of trade and industry, but in a study of the rules laid down by the various craft gilds and of the customs in connection with them, the life of the Middle Ages stands out in its community and corporate aspect. The Middle Ages regarded religion and education, industry and art, the business of the community and the craft gilds touched most of these.

The rules of the craft gild were very strict about the quality of the materials used in industry, and the penalties for bad or slovenly workmanship were severe. As a rule night work was prohibited,

by reason that no man can work so neatly by night as by day. And many persons, who compass how to practise deception in their work, desire to work by night rather than by day; and then they introduce false iron, and iron that has been cracked, for tin, and also they put on false copper, and cracked. . . .

By reason thereof it seems that working by night should be put an end to, in order to avoid such false work, and therefore the mayor and the aldermen do will, by the assent of the good folk of the said trade and for the common profit, that from henceforth such time for working shall be forbidden.[1]

Fines were to be laid on those who violated the ruling. No work was allowed on Saturday afternoons, Sundays or other holy days.

Craft gilds had their definitely religious characteristics. Nearly every gild had its own patron saint and kept a light burning before that saint's altar in the church. The White Tawyers (a certain kind of leather worker) of London

ordained that they will furnish a wax candle, to burn before our Lady, in the Church of All-hallows, near London wall.

Each year the festival of the patron saint was observed by the gild. The members attended Mass in the chapel dedicated to that saint and which was very often supported by the gild. They wore their own livery. When the Haberdasher and the Carpenter, the Weaver, and the Dyer, and

[1] From Articles of the Spurriers, London 1345.

the Upholsterer started on their pilgrimage to Canterbury, Chaucer tells us how

> . . . they were clothed alle in o liveree,
> Of a solempne and greet fraternitee.
> Ful fresh and newe hir gere apyked was;
> Hir knyves were y-chaped noght with bras,
> But al with silver wroght ful clene and weel,
> Wel semed ech of hem a fair burgeys,
> To sitten in a yeldhalle on a deys.
> Everich, for the wisdom that he can,
> Was shaply for to been an alderman.[1]

The social side of the craft gild was similar to that of
the Gild Merchant. Members were under an obligation to
give assistance to fellow members who were in need or to
their widows and orphans and to see that proper provision
was made, if necessary, for funerals.

Also, if by chance any one of the said trade shall fall into
poverty, whether through old age or because he cannot labour or
work, and have nothing with which to keep himself, he shall
have every week from the said box (a box belonging to the gild
in the church) sevenpence for his support, if he be a man of
good repute. And after his decease, if he have a wife, a woman
of good repute, she shall have weekly for her support sevenpence
from the said box, so long as she shall behave herself well and
keep single.

And if any one of the said trade shall have work in his house
that he cannot complete, or if for want of assistance such work
shall be in danger of being lost, those of the said trade shall aid
him, that so the said work be not lost.

And if any one of the said trade shall depart this life, and
have not wherewithal to be buried, he shall be buried at the expense of the common box. And when any one of the said trade

[1] Chaucer, Prologue to *Canterbury Tales*. Oxford University Press,
London and New York.

shall die, all those of the said trade shall go to the vigil, and make offering on the morrow.[1]

The craft gild was an essential part of the life of the medieval town, for it was concerned not only with the teaching of the craft itself, but with the developing of good citizens. Comparisons have been made sometimes between the medieval craft gild and the modern trade union. Both associations were concerned with industry and with the standards of living, but the trade union is an association of workers in the same industry all over a country, whereas the members of a craft gild were the workers in one town and each industry had its own gild in each town. The trade union is an organization of workers only, and is concerned with their economic well-being and not with the quality of their work; the craft gild, on the other hand, included employers, the masters, as well as men; it took notice of the standard of the work produced; and it was concerned also in safeguarding the interests of the consumer. There were dangers, however, in the craft gild of the Middle Ages. The monopoly of a craft in the hands of one gild did not always allow for the introduction of new ideas that might have been brought by alien workers. The result was often an intolerance towards craftsmen who were not members of that particular gild.

The craft gilds belonged to a period when all work was done by hand. Their decline came at a later period and for a variety of reasons. They have, however, given to the world of today ideals, not only of good workmanship, based on a thorough knowledge of the craft, but also of a recognition of the duties and obligations owed to each other by both producer and consumer.

[1] *Ordinances of the White Tawyers.*

4. *The Medieval Drama*

THE medieval drama is closely bound up with the craft gild, especially in England, for by the fourteenth century the craft gilds had become responsible for the Mystery Plays that were given regularly in most English towns. These plays were given originally in churches, first at Christmas and Easter, and then at other festivals. They were plays that represented in dramatic form the Nativity and the Passion of Christ and other subjects taken from the Bible. As long as they were performed in the church, the clergy, the choristers and the clerks were the chief performers.

These dramatic representations of the Bible were called Mystery Plays and at first they were very simple. But they became very popular and from the simple dramatizing of the words of the Bible, there gradually developed a real religious drama. Plays were grouped together in such a way as to give a complete religious story, and they were presented in Cycles at the great festivals.

As time went on, instead of giving them inside the church, these plays were performed outside in the church-yard, so that more people could see them. Then, because people thronged to them in great numbers, still larger and more convenient places were chosen. As the places in which these plays were given were unconnected with the church, the clergy gradually ceased taking part, and in time, though the plays remained religious in subject and were performed at the great religious festivals, they were produced entirely by the laity.

The place of the clergy in producing the Mystery Plays was taken by the craft gilds. In the Middle Ages there must have been a great many Cycles performed each year in different places, but today we know only four. These are not complete, but the York, Chester, Wakefield (or Towneley) and Coventry plays give us a good idea of what the Cycles must once have been.

When the plays were presented in the churchyard a temporary stage, a "scaffold hye," was built and the plays were given only in one place. A walled town, however, did not have many wide open spaces where very large numbers of people could congregate, so when the churchyard could no longer accommodate the spectators, the custom arose of giving the plays in a number of different places called stations. To do this portable stages were built and placed on wheels. These stages were called pageants, and they consisted of two parts, an upper part, on which the action took place, and a lower, hidden to view by curtains, in which the actors dressed and waited their turn to appear.

Each craft gild in a town had charge of one scene in the cycle of plays, it had its own stage and performers. The stations where the plays were to be given were appointed and then each gild arrived in turn, performed its scene, and moved on to the next station. During the performance of a cycle of plays, it must have seemed as if a great pageant were passing through the town, for the processions went from station to station with pomp and ceremony, with music and singing. Some scenes were so elaborate and costly that several gilds joined together to produce them. The most popular festival for these plays was that of Corpus Christi, a feast of the early summer when the days were long and the weather often radiant.

The medieval Mystery Plays are important in the history of the English drama, but they are also important in the history of the life of the town. The study of how they were produced is a study of one side of the work of the craft gilds, and the plays themselves carry us back to the daily toil and cares, the wit and humour, the joys and sorrows of the medieval town. The stories may be taken from the Bible, but the setting is of the Middle Ages.

CHAPTER XV

MEDIEVAL TRADE AND COMMERCE

FROM very ancient times commerce has been regarded as one of the great occupations in the world. The Hebrew prophet described the merchants who were engaged in it as "princes and its traffickers the honourable of the earth."[1] Primitive commerce arose as soon as groups of people began to exchange their products. As civilization has advanced, so have the needs of people increased, until today many of the necessities of life come from afar.

As far as the daily needs of life were concerned, the medieval manor was self-sufficing, but from quite early times in medieval Europe merchants were to be met travelling from place to place. They brought with them wares from distant places, luxuries unknown to castle or manor, for which there soon grew a demand.

Their trading was often hindered by the endless tolls they were required to pay as they went through the lands of feudal barons, and as they went from their own country into foreign lands they were often in need of protection. In the time of Charlemagne English merchants were met with in the empire, and in 796 the emperor wrote a letter concerning them to Offa, King of Mercia.

Concerning the pilgrims who for the love of God and the salvation of their souls desire to visit the precincts of the Apostles, we have granted as of old that they may journey in peace, free

[1] Isaiah XXIII, 6.

from all disturbance, taking with them what they need. But we have discovered in their midst traders who pass themselves off as pilgrims, pursuing gain and not serving religion; if these are found among them, they must pay the fixed tolls in the regular places. You have also written to us about your merchants. We would have them enjoy our protection and defence within our realm as we have ordained, according to the ancient custom in commerce, and if in any place they are distressed by unjust oppression let them appeal to us or our judges, and we will order justice to be done to them. Show like favour to our merchants, and if they suffer wrong within your realm let them appeal to your justice, so that disturbance may nowhere arise between us.

That English merchants were engaged in foreign trade in the tenth century is shown by an old Saxon dialogue:

I am useful to the king and to the lords, to the rich, and to everybody. I go aboard my ship with my goods, and sail to distant lands, to sell them. I buy precious things which are not found in this country, and I bring them back to you with much danger across the sea; and sometimes I am shipwrecked, with the loss of all my goods, and at the peril of my life.

What do you bring back?

I bring back purple and silk, precious stones and gold, and many garments and scents, wine and oil, ivory, latten and brass and tin, sulphur and glass, and things of that sort.

Will you sell your things here as you bought them there?

I will not, what would my labour profit me? I will sell them here, dearer than I bought them there, that I may get some profit to feed me, my wife and children.[1]

All through the Middle Ages travelling merchants and pedlars carried their wares on foot from place to place, but after the eleventh century there had developed three important ways by which trading was carried on: at markets and fairs, by the commercial league known as the Hansa, and by the great Italian trading cities.

[1] See p. 174 note.

1. *Markets and Fairs*

Most large manors produced more than was necessary for the manor itself, and the surplus produce was usually sent to the nearest market or fair to be disposed of. Markets were held in the open market square of towns. As a rule they were held every week, and it was to these that most manors sent their surplus produce. At a market could generally be found all that the surrounding country supplied in the way of food, and at early markets not much else was sold. It was at the great fairs that other things besides food and farm produce in general were bought. Castles and monasteries needed many things that had to be bought, and supplies for such communities for a whole year were often obtained at the yearly fair.

The word fair comes from the Latin *feria,* a holiday, and in the Middle Ages most of the important fairs were held on Saints' Days. The earliest fairs lasted for three days: the eve of the feast day, the day itself, and the day after. Later, a fair lasted longer. At Winchester it lasted for sixteen days, and the Stourbridge Fair in Cambridge, one of the most famous of the English medieval fairs, went on for three weeks.

The places chosen for fairs were those which would most easily attract large numbers of people. Often they were places of pilgrimage, or centres to which people could easily come from many districts, or places through which travellers often passed.

Before a fair could take place a charter had to be obtained from the lord or bishop on whose land it was to be held. The oldest of such charters still in existence is that of the fair of St. Denis in Paris, which was granted by King Dagobert in 642. In these charters were certain regulations that had to be observed within the fair itself, and certain privileges for those attending them. At Frankfurt, for example, for eighteen days before and for eighteen days after, merchants going to and from the fair were exempt from imperial taxation and from arrest for debt. The organizers of a fair were required to see that everything was sold according to a just weight and measurement. As a rule no two fairs might be set up within seven miles of each other. Sometimes the regulations were a hardship for neighbouring towns. During the fair of St. Giles, near Winchester, all shops in both Winchester and Southampton had to be closed. This fair of St. Giles went back to the eleventh century. William I had given a charter permitting it to be held to the Bishop of Winchester, to whom it was a source of considerable revenue. By the charter the bishop was allowed to take tolls from all goods that passed through the city of Winchester to the fair, and on St. Giles's Eve the chief burghers of Winchester were required to hand over the keys of the city to the bishop, who appointed his own officials to keep order in the city until the fair was over.

In towns, members of one craft gild tended to live and carry on their trade in the same street, or if the town were large, in the same neighbourhood. The larger fairs were arranged on the same plan. Instead of shops there were booths and the goods to be sold were displayed where every one could see them. Robbery from booths was very severely punished, but it seems to have been a frequent offence.

Nearly every charter granted for the holding of a fair contains some reference to the regulation that everything shall be sold according to just weight and measurement. Yet we read in *Piers Plowman:*

I've been covetous. . . . I confess it here;
For some time I served old Sim-at-the-Stile,
And was plighted his 'prentice, his profit to serve.
First learned I, in lying, a lesson or twain;
Wickedly to weigh was my first lesson;
To Weyhill and Winchester I went to the fair
With all manner of wares, as my master bade;
If Guile had not given some grace to my ware,
It had still been unsold, were it seven years since!

Then I drew me to drapers, my duties to learn,
To stretch out the stuff, till it looked the longer.
One lesson I learned as to long striped cloths;
To pierce them with a needle, and piece them together,
Put them in a press, and press thereunder
Till ten yards or twelve were turned to thirteen! [1]

A great medieval fair must have been a wonderful
sight. In addition to local produce, which perhaps did not
differ very much in many parts of northern Europe where
the greater fairs were held, there were articles from almost every part of the medieval world. Flemish weavers
brought linen, Italian merchants silks and velvet as well
as their eastern produce, their spices and perfumes, dyes
and drugs. From the south of France came merchants with
their wines, Spaniards brought armour and weapons, and
from the north came Hansa merchants with furs and
amber. Much of the trade in the earlier Middle Ages was
carried on by barter, but when money became more common it was the medium of exchange most often used, and
at every fair there would be found Jewish and Lombard
money-changers carrying on a brisk trade in the exchange
of money.

Trade within the towns was very rigidly controlled and

[1] From *The Vision of Piers the Plowman*, by William Langland.

regulated in the interests of the townspeople, but the fair welcomed merchants and traders from foreign lands. Safe passage through England was assured to foreign merchants in Magna Carta.

All merchants shall have safe and secure exit from England, and entry to England, with the right to tarry there and to move about as well by land as by water, for buying and selling by the ancient and right custom, quit from all evil tolls except (in time of war) such merchants as are of the land at war with us. And if any such are found in our land at the beginning of the war, they shall be detained, without injury to their body or their goods, until information be received by us, or by our chief justiciar, how the merchants of our land found in the land at war with us are treated; and if our men are safe there, the others shall be safe in our land.[1]

A fair brought together men from different parts of a country and from different lands. In days of slow and difficult travel, the yearly fair must have afforded to many people of the towns and manors opportunities to learn more not only of their own world that lay about them, but of lands and countries that were far beyond their borders.

2. *The Hansa*

THE Hansa or Hanseatic League was a trading confederacy formed during the twelfth and thirteenth centuries by the northern German trading towns as a protection against the difficulties and dangers which interfered with and hindered their trade. At sea there were the ships of the Norsemen, a constant menace to those who sailed the Northern seas. There was also the old custom of *Strand-*

[1] Article 41. James Harvey Robinson, *Readings in European History*, Vol. I. Ginn and Company, Boston.

gut, a custom which allowed all goods washed up on the shore to become the property of the owner of the land, and not a few landowners followed the trade of wrecking. On the land were endless dangers on the roads where neither life nor property was safe from robber barons. Early in the thirteenth century separate towns began to make agreements for mutual aid and protection. In 1253 four north German towns made such an alliance.

The magistrates, consuls, and the whole community of burghers and citizens in Munster, Dortmund, Soest, and Lippstadt, to all who may read this document, greeting:

We hereby make known to all men, now and in the future, that because of the manifold dangers to which we are constantly exposed, of capture, robbery, and many other injuries, we have, by common counsel and consent, decided to unite in a perpetual confederation under the following terms, and we have mutually given and received word and oath:

First, that if any man shall take captive one of our citizens, seize his goods without just cause, we will altogether deny to him opportunity to trade in all our cities aforesaid. And if the castellan of any lord shall be the author of an injury that has been done, the afore-mentioned privileges shall be altogether withheld from the lord of that castellan, and from all his soldiers and servants, and all others dwelling with him in his castle. . . .

If any robber has taken goods from one of our citizens . . . and the injured man shall go to any one of our cities seeking counsel and aid, in order that justice may be done upon the malefactor, the citizens of that city shall act as they would be obliged to act if executing justice for a similar crime against one of their own fellow-citizens.

And if any of our burgesses shall chance to go to any of our cities and fear to go forth because of peril to life and property, the burgesses of that city shall conduct him to a place whence his fellow-citizens can receive him in safety. . . .

If any one of us shall buy goods taken from any of our confederates by theft or robbery . . . he shall not offer the goods at retail anywhere and shall be held guilty with the thief and robber.[1]

By degrees these alliances spread until by the thirteenth century they had developed into the great confederacy of the Hansa. This league included all the important German and Flemish towns and a very large number of smaller ones. Lübeck, Hamburg and Bremen were the most important cities, and Lübeck was the capital. Every year an assembly or Diet of the league was held, and representatives from all the Hansa cities attended. The business of the assembly was to admit new members, to determine trading policies, to settle disputes, and sometimes to expel cities from the league, or to un-Hanse them as it was called. To be un-Hansed was a very serious thing. It was done to any city that had violated any of the Hansa laws; there are records which show that sometimes cities were un-Hansed for selling goods below the standard required of Hansa merchandise, and a city would be un-Hansed if it repeatedly failed to send a representative to the Diet.

Hansa merchants travelled all over Europe, and in most of the foreign cities they established factories. These were settlements where they could live securely, which were good centres for trade, and where it was possible for the trading methods to be supervised, so that they might conform to Hanseatic methods of conducting business. One of the best known of these factories was the Steelyard in London.

In the Middle Ages the most important trade of Flanders was the wool trade. Flemish weavers were famous for the finely woven materials they produced, and through the Hansa much of this went all over Europe.

[1] James Harvey Robinson, *Readings in European History*, Vol. I. Ginn and Company, Boston.

The chief Flemish trading towns were Antwerp, Ghent and Bruges, Ypres and Arras.

The Hansa had its own fleet, and a Hansa captain had strict rules laid down for him on every subject that could possibly concern a ship, from instructions as to the delivery of his merchandise, the care of sick sailors, the aid he should give to other vessels in distress, down to what is to be done to "goods damaged by rats, when there was no cat on board."

Some of the sea laws of the Hansa were:

If a Captain be safe in any port and sees that another Captain cannot, on account of distress, make port, the Captain already in port has the right, if he so think fit, to order his sailors to aid the one in distress to enter harbour. If a sailor shall refuse he is to be deprived of his pay, put ashore, and from thenceforth no other Hansa ship shall hire him.

The Master must take the advice of the majority of the ship's company with regard to setting sail; if he does not, he is responsible for any loss and must make it good.

Mariners hire themselves out to their master and some of them go ashore without leave and get drunk and make a disturbance and some be hurt. The Master is not under obligation to have them healed . . . he may put them ashore and hire others in their place.

If a mariner be sick (or hurt in the business of the Master), he shall send him ashore, give him a ship's boy to tend him, or engage a nurse.

The Hansa set a very high standard for all the merchandise it handled, and it obtained for itself the monopoly of the trade of northern Europe. It became so powerful that it waged war against rivals, and through its wealth claimed equality with kings and princes. But what had made its strength in the fourteenth and fifteenth centuries proved its weakness in the sixteenth. The Hansa could tolerate no rivals, but it was slow to change its methods or adjust itself to changing conditions. As the countries of Europe grew more united and developed stronger national governments, the free cities of the Hansa, already weakened by jealousies and rivalries amongst themselves, declined in power.

After the discovery of the New World, new trade routes were discovered and new trading companies were formed which gradually took the place of the Hansa. As out of many alliances between towns it had developed slowly and quietly, so did it disappear. It had done its work. It had made trading in the northern seas safe, it had secured trading rights for merchants in every important city of Europe, it had set high standards for merchandise. The merchants of the Hansa had set an example of devotion and loyalty to all civic obligations. But the narrow intolerance of the league towards outsiders, its determination to secure and keep for itself a trade monopoly, was a weakness that led in time to its decline and final disappearance.

3. *Venice, the Bride of the Adriatic*

IN the north of Europe the most important centres of medieval commerce were the Flemish and German cities of the Hansa. In the south they were the Italian city-states, and of these Venice was the greatest.

Venice was built on the islands in the lagoons at the head of the Adriatic, and in the early Middle Ages when other cities around her were struggling to maintain their independence, she was secure. The Venetians of the time said: "God, who is our help and protection, has saved us in order that we may dwell upon these watery marshes.

This Venice which we have raised in the lagoons is a mighty habitation for us. No power of emperor or of prince can reach us save by the sea alone, and of them we have no fear." An old legend of Venice told how once St. Mark had landed there, and that an angel had appeared to him saying, "Peace to thee, Mark, thy body shall rest here." When in the ninth century the body of the saint was brought to Venice, the Venetians regarded it as the fulfilment of the promise, and St. Mark became their patron saint.

Venice was called a republic, but in reality she was an oligarchy. The chief power was in the hands of the Council of Ten at the head of which was the Doge. The office was not hereditary, but as time went on it became more and more the practice to elect the Doge from the same powerful family. The office was held for life, but the people had the power to depose a Doge, and in the turbulent days of the early Middle Ages they often availed themselves of the right.

The power and wealth of Venice came from her command of the sea. She knew this and called herself the Bride of the Adriatic. Every year on Ascension Day her sea-power was celebrated in a gorgeous pageant. The Doge, magnificently robed, went in procession to the sea, where he prayed: "Grant, O Lord, that for us and for all who sail on it, the sea may be calm and quiet; this is our petition. Lord, hear us." Then he entered his state galley from which floated the banner of St. Mark, and sailing out to the Adriatic, he dropped a ring into the sea, saying: "We wed thee, O Sea, in sign of our true and perpetual dominion."

The Venetians were a people who loved beauty and magnificence and they made of their city one of the loveliest of medieval Italy. They were also practical, shrewd and far-seeing men of affairs. At the time of the Crusades they had already been trading with the east, and they found it difficult to look upon the Saracens as enemies. But when the crusaders set up feudal kingdoms in Syria, the Venetians saw at once how they could turn this to their profit. They provided a great many of the ships that carried the Franks to Asia Minor and Syria, and as a reward they bargained for concessions in the cities the crusaders conquered. In each city they were to have their own quarter, it was to be free from taxation, administered according to their own law, and Venetian weights and measures were always to be used.

By the beginning of the fifteenth century Venice had no serious rival in the Mediterranean except Genoa. She had built great fleets, over three thousand Venetian ships carried her commerce all over the Levant and from the Adriatic to the North Sea. Everything she did was well organized. All the ships owned by the state were built in the Arsenal at Venice and in every port to which they sailed, there were Venetian offices and warehouses where repairs could be promptly attended to.

The wealth of the medieval world from the eleventh to the fifteenth centuries passed through Venice, just as earlier it had passed through Constantinople. Then, in the fifteenth century, two things happened. In 1453 the Turks captured Constantinople, and Venice was no longer the mistress of the Eastern Mediterranean, her ships were not even safe there. In 1497 Vasco da Gama discovered the Cape Route to India, and Venice lost her carrying trade. When the maritime countries of northern Europe could send their ships directly to the east, the sea power of medieval Venice was no longer needed. The rest of her story belongs to the great period of the Italian Renaissance.

4. *The Trade Routes*

a. Land Routes

THE medieval merchant who travelled by land had great difficulties to contend with. The roads were often in poor condition, there was a lack of good bridges, he had to cross the mountains and face all kinds of weather. In feudal Europe travelling by road was made more difficult and dangerous by the violence of private warfare. Added to all these difficulties travelling from one country to another, from one feudal domain to another, even from one part of a feudal domain to another part of the same domain, and from one town to another, was hindered by the frequent and excessive tolls that had to be paid.[1]

There were three great land routes between northern and southern Europe. Two went from Venice, one across the Alps to the Rhine and Bruges, the other to Nuremburg and north to Hamburg. The third, known as the Danube Route, went from Constantinople to Vienna and then to Nuremburg, where it joined the other routes and the merchant could travel either to Bruges or Hamburg.

b. Sea Routes

IN the north of Europe most of the sea trade was carried in the Hansa ships, in the south, the great fleets were those of Venice. There were four recognized routes of the Venetian ships. The Black Sea Fleet sailed down the Adriatic, touched in Greece and at Constantinople, and

[1] See also p. 230.

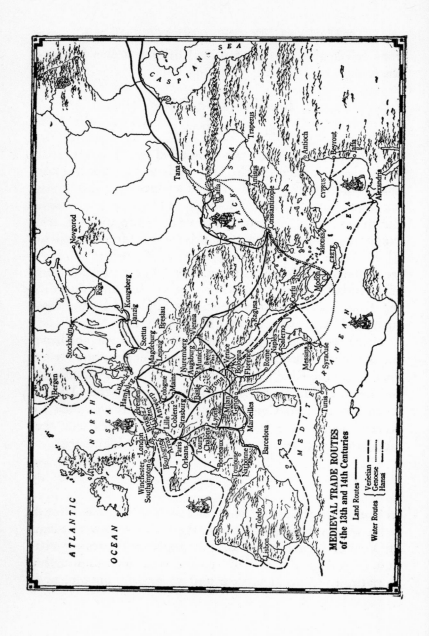

MEDIEVAL TRADE ROUTES
of the 13th and 14th Centuries

Land Routes ———
Water Routes { Venetian ———
Genoese ·········
Hansa —·—·—

then sailed into the Black Sea. The ports at which the ships stopped were all connected with the chief caravan routes across eastern Asia and the Venetians met traders from Damascus, from Bagdad, and from Basra at the head of the Persian Gulf. The Syrian Fleet carried on trade in the Levant. The ships went to Crete and Rhodes and Cyprus, and then on to the ports of Syria. The Egyptian Fleet went to Alexandria, the city in Egypt founded by Alexander the Great because of its unrivalled position as a seaport through which the civilization of east and west might pass. The North Sea Fleet sailed away from the Mediterranean through the Strait of Gibraltar, and keeping close to the coasts of Portugal and France, sailed on through the English Channel to the Flemish ports of Antwerp and Bruges.

These ships were small, they sailed to distant places, but none of them went very far from land or into unknown seas, and there were frequent stops at ports of call along all the routes. There were regulations determining when the voyages should take place, and the stormy months of the year were avoided. The ships sailed in fleets, for the sailor ran the same danger from violence as the traveller by land. Pirates sailed every sea, and a single ship was always in danger.

The real difficulties of travel by sea were great, but the imagined ones were greater. The ideas held by medieval sailors about the dangers of the unknown were enough to frighten any one from putting out to sea. But in spite of dangers and difficulties, known and unknown, ships of the Hansa and of Venice, carrying with them the products of north and south, of east and west, sailed into every port known to medieval Europe.

CHAPTER XVI

MEDIEVAL TRAVELLERS

1. *The Highways*

ALL medieval travellers used the road, and one of the most important functions of landlords was to keep the highways and bridges in repair. All through the Middle Ages, repairing roads and building bridges were amongst the tasks undertaken as acts of piety. In the *Vision of Piers the Plowman,* Truth bids wealthy merchants:

> ". . . Roads that are rotten full rightly repair,
>   Or bridges, when broken, to build up anew."

Bridges were usually placed under the protection of some saint and chapels were erected on them dedicated to the patron. London Bridge was the most famous English bridge of the Middle Ages. It had houses built on it, a chapel dedicated to St. Thomas of Canterbury and it was protected by towers.

The building of a bridge was in many cases a pious act, but its maintenance when built was not always provided for. In the case of bridges on which houses were built, the rents were a source of revenue, and tolls were always demanded of those who crossed the bridge. These tolls were exacted not only from persons crossing the bridge for themselves and their vehicles, but for all merchandise that was taken across. Such tolls were exacted on roads as well as on bridges, and were the cause of endless hindrances and delays. Travellers in some places were required to pay a toll, not only on entering the land of a lord, but also on leaving it, whether by road or river, on going under as well as across a bridge. On the river Loire in France from Orleans to the sea no less than seventy-four tolls had to be paid.

Other difficulties confronting the wayfarer were those of roads in bad repair. They were often full of holes into which the wheels of vehicles sank, and hours were spent in extricating them. There were rivers in flood and the bridges had been swept away. There were dangers from robbers and outlaws, and it was an unwise traveller who found himself without shelter at night.

Along these roads travelled a great variety of people. Most of the travel was either on horseback or on foot, though there were carriages, clumsy, heavy vehicles, for the very great personages and sometimes for ladies. There were carts of all kinds bound for markets and fairs, but most people who did not go on foot preferred to ride on horseback.

When a king travelled, a tremendous escort went with him, for not only did all the officials of his household accompany him, but his chancellor and ministers of state, for state business in those days was transacted wherever the king happened to be. Knights on horseback, singly or in companies, were always to be met with on the roads, so were pilgrims, friars, merchants and pedlars, minstrels and tumblers, beggars and vagabonds of all descriptions.

Looked at across the centuries, medieval travellers seem a gay and picturesque company, though they probably did not regard themselves as such. Travel was so slow, the difficulties and dangers so great, that they must have rejoiced when they found themselves safely at the journey's end. The poorer wayfarers probably slept at night under the stars, except in the winter when they would try to arrive at some monastery before dark. Most of the larger monasteries had halls for the penniless wayfarer, where all were received. No one was questioned, no one was turned away, and food was always provided. The monastery guest-house provided for the better class of traveller or pilgrim and distinguished pilgrims were entertained by the abbot or prior. Monastic hospitality was given freely to rich and poor alike. Like some religious houses today where the stranger is welcomed, no recompense was asked save what the guest offered as a gift for the needs of the house.

Castles also dispensed hospitality. Passing knights or minstrels were welcomed, and repaid their hosts with tales of the great world or with song.

There were inns for the merchant and pedlar, neither too clean nor too comfortable, and there were hermits who provided shelter in wild and stormy weather for those who had lost their way. The hermits often did good service to the traveller in setting him on the right road and sometimes in ferrying him across the rivers.

Perhaps the most inhospitable situation in which a medieval traveller found himself was to arrive outside the wall of a city after the gate was shut. It was not easy to get it opened, for the townspeople disliked letting strangers into the dark streets after nightfall, fearing lest they might be of evil intent. But nearly all other medieval hospitality was marked by a friendly courtesy. Monasteries never, and castles in time of peace very seldom, refused to open their gates to the wayfarer.

2. *Pilgrims*

IN the Middle Ages places where holy men had lived and died, churches which had relics of saints and above all the Holy Land were objects of pilgrimage. Some people went to these holy places to expiate a sinful life, some went in the hope of healing, some from a deep sense of the holiness of the place to which they went and the desire to see it and to worship there. Some, too, went for less pious reasons. There was adventure in the thought of a journey to a strange new place, the restlessness that comes in spring and yearns for the open air and an outdoor life was satisfied by a pilgrimage.

> Whan that Aprille with his shoures sote [1]
> The droghte of Marche hath perced to the rote,
> And bathed every veyne in swich licour,
> Of which vertu engendred is the flour;
> Whan Zephirus eek with his swete breeth
> Inspired hath in every holt and heeth
> The tendre croppes, and the yonge sonne
> Hath in the Ram his halfe cours y-ronne,
> And smale fowles maken melodye,
> That slepen al the night with open yë,
> (So priketh hem nature in hir corages): [2]
> Than longen folk to goon on pilgrimages,
> And palmers for to seken straunge strondes,
> To ferne halwes,[3] couthe [4] in sondry londes;
> And specially, from every shires ende
> Of Engelond, to Caunterbury they wende,
> The holy blisful martir for to seke,
> That hem hath holpen, whan that they were seke.[5]

[1] sweet.   [2] mind.   [3] shrines.   [4] well-known.
[5] Chaucer. From the Prologue to the *Canterbury Tales*. Oxford University Press, London and New York.

Special privileges were accorded pilgrims. A priest on a pilgrimage drew all his stipend if he were not away for more than three years; a layman was exempt from all taxes, and the property of pilgrims was secure from confiscation whilst its owner was away on a pilgrimage.

Pilgrims were constantly seen on the roads, sometimes singly, sometimes in groups. They were recognized by their dress. A pilgrim wore a long robe and a wide-brimmed hat, he was often barefoot and he carried a staff and scrip, the latter being a small bag slung at his side by a cord over the shoulder containing food and a few necessaries. Every shrine had its own particular token which a pilgrim was entitled to wear, such as the ampulla or small flask of holy water from St. Thomas of Canterbury, or the scallop shell from St. James of Compostella. On his return from the Holy Land, a pilgrim was entitled to wear the palm, hence the word *Palmer*. A pilgrim who had been to several shrines often came back with a number of tokens or badges hanging on him. These tokens were eagerly sought after by beggars, who would collect a number and pretending that they had been on all the pilgrimages they represented would collect alms from good people who believed them. In *Piers Plowman* there is a description of such a beggar:

> He bare him a staff, with a broad strip bound,
> That round it was twined like a woodbine's twist;
> A bowl and a bag he bare by his side;
> A hundred of vials was set on his hat,
> Signs from Sinai, Gallician shells;
> With crosses on his cloak, and the keys of Rome,
> And the vernicle before, for that men should discern
> And see by his signs what shrines he had sought.

Then fain would this folk know from whence he had come?
"From Sinai," he said, "and the Sepulchre Holy,
Bethlehem and Babylon, I've been in them both,
Armenia, Alexandria, and other like places.
Ye may see by the signs that here sit on my hat
I have walked full widely, in wet and in dry,
And sought out good saints for the health of my soul." [1]

The most famous medieval pilgrimages were to the shrines of Our Lady at Walsingham and at Chartres, of St. Thomas at Canterbury, and of St. James at Compostella in Spain. Pilgrimages were made, too, to Glastonbury, founded, according to the legend, by St. Joseph of Arimathea; to Rocamadour, to which Roland was said to have made a pilgrimage before starting out for Roncesvalles; to Rome, full of shrines and relics; and above all other places, to the Holy Land.

For whatever reason a pilgrimage was undertaken, it was regarded as a deeply religious thing, and even the most light-hearted must have caught something of the seriousness that underlay the journey. Before starting pilgrims usually sought the blessing of the Church, a blessing that was often given with a good deal of ceremony.

Then the pilgrim, having received his scrip with cross and holy water in the parish church, is conducted in procession outside the parish, to seek Jerusalem, Rome, or St. James, or to go on another pilgrimage, "per Cruce Signationem." [2]

3. Medieval Travellers to the East

SOME mention must be made of another kind of traveller of the Middle Ages, the traveller who left Europe behind

[1] From the *Vision of Piers the Plowman*, by William Langland.
[2] From the *Coutume de Normandie*. Joan Evans, *Mediæval France*. Oxford University Press, London and New York.

him and set out for the far east. Three things took such men to Asia: missionary enthusiasm, both Christian and Moslem, the desire to increase trade, and the love of adventure.

If travelling by road in Europe was difficult, it was easy compared with the dangers and difficulties that confronted the traveller who set out for China. Yet beginning in the seventh century and continuing throughout the Middle Ages, there are records of such men. Conditions varied very little during the period, and descriptions given in the seventh century were probably equally true of the thirteenth and even the fourteenth. Some of our knowledge of these conditions comes, not from Europeans who set out for the east, but from men of the east who set out across Asia towards the west.

One of these early travellers was a Chinaman, Hiuen-tsiang, whose journey took him to India where he hoped to find copies of some of the original sacred writings of the Buddhists. On his return home he wrote a book describing his travels and the difficulties of the road. He described the icy cold, the tempest and the snow as he crossed the mountains, and the lack of water and the hot winds that were the terror of the desert. Though he attributed every danger to the work of demons and evil spirits, he probably gives a fairly accurate picture of the conditions themselves.

In the ninth century a Mohammedan traveller, Ihn Batuta, set out from Tangiers on a pilgrimage to Mecca. But he was very adventurous and went much further. He went first to Alexandria and there he met a learned man who asked him if it was his purpose to visit strange and distant countries. When he heard that it was, he said to Ihn Batuta that he must not fail to visit his three brothers, one of whom lived in Persia, one in India, and one in China, and in the book he wrote of his travels, Ihn Batuta assures us that he saw them all. His book is not always trustworthy as he seems to have believed everything he was told, but he was much impressed with all that he saw in China, especially with the size of the Chinese ships and with the great wealth he found everywhere.

At the time when they were crossing Asia the west knew nothing of these Chinese and Moslem travellers and of the ancient civilizations they were seeing. In the middle of the ninth century the sons of Charlemagne were trying in vain to rule the empire their father had created. Norsemen were invading England and settling in France. If rumours ever reached the west of the civilization of the far east, they were faint and unreal as a dream. The period of the Crusades brought the east much nearer to Europe, but it was still mysterious. Europeans had not themselves been further than Constantinople or Syria or to the shores of the Black Sea. They were beginning to know something more of the silks and brocades, the jewels, the spices and the rare woods that came from the east, but these things were brought to them by traders, they had not themselves been in the lands whence such treasures came. In the thirteenth century three Italians made the journey to China, one of the famous journeys of history.

In 1260 Nicolo Polo and his brother, two Venetian traders, set out on a journey that took them finally to China, where they were received at the court of Kublai Khan, one of the great medieval rulers of China. He was much interested in them, asked endless questions about Europe, about the pope and the emperor and the Christian religion.

Being introduced to the presence of the Grand Khan Kublai, the travellers were received by him with the condescension and affability that belonged to his character, and as they were the first Latins who had made their appearance in that country, they were entertained with feasts and honoured with other marks of distinction. Entering graciously into conversation with them, he made earnest inquiries on the subject of the western parts of the world, of the emperor of the Romans, and of other Christian kings and princes. He wished to be informed of their relative consequence, the extent of their possessions, the manner in which justice was administered in their several kingdoms and principalities, how they conducted themselves in warfare, and above all he questioned them particularly respecting the Pope, the affairs of the church, and the religious worship and doctrine of the Christians. Being well instructed and discreet men, they gave appropriate answers upon all these points, and as they were perfectly acquainted with the Tartar (Moghul) language, they expressed themselves always in becoming terms; insomuch that the Grand Khan, holding them in high estimation, frequently commanded their attendance.[1]

When the Grand Khan had heard all that they had to tell him, he begged them to return to Europe and ask the Pope to send him a hundred missionaries who would convert his people to the Christian faith. The Venetians returned, but they found that the Pope had died and his successor was not yet elected. After a time they decided to return to China, though without the hundred missionaries. Two friars went with them, but they grew fearful in Armenia and turned back. The Polos had procured some of the oil from the Holy Sepulchre in Jerusalem and this they took back with them to China.

Nicolo Polo and his brother were accompanied this time by Marco, the seventeen year old son of Nicolo.

Upon their arrival they were honourably and graciously received by the Grand Khan, in a full assembly of his principal officers. . . .

[1] *The Travels of Marco Polo.*

Upon his observing Marco Polo, and inquiring who he was, Nicolo made answer, "This is your servant and my son"; upon which the Grand Khan replied, "He is welcome, and it pleases me much," and he caused him to be enrolled amongst his attendants of honour. And on account of their return he made a great feast and rejoicing; and as long as the said brothers and Marco remained in the court of the Grand Khan, they were honoured even above his own courtiers. Marco was held in high estimation and respect by all belonging to the court. He learned in a short time the manners of the Tartars, and acquired a proficiency in four different languages, which he became qualified to read and write. Finding him thus accomplished, his master was desirous of putting his talents for business to the proof, and sent him on an important concern of state to a city named Karazan, situated at the distance of six months' journey from the imperial residence; on which occasion he conducted himself with so much wisdom and prudence in the management of the affairs intrusted to him, that his services became highly acceptable. On his part, perceiving that the Grand Khan took a pleasure in hearing accounts of whatever was new to him respecting the customs and manners of people, and the peculiar circumstances of distant countries, he endeavoured, wherever he went, to obtain correct information on these subjects, and made notes of all he saw and heard, in order to gratify the curiosity of his master. In short, during seventeen years that he continued in his service, he rendered himself so useful, that he was employed on confidential missions to every part of the empire, and its dependencies; and sometimes also he travelled on his own private account, but always with the consent, and sanctioned by the authority, of the Grand Khan. Under such circumstances it was that Marco Polo had the opportunity of acquiring a knowledge, either by his own observation, or what he collected from others, of so many things, until his time unknown, respecting the eastern part of the world and which he diligently and regularly committed to writing.[1]

In 1295 the Polos returned to Venice. The journey home had been long, they were wearing curious Chinese

[1] *The Travels of Marco Polo.*

garments, they had spoken the Tartar languages for so long, that Italian came back to them haltingly, and the tale is told that on their arrival no one at first recognized them. They arrived to find Venice at war with Genoa, and Marco Polo immediately took part, but unsuccessfully, for he was taken prisoner and kept in Genoa for three years. During this captivity he wrote an account of his travels, and this book of Marco Polo's became one of the most famous of all travel books.

To Marco Polo the west owes its first real knowledge of China. He described its teeming population, its cities with their wealth, its birds and beasts and flowers, and above all the great ruler Kublai Khan. His book is full of the mystery and romance, of the wonders and the marvels of the east, yet he wrote only of what he had himself seen.

Other European travellers followed Marco Polo. The curiosity of the west was aroused and no tale was too strange to be believed. In the fourteenth century another medieval book was written by a traveller calling himself Sir John Mandeville. The book was so full of wonders that it was eagerly read and believed, and the tales that were told in it, impossible to believe as some of them were, became part of the medieval legend of the east. It was Sir John Mandeville who told the tale of Prester John, Emperor of India, and the greatest king on earth, who carried a sceptre of emeralds and wore a robe woven by salamanders. He was waited on by seven kings, sixty dukes and a different count for every day in the year.

Pilgrimages, crusades and travels, to each of these the west owes something of its knowledge of the east. By degrees a new continent was opened out before the eyes of Europe. The horizons of the west were widened, the imagination was quickened. Contact with the east brought to the European mind not only something of the mystery of ancient ways and ancient traditions, of what man had done and thought in a strange and distant past, but of strange and unfamiliar things that men were doing and thinking in the present. In the thirteenth century Europe discovered a world in which the traditions were more ancient than her own. At the end of the fifteenth century the discovery of a new world was to bring to her the adventure of something in which tradition was to be made.

CHAPTER XVII

THE FRIARS

THE thirteenth century was a period when the Church was very powerful. It was rich both in land and in magnificent church and monastic buildings. Bishops and other clergy were amongst the advisers of many of the kings and rulers, and since the days of Gregory VII the Pope had wielded immense power and influence. It is true that with all this power there was much in the Church that was amiss. The leaders often forgot that their chief work was with the souls of men, with right and wrong, with holding up ideals of righteousness and holiness. Popes and emperors quarrelled, and kings and emperors were excommunicated, any questioning of the orthodox beliefs of the Church resulted in ruthless persecution. But there were a great many people who knew nothing of these things: serfs and peasants, the poor who had no place in the organized life of the manor or town and who lived huddled together outside the walls, and the sick, lepers and maimed, who, unless a friendly monastery took them in, were uncared for.

Into this thirteenth century world came two men, St. Francis and St. Dominic, both of whom founded religious orders. These orders followed some of the same rules as the monastic orders, but the members lived in the world. They were called *Friars* (from the Latin *frater*, a brother), they lived a life of poverty and their aim was to bring to all men, but especially to the poor and suffering, a quickening of spiritual ideals.

1. *St. Francis of Assisi*
1182-1226

ST. FRANCIS was born in 1182 in Assisi, one of the small independent hill towns in Umbria. His father, Pietro Bernadone, was a wealthy cloth merchant, whose business often took him to France; his mother, the Lady Pica, was probably of noble birth, so the young Francis grew up surrounded with all that money could give him and welcome in the gay society of the young nobles of Assisi. He was popular, but vain and loved to be admired, boastful and extravagant, loving fine clothes and all the pageantry that the times loved. But with all his faults he was generous and chivalrous. The story is told of him that one day when he was busy selling to customers in his father's shop, a beggar came in asking for alms in the name of God. Francis was irritated and sent him away and then suddenly said: "What would I not have done if this man had asked something of me in the name of a count or baron? What ought I not to have done when he came in the name of God? I am no better than a clown," and running after the beggar, he brought him back and heaped gifts upon him.

When he was twenty-two years old, Francis fell ill and when he had recovered a change had taken place in him. Silent and thoughtful, where he once had been lively and gay, his friends asked him if he were in love. "Yes," said Francis, "but I shall marry a fairer and nobler bride than you ever saw, who shall surpass all others in beauty and excel them in wisdom." His bride was to be the Lady Poverty. Against his father's will, he gave up all he possessed and with two friends who joined him began a life in which he carried out to the letter the commission given in the Gospel to the twelve apostles: To preach the Gospel, to heal the sick and cleanse the lepers, to take nothing for their journey, neither staves, nor scrip, nor bread, nor money, to have neither shoes nor two coats apiece.

Soon the three were joined by others. The Benedictines of Monte Subasio, on the slope of which Assisi is built, gave Francis for himself and his brothers for ever a little chapel, Santa Maria degli Angeli or the Portiuncula (the Little Portion). This chapel stood in the plain below the town and was already much beloved of Francis and to it he always returned from his journey as to his home. With all their poverty and hardships, Francis and his Brothers were always so merry and gay that they were known as the Jongleurs of God. His biographer said of Francis:

Aside from prayer and the divine service, the blessed Francis was most zealous in preserving continually an inward and outward spiritual gladness. And this he specially cherished in the brothers, and would reprove them for sadness and depression. For he said that if the servant of God would study to preserve, inwardly and outwardly, the spiritual joy which rises from purity of heart, and is acquired through the devotion of prayer, the devil could not harm him, for they say: So long as the servant of God is joyful in tribulation and prosperity, we cannot enter into him or harm him. . . . To our enemy and his members it pertains to be sad, but to us always to rejoice and be glad in the Lord.

By 1209 the friars had increased so greatly in numbers that Francis, taking twelve friars with him, went to Rome, where the Pope Innocent III recognized the brothers as an order and gave his permission for them to follow a rule of poverty, to wear a grey habit and to walk barefoot.

Francis spent endless thought and care on a written Rule for the order, but it was not officially accepted and authorized by the pope until 1223.

The first ten years of the order were years of great happiness for Francis. The friars lived by their own work, they served all who were in need, especially the lepers, they preached, they spent nights in prayer. They were all men who had heard the call, *Follow me*, and they had left all that they possessed and followed Christ.

In 1212 St. Francis was able to establish the order of the Poor Clares. A maiden of Assisi, afterwards known as St. Clare, had fled from her home to the Portiuncula where she begged Francis to receive her as one who would live the same kind of life. He took her to a convent of Benedictine nuns where she stayed for a time. Later, when a number of companions had joined her, she went to the convent of San Damiano, where she and her nuns devoted themselves to a life of work for the poor and sick.

Francis had many of the characteristics of the medieval knight. He was courteous and chivalrous, and he loved adventure. It was this perhaps that sent him and his friars on expeditions to convert the infidels. He went himself with one of the crusading armies to Syria, and before his death Franciscan friars had gone to the Moors in Spain, to Hungary and the East. Singleness of heart, humility, obedience to the Lady Poverty were the characteristics of Francis and the early friars, and few men of whom history has preserved a record were as completely possessed as Francis by a spirit of love. This love was given to everything that had life, and many are the tales told of how animals heeded him and became gentle and quiet at his bidding. Because they were small and fragile, he especially loved birds.

The most blessed father Francis was journeying through the valley of Spoleto, and came to a spot near Bevagna where a very great number of birds were gathered together. When he saw them, being a man of the most fervent temper and also very tender and affectionate toward all the lower and irrational creatures, Francis the most blessed servant of God left his companions in the way and ran eagerly towards the birds. When he was come close to them and saw that they were awaiting him, he gave them his accustomed greeting. But, not a little surprised that the birds did not fly away (as they are wont to do) he was filled with exceeding joy and humbly begged them to hear the word of God: and, after saying many things to them he added: "My brother birds, much ought ye to praise your Creator, and ever to love Him who has given you feathers for clothing, wings for flight, and all that ye had need of. God has made you noble among His creatures, for He has given you a habitation in the purity of the air, and, whereas ye neither sow nor reap, He himself doth still protect and govern you without any care of your own." On this (as he himself and the brethren who had been with him used to say) those little birds rejoicing in wondrous fashion, after their nature, began to stretch out their necks, to spread their wings, to open their beaks and to gaze upon him. And then he went to and fro amidst them, touching their heads and bodies with his tunic. At length he blessed them, and having made the sign of the Cross, gave them leave to fly away to another place. But the blessed father went on his way with his companions, rejoicing and giving thanks to God Whom all creatures humbly acknowledge and revere.

On another occasion Francis was about to preach to the people who had assembled to hear him, and he asked for silence.

But though all the company held their peace and stood reverently by, a great number of swallows who were building their nests in that same place were chirping and chattering loudly. And as Francis could not be heard by the men for their chirping, he spoke to the birds and said: "My sisters, the swallows, it is now time for me to speak too, because you have been saying enough all this time. Listen to the word of God and be in silence, and quiet, until the sermon is finished." And those little birds (to the amazement of all the bystanders) kept silence forthwith, and did not move from that place till the preaching was ended.[1]

In the last years of his life Francis became almost blind. He was tended for a time in the house of the Bishop of Assisi, but when he realized that he was dying, he asked to be taken to the Portiuncula. On the way, as they came to a turn in the road from which there was a view of the town of Assisi, Francis asked that his face might be turned to it, and then, raising his hand, he blessed the little city that had been his birthplace:

Blessed be thou of God, holy city, for many souls shall be saved because of thee, and in thee shall dwell many of God's servants; and from thee many shall be chosen to the kingdom of life everlasting.

The work of the Franciscan friars grew in importance after the death of Francis. But it was soon found that the early rule which forbade them to own houses was almost impossible to keep, and they were allowed to have friaries when such were given to them. The Franciscan houses in some of the universities became famous, for though Francis had never encouraged learning amongst the friars who had been his immediate companions, in later years Franciscan friars made very notable contribution to medieval scholarship.

Francis had had dreams of converting the infidel, but though he had not been successful, after his death Franciscan friars set out on missions to the heathen. They went not only to Africa, to Morocco and Tunis and Algiers, to Egypt and the Holy Land, but also across Asia from

[1] From Thomas of Celano, *First Life of St. Francis of Assisi.*

Persia to Tibet and China. The account of one such mission has been preserved in the letters of a friar, Brother John, who, at the end of the thirteenth century, went to Peking. He laboured there for eleven years all alone, the friar who started with him having died on the way.

I was alone in this pilgrimage, he writes, without confession, for eleven years, till there came to me brother Arnold, a German of the province of Cologne, last year. I have built a church in the city of Khanbalig, where the king has his chief residence: this I completed six years ago. . . . I have baptized there, as I reckon, up to this time about 6,000 persons; and I am often engaged in baptizing. Also I have bought, one after another, forty boys, the sons of pagans, aged between seven and eleven years, who so far knew no religion. And I have baptized them and taught them to read Latin, and our ritual; and I have written for them thirty psalters with hymn-books, and two breviaries, with which eleven boys now say our office, and attend service, and take their weekly turn in the convent, whether I am present or not. . . . And the emperor is greatly delighted at their chanting. I strike the bells at all the hours, and with this congregation of babes and sucklings I perform divine service: but we sing by ear, because we have no service-books with the notes.

Brother John then pleaded that books might be sent to him and he added: Now I am building another church, so as to distribute the boys in more places than one. I am now old and grey, more from toil and trouble than age, for I am fifty-eight years old. I know the Tartar language and writing, and I have now translated into that language and writing the whole New Testament and the psalter . . . which I keep and read and preach from openly.

Not only were books sent to him, but seven other friars were commissioned by the pope to join Brother John in Peking. The mission prospered for about fifty years. It came to an end when an unfriendly king came to the throne and the surviving friars were put to death.

Of all that has come down to us of St. Francis, the story

of his life written by Thomas of Celano who knew him, the collection of stories known as the *Little Flowers of St. Francis* and many other tales and legends, none is perhaps more characteristic than the hymn he composed and sang, called the *Canticle of the Sun*.

O most high, almighty, good Lord God, to thee belong praise, glory, honour, and all blessing.

Praised be my Lord God with all his creatures, and specially our brother the sun, who brings us the day and who brings us the light; fair is he and shining with a very great splendour: O Lord, he signifies to us thee.

Praised be my Lord for our sister the moon, and for the stars, the which he has set clear and lovely in heaven.

Praised be my Lord for our brother wind, and for air and cloud, calms and all weather by the which thou upholdest life in all creatures.

Praised be my Lord for our sister water, who is very serviceable unto us, and humble and precious and clean.

Praised be my Lord for our brother fire, through whom thou givest us light in the darkness; and he is bright and pleasant, and very mighty, and strong.

Praised be my Lord for our mother the earth, the which doth sustain us and keep us, and bringeth forth divers fruits, and flowers of many colours, and grass.

Praised be my Lord for all those who pardon one another for his love's sake, and who endure weakness and tribulation; blessed are they who peaceably shall endure, for thou, O most Highest, shalt give them a crown.

Praised be my Lord for our sister, the death of the body, from which no man escapeth. Woe to him who dieth in mortal sin! Blessed are they who are found walking by thy most holy will, for the second death shall have no power to do them harm.

Praise ye, and bless ye the Lord, and give thanks unto him, and serve him with great humility.

2. *St. Dominic*
1170-1221

ST. DOMINIC was a Spaniard, different not only in nationality but in temperament and in ideals from St. Francis. But they were alike in their enthusiasm and whole-hearted devotion to God and in the methods by which they sought to attain their ideal. St. Francis cared deeply for the poor, he had compassion on the suffering and the needy, he touched the hearts of people. St. Dominic, on the other hand, was concerned with ignorance and heresy, he sought to win the mind and the intellect to the service of God. He had entered the Church as a young man and had been sent by the pope to Provence in the south of France at the time of the crusade against the Albigenses, a group of people who were rejecting the orthodox teaching of the Church.

In his work in Provence St. Dominic came to the conclusion that one of the causes of the heresies which were springing up there and in other places was that many of the parish priests were very ignorant and knew little about preaching. As a result, he founded an order of friars, in its rule of life not unlike that of St. Francis, except that the chief work of the Dominicans was to teach and preach. The Rule was authorized by the Pope in 1220 and study was made binding on all who entered the order. Clad in a white habit with a short black cape, from which came their name of *Black Friars*, the Dominican wandered over Europe and the Preaching Friar was as well known as the Franciscan. Because of the share the Dominicans had had in fighting heresy, they were known as *Domini canes*, the Watch-dogs of the Lord. The ideal of St. Dominic was that of a friar trained in preaching who would combat ignorance and so keep watch over the preservation of the doctrine of the Church.

The influence of the friars, both Franciscan and Dominican, in the thirteenth century was wide. Unlike the monks, they lived among the people they served, and bound by their vows of poverty and obedience they worked amongst the poorest and most oppressed, and with nothing to gain for themselves their sympathy often made them the champions of those who were struggling for justice.

Later, when because of the popularity of their work and example, wealth came to them at first in the form of gifts of houses and splendid churches, the earlier spirit of the friars gave way before the subtle temptations that wealth brought in its train. But amongst the Franciscans there was always one group that insisted on keeping to the old rule of absolute devotion to the Lady Poverty, and the influence of the early friars was always in the direction of a more spiritual religion, of real piety and of a love of God, a love that showed itself in acts of mercy and compassion, and in active sympathy with all forms of suffering and need.

NOTE. The quotation on p. 244 is from Henry Osborn Taylor, *The Mediæval Mind*. By permission of the Macmillan Company, publishers.

CHAPTER XVIII

MEDIEVAL EDUCATION

THE wise man of old said that "where there is no vision the people perish." The vision that any age holds of supreme importance can generally be seen in the education of the time. For education will do two things: it will prepare a child to live intelligently in the world, and what is of more importance, from the ideals and motives it sets up, from the kind of hero it exalts, from the ideas it spreads, education will train and develop character and will give that vision that is needed if the people are not to perish.

In the Middle Ages, the peasant was given little or no education as we understand the word today. He learned to handle plough and spade, to sow and reap, to look after animals, to become a good agricultural labourer. It was his duty in life to provide the food and all the material necessities for those whose business it was to fight and to protect others and for their families.

The ideals which underlay the education of the knight and the education itself have already been described; for other boys there were schools and universities. Originally schools and universities were founded for those who intended to enter the Church in some capacity or other, but not every boy who went to school intended to become either a priest or monk. As medieval education was in the hands of the Church, those who received such education were generally admitted to a lower order. These men were called *clerks* and a number of careers were open to them. They could become high officials under kings or princes, they could be lawyers, judges, diplomats, scholars and teachers, both in schools and universities.

1. *Children and Schools*

UNTIL a child was seven years old he stayed at home, where he was sometimes so strictly brought up that medieval writers on education urged that the discipline be tempered with gentleness. An Italian writer (Mafeo Vegio of Lodi, who died in 1457) advised that from the time children were small babies they should be accustomed to the cold so that they might grow into hardy, healthy children. He went on to say that

it is a mistake for parents to frighten their children with threats or beatings. Beatings may stupefy a child more than enlighten him. . . . They are to be considered as children not as slaves. Whatever there is of generosity in them can easily be touched by kindness. . . . This must not be taken to mean lack of discipline, for in these modern days children are being spoiled by softness of education.

It was at home that children were given their first religious education. Joinville in his biography of St. Louis describes how the king taught his sons:

Before he lay down in his bed he would cause his children to come to him, and bring to their minds the deeds of good kings and emperors, telling them it was of such men they should take example. And he would bring to their minds also the deeds of great men who were wicked, and by their ill-doing, and their rapine, and their avarice, had brought their kingdoms to ruin. . . .

He made them learn the Hours of Our Lady, and say before him the Hours of the Day, so as to accustom them to hear the Hours when they ruled over their own lands.[1]

Children were also taught manners at home, especially those children who were brought up in castles and in the manor houses. At seven years of age those who were to be trained as knights became pages and later squires, those who wished to become clerks, went to school.

Charlemagne at Aix and Alfred the Great in England had both established schools in order that the young sons of their nobles might have some knowledge of reading and writing, but it was not until the eleventh century that in most places schools became at all common.

These schools were connected with cathedrals and monasteries, with gilds and with chantries. They varied, of course, in different places and in different countries, but they had certain things in common. The discipline was severe, the hours were long, often ten to twelve hours a day, and the holidays were short, about twelve days each at Christmas, Easter and Whitsuntide.

The subjects taught were those known as the *seven liberal arts,* grammar, rhetoric, logic, arithmetic, geometry, astronomy and music. The first three of these were called the *Trivium,* the remaining four the *Quadrivium.* In the school these were taught in an elementary form and some boys were content to go no further than the Trivium, but those who wanted to go to the university usually studied the Quadrivium.

In the Middle Ages Latin was the universal language of learning in Europe, it was the language of the Church, of the law and of philosophy, so in the schools boys were taught Latin grammar very thoroughly. There were only

[1] Joinville's *Chronicle of St. Louis.*

a few textbooks in use and not many copies of them, and most of the teaching was given orally.

2. *Universities*

THE university occupied a very important place in the intellectual life of the Middle Ages, but it was very different from what we think of as a university or college today. All the medieval university needed for its work were teachers and scholars. It had no equipment, no museums, no science laboratories, and often no class-rooms. Scholars met their teachers wherever it was most convenient, and listened to their lectures.

The studies in a medieval university were divided into four groups: arts, theology, law and medicine. The arts had already been studied in an elementary form in the schools, but scholars were not allowed to go on to higher branches of learning until they had covered the ground of the seven liberal arts. In the classes a text would be studied, then the master would explain it in great detail, after which would follow a formal discussion. Examinations were not compulsory, but at the end of seven years a candidate could present himself for the degree of Master of Arts, which qualified him to teach the seven liberal arts.

The earliest universities grew out of the cathedral schools and were groups of masters and scholars associated under the authority of the Chancellor for the pursuit of knowledge. No one could teach without the permission of the Chancellor. The earliest universities date from the thirteenth century and were at Salerno and Bologna, at Montpellier and Paris, at Oxford and Cambridge. Scholars flocked to them from all over Europe, they were young and often boisterous, they were of all the nations of Europe and conflicts between them were frequent. By degrees colleges were built and endowed in which the scholars lived and were under a certain amount of restraint. These colleges have long been done away with on the continent, but at Oxford and Cambridge the system of colleges, founded for the most part in the Middle Ages, is still preserved.

By degrees a certain amount of discipline was introduced into university life. Lectures were given in the morning, generally between 6 and 10 A.M. At Toulouse there was a rule that "since study was a vehement application of the mind and requires the whole man, the scholars are forbidden to attend more than two or three lectures a day." At Oxford fines were imposed if the scholar missed a daily attendance at Mass, if he indulged in gambling or sword practice, if he brought an unsheathed knife to table, or if he "sinned with his tongue or shouted or made melody when others wished to study or sleep." At one college in Cambridge no scholar might keep either a dog or a falcon for "if one can have them in the house, all will want them and so there will arise a constant howling to disturb the studious." Musical instruments do not seem to have been looked on by the authorities with much favour because of the disturbance they might cause. One German university, however, allowed them at certain hours, "provided they were musical."

In some universities the teachers as well as the scholars were subject to fines. At Bologna a teacher was fined if he were late, if he skipped a chapter in the text that was being studied, or if he failed to reach certain points in the work by certain dates. If he wished to be absent, he was required to obtain permission from his scholars as well as from the head of the university.

The medieval scholar seems always to have been poor and his letters were full of requests for money. Scribes composed models for such letters, with a variety of ways in which the subject might be approached.

To their dear and respected parents, their sons send greeting and filial obedience.

This is to inform you, that by divine mercy, we are living in good health in the city of Orleans and are devoting ourselves wholly to study, mindful of the words of Cato: "To know anything is praiseworthy." We occupy a good dwelling, next door but one to the schools and market-place, so that we can go to school every day without wetting our feet. We have also good companions in the house with us, well advanced in their studies and of excellent habits—an advantage which we well appreciate, for as the Psalmist says, "With an upright man thou wilt show thyself upright."

Then follows a request for money. Another wrote:

This is to inform you that I am studying at Oxford with the greatest diligence, but the matter of money stands greatly in the way of my promotion, as it is now two months since I spent the last of what you sent me. The city is expensive and makes many demands; I have to rent lodgings, buy necessaries, and provide for many other things which I cannot now specify. Wherefore I respectfully beg your paternity that by the promptings of divine pity you may assist me, so that I may be able to complete what I have well begun.[1]

In the fourteenth century Eustache Deschamps made these requests famous in verse.

[1] Charles H. Haskins, *The Rise of Universities*. Henry Holt and Company, New York.

Lettres des escoliers d'Orliens:
Treschiers peres, je n'ay denier,
Ne sanz vous ne puis avoir riens;
Et si fait a l'estude chier,
Ne je ne puis estudier
En mon Code n'en ma Digeste:
Caduque sont. Je doy de reste
De ma prevosté dix escus,
Et ne treuve homme qui me preste:
Je vous mande argent et salus!

Trop fault, qui est estudiens;
Se son fait veult bien advancier,
Il fault que son pere et les siens
Lui baillent argent sanz dangier,
Par quoi cause n'ait d'engagier
Ses livres, ait finance preste,
Robes, pannes, vesteure honneste,
Ou il sera un malostrus;
Et qu'om ne me tiengne pour beste,
Je vous mande argent et salus.

Vins sont chiers, hostelz, autres biens;
Je doy partout; s'ay grant mestier
D'estre mis hors de tels liens:
Chiers peres, vueillez moy aidier.
Je doubte l'excommunier,
Cité suy; cy n'a n'os n'areste:
S'argent n'ay devant cette feste
De Pasques, du moustier exclus
Seray. Ottroiez ma requeste
Je vous mande argent et salus.

L'Envoy

Treschiers peres, pour m'alegier
En la taverne, au boulengier,
Aux docteurs, aix bediaux, conclus,
Et pour mes colectes payer
A la burresse et au barbier,
Je vous mande argent et salus.

(Thus runs the Orleans scholar's letter: Well beloved father, I have not a penny nor can I get any save through you, for all things at the university are so dear; nor can I study in my Code or my Digest, for their leaves have the falling sickness. Moreover, I owe ten crowns in dues to the Provost, and can find no man to lend them to me; I ask of you greetings and gold.

The student has need of many things if he will profit here; his father and his kin must needs supply him freely, that he be not compelled to pawn his books, but have ready money in his purse, with gowns and furs and decent clothing; or he will be damned for a beggar; wherefore, that men may not take me for a beast, I ask of you greetings and gold.

Wines are dear, and hostels and other good things; I owe in every street, and am hard bestead to free myself from such snares. Dear father, deign to help me. I fear to be excommunicated; already I have been cited, and there is not even a dry bone in my larder. If I find not the money before this feast of Easter, the church will be shut in my face; wherefore grant my supplication. I ask of you greetings and gold.

Envoi.

Well beloved father, to ease my debts contracted at the tavern, at the baker's, with the professors and the bedels, to pay my subscriptions to the laundress and the barber, I ask of you greetings and gold.)[1]

All scholars at the universities, however, did not take examinations, and the "wandering scholar" as he was called, was a familiar sight. He would go from one university to another, sometimes in search of learning, sometimes to listen to the great teachers, such as Peter Abelard in the twelfth century at Paris, sometimes he wandered from restlessness, sometimes from a desire to see the world. A twelfth century monk writes of the Wandering Scholars:

[1] Joan Evans, *Mediæval France*. Oxford University Press, London and New York.

They are wont to roam the world and visit all its cities, till much learning makes them mad; for in Paris they seek liberal arts, in Orleans classics, at Salerno medicine, at Toledo magic, but nowhere manners or morals.

These scholars wandered about, begging their way, always merry, and often singing.

I, a wandering scholar lad,
  Born for toil and sadness,
Oftentimes am driven by
  Poverty to madness.

Literature and knowledge I
  Fain would still be earning,
Were it not that want of pelf
  Makes me cease from learning.

These torn clothes that cover me
  Are too thin and rotten;
Oft I have to suffer cold,
  By the warmth forgotten.

Scarce I can attend at church,
  Sing God's praises duly;
Mass and vespers both I miss,
  Though I love them truly.

O, thou pride of N——,
  By thy worth I pray thee
Give the suppliant help in need,
  Heaven will sure repay thee.

Take a mind unto thee now
  Like unto St. Martin;
Clothe the pilgrim's nakedness,
  Wish him well at parting.

So may God translate your soul
  Into peace eternal,

And the bliss of saints be yours
In his realm supernal.[1]

The medieval scholar was the subject of many a sermon, and from them most of their failings can be learnt,
how lazy and idle they were, how quarrelsome and insolent, how dishonest and deceitful. But there were others
besides these, scholars like Chaucer's Clerk of Oxenford.

A Clerk ther was of Oxenford also,
That un-to logik hadde longe y-go.
As lene was his hors as is a rake,
And he was nat right fat, I undertake;
But loked holwe, and ther-to soberly.
Ful thredbar was his overest courtepy;
For he had geten him yet no benefice,
Ne was so worldly for to have office.
For him was levere have at his beddes heed
Twenty bokes, clad in blak or reed
Of Aristotle and his philosophye,
Than robes riche, or fithele,[2] or gay sautyre [3]
But al be that he was a philosophre,
Yet hadde he but litel gold in cofre;
But al that he mighte of his frendes hente [4]
On bokes and on lerninge he it spente,
And bisily gan for the soules preye
Of hem that yaf him wher-with to scoleye.
Of studie took he most cure and most hede.
Noght a word spak he more than was nede,
And that was seyd in forme and reverence,
And short and quik, and ful of hy sentence.
Sowninge in moral vertu was his speche,
And gladly wolde he lerne, and gladly teche.[5]

[1] Charles H. Haskins, *The Rise of Universities*. Henry Holt and
Company, New York.
[2] fiddle.   [3] psaltery.   [4] get.   [5] From Chaucer's Prologue.
Oxford Univerity Press, London and New York.

3. *The Education of Girls*

As the medieval boy who was educated at all was trained
either to become a knight and to understand all the duties
and obligations of knighthood, or to become a monk or
a clerk, so was the medieval girl educated to become either
the wife of a knight or a lord, to undertake the duties of
a nun in a cloister, or to become the wife of a townsman.
The medieval girl did not receive the same kind of education as the boy. In some ways she was better educated and
she was generally well prepared for whatever life lay
ahead of her.

In the convent a nun learned to read and write, to sing
the services of the Church and to do very fine and beautiful tapestry and embroidery. Sometimes she worked as a
scribe and became a skilled illuminator. Sometimes she
learned French. She was taught to care for the sick. If
she showed any ability for administration, she would learn
the business of superintending the convent with its estates
and its many money matters, so that if she were called
to preside over it as abbess or prioress, she would know
how to conduct its business. To be abbess of a great medieval convent was to be a very great lady. She was just as
much a part of the feudal system as an abbot, she was the
overlord of feudal vassals, she was the equal of princes
and barons. Only a woman who was well educated, who
had read widely of the literature that was at her command,
who understood the medieval world of affairs could occupy such a position.

Not all medieval women learnt Latin. All nuns knew
enough to follow the services of the Church and to chant
the psalms; if they knew more, whatever books of history,

philosophy or science the convent possessed were at their disposal.

The girl who lived in the castle was either trained at home by her mother, or she was sent to another castle where with a group of maidens she was taught the things that a medieval lady would be expected to know and do. Most of these girls could read and write, and they were taught to read aloud, they learnt music, they could both sing and play on some instrument, they were trained to become skilled needlewomen. They learnt, too, a great deal about the art of healing and the medicinal virtues of herbs, for it was the task of the lady of the castle to care for the sick in her household, and to tend wounded knights who might be brought into her house either after a tournament, or after meeting with some mishap on the road. The medieval girl had to learn how to manage her household, and sometimes she was trained in the management of estates, for in the absence of her husband it would fall to her to look after them.

The girl who was brought up in a castle learnt a great deal from the conversation she heard about her. There was not much privacy in a castle and little could have been talked about that she did not hear. Passing travellers, knights and serving-men, minstrels and jongleurs, pilgrims and other wayfarers must all have contributed to the education of the girl by their news of the world outside the castle walls and their tales of distant lands.

The girl brought up in the town was taught how to manage her household, and in a poem of the fifteenth century we are given details as to what was expected of her.

How the Good Wife Taught Her Daughter
c. 1430

The good wife taught her daughter,
 Full many a time and oft,
A full good woman to be;
For said she: "Daughter to me dear,
Something good now must thou hear,
 If thou wilt prosper thee.

Daughter, if thou wilt be a wife,
 Look wisely that thou work;
Look lovely and in good life,
 Love God and Holy Kirk.
Go to church whene'er thou may,
 Look thou spare for no rain,
For best thou farest on that day;
 To commune with God be fain.
  He must needs well thrive,
  That liveth well all his life,
   My lief (dear) child.

Gladly give thy tithes and thy offerings both,
To the poor and the bed-rid,—look thou be not loth.
Give of thine own goods and be not too hard,
For seldom is the house poor where God is steward.
  Well is he provéd
  Who the poor hath lovéd,
   My lief child.

When thou sittest in the church, o'er thy beads bend;
Make thou no jangling with gossip or with friend.
Laugh thou to scorn neither old body nor young,
But be of fair bearing and of good tongue.
  Through thy fair bearing
  Thy worship hath increasing,
   My lief child.

And wisely govern thy house, and serving maids and men,
Be thou not too bitter or too debonaire with them;
But look well what most needs to be done,
And set thy people at it, both rathely and soon.
>   For ready is at need
>   A foredone deed,
>   My lief child.

Whate'er thy household doth, about them must thou wend,
And as much as thou mayest, be at that one end,
If thou find any fault, make them soon amend,
As they have time and space, and may them defend.
>   To compel a deed be done, if there be no space,
>   It is but tyranny, without temperance and grace,
>   My lief child.

And give your household their hire at their term-day,
Whether they dwell still with thee, or they wend away.
Do well by them of the goods thou hast in hold,
And then shall they say well of thee, both the young and old.
>   Thy good name to thy friends
>   Great joy and gladness lends,
>   My lief child.

Housewifely thou shalt go on the working day,
For pride, rest and idleness take thrift away;
But when the Holy Day is come, well clothed shalt thou be,
The Holy Day to honour, and God will cherish thee.
>   Have in mind to worship God alway,
>   For much pride comes of the evil day,
>   My lief child.

When thou art a wife, a neighbour for to be,
Love then well thy neighbours as God hath commanded thee.
It behoveth thee so for to do,
And to do to them as thou wouldest be done to.
>   If any discord happen, night or day,
>   Make it no worse, mend it if thou may,
>   My lief child.

And if thou art a rich wife, be not then too hard,
But welcome fair thy neighbours that come to thee-ward
With meat, drink, and honest cheer, such as thou mayest bid,
To each man after his degree, and help the poor at need.
    And also for hap that may betide,
      Please well thy neighbours that dwell thee beside,
        My lief child.

And if thy children be rebel and will not bow them low,
If any of them misdo, neither curse them nor blow (scold);
But take a smart rod and beat them in a row,
Till they cry mercy and their guilt well know.
    Dear child, by this lore
      They will love thee ever more,
        My lief child.

Now have I taught thee, daughter, as my mother did me;
Think thereon night and day, that forgotten it not be.
Have measure and lowness, as I have thee taught,
Then whatever man shall wed thee will regret it naught.
    Better you were a child unbore
      Than untaught in this wise lore,
        My lief child.

The blessing of God may'st thou have, and of His mother bright,
Of all angels and archangels and every holy wight (creature)!
And may'st thou have grace to wend thy way full right,
To the bliss of heaven, where God sits in His might!
                      Amen.

CHAPTER XIX

MEDIEVAL LEARNING

1. *The Schoolmen*

IN the Middle Ages the two higher branches of learning that were most often studied were theology and philosophy. Theology is the study that seeks to know and understand the nature of God and to answer the questions that are always being asked concerning the soul, and life, and death. Philosophy is the study that seeks to find a way of life that commends itself to the mind and reason of man. It is not very easy to study these subjects apart from each other, and the way in which they were combined in the Middle Ages was called Scholasticism.

The authority in philosophy on whom the medieval scholar relied was Aristotle, and nearly all the teaching on philosophy was an explanation in great detail of his works. The medieval scholar was much concerned in the effort to reconcile the teaching of Aristotle with the doctrines of the Church, for the thought and philosophy of the time was inspired by the belief that all knowledge should be brought into one harmonious whole. The veneration that was given to Aristotle is well summed up by Averroës, the Spanish scholar at Cordova who died in 1198.

Aristotle was the wisest of the Greeks and constituted and completed logic, physics, and metaphysics. I say that he constituted these sciences, because all the works on these subjects previous to him do not deserve to be mentioned and were completely eclipsed by his writings. I say that he put the finishing touches on these sciences, because none of those who have succeeded him up to our time, to wit, during nearly fifteen hundred years, have been able to add anything to his writings or find in them any error of any importance. Now that all this should be found in one man is a strange and miraculous thing, and this privileged being deserves to be called divine rather than human.[1]

The teaching of Aristotle and the doctrine of the Church did not always agree and as both these authorities were held to be infallibly true, medieval scholars often got into difficulties. But the results of the methods of their reasoning were accepted as final and as an unquestioning and unquestioned guide in all matters of the intellect and conduct.

The most famous of the scholastic scholars, or School-men, as they were called, was St. Thomas Aquinas. He was not only celebrated for his great learning during his lifetime, but for centuries afterwards his teaching was considered authoritative and to question it was a heresy.

St. Thomas Aquinas was born in Italy about the year 1225. His parents were rich and his family was said to have royal blood in it. He was educated at the Benedic-tine monastery at Monte Cassino and then at Naples, where his teachers were amazed at the brilliance he showed, at the keenness of his mind and his extraordinary memory. Expecting of such a youth that he would make his mark in some secular occupation, his parents were dismayed when he announced his intention of becoming a monk and entering the Dominican order. He had his way, however, and he studied and taught in Paris and Rome, in Bologna and Orvieto. Once he went to London to be

[1] James Harvey Robinson, *Readings in European History*, Vol. I. Ginn and Company, Boston.

present at a chapter of his order that was held there. He died in 1274, still young, for he was not yet fifty years old.

St. Thomas Aquinas, the Angelic Doctor, as he was called, left as his chief work the *Summa Theologica*. In his philosophy he recognized as the two sources of all knowledge, the Christian faith which was authoritative in the form handed down by the Scriptures, the Fathers of the Church and the ancient Christian tradition, and the truths that come from human reasoning. Both came from God, therefore both must be true, and they could not contradict one another. This learning of the Schoolmen was weakened by their uncritical acceptance of dogma as being once for all authoritative, and the lesser Schoolmen who followed St. Thomas spent much time on subject matter that seems profitless to us today, but the modern world owes them a real debt. They insisted on a severe intellectual discipline in the use of words, a discipline which resulted in a clear and logical expression of ideas.

St. Thomas Aquinas was not only a learned Schoolman, he was also a poet. In 1264 the Pope instituted the festival of Corpus Christi, for which St. Thomas wrote the office, and in connection with this feast he wrote some Latin hymns. Some of these, such as the *Pangue lingua*, the *Adoro te devote*, and *O salutaris hostia* have been sung and treasured by the Christian Church for over seven hundred years.

2. *Roger Bacon*
1214-1292

Not all scholars insisted on an unquestioning acceptance of Aristotle as the source of all knowledge. At Paris in the twelfth century, Peter Abelard had declared that "doubt is the way to enquiry," and that "by enquiry we perceive the truth." He is also reported to have said that "a doctrine is not to be believed because God has said it, but because we are convinced by reason that it is so." Peter Abelard got into trouble with the authorities in Paris, his opinions were regarded as heretical and probably few people shared them. It was Roger Bacon, whose long life covered most of the thirteenth century, whose teaching was a real forecast of the modern attitude towards scientific knowledge.

Roger Bacon was a Franciscan friar at Oxford. He taught that human error was due to an undue regard to authority, to a false idea of what knowledge was, to prejudice and to habit which encouraged mental laziness. He declared that the only way to find out the truth was not merely to argue, but to observe and experiment, because it is by observation and experiment that conclusions can be tested. From Oxford he went to Paris, where he spent all the money he possessed on experiments. "Without mathematical instruments no science can be mastered," he said, but they were not to be had and to have them made was very costly. "They are worth a king's ransom," he lamented, "and could not be made without a vast expense." It was difficult to get books. Some of those he wanted had not been translated into Latin and were not to be found in libraries. He went back to Oxford and his order forbade him to teach his new methods. Then some one showed something of his work to the pope, Clement IV, who was interested and told him to write, but sent him no money, and his need for instruments with which he could continue his work on optics and physics was as great as ever. Clement IV died in 1277 and Roger Bacon was imprisoned because of his teaching. He was kept in prison till 1290, two years before his death. He described himself as "unheard, forgotten, buried," but though the recognition did not come in his life-time, his influence on thinking makes him the first modern scientific thinker.

In the Middle Ages mathematics was a term used to include physical science in general. Roger Bacon regretted the general neglect of mathematics by scholars, a neglect, he said, which "for nearly thirty or forty years hath nearly destroyed the entire studies of Latin Christendom. For he who knows not mathematics cannot know any other sciences; and what is more, he cannot discern his own ignorance or find its proper remedies."

As a result of his scientific experiments Roger Bacon foretold many things which, seemingly impossible in the thirteenth century, have been fulfilled in the nineteenth and twentieth.

1. A vessel may be so constructed, and oars therein so disposed, as to make more way with one man in her than another vessel fully manned.

2. It is possible to make a chariot which, without any assistance of animals, shall move with that irresistible force which is ascribed to those scythed chariots in which the ancients fought.

3. It is possible to make instruments for flying, so that a man sitting in the middle thereof, and steering with a kind of rudder, may manage what is contrived to answer the end of wings, so as to divide and pass through the air.

4. We can so shape transparent substances, and so arrange them with respect to our sight and objects, that rays can be broken and bent as we please, so that objects may be seen far off or near, under whatever angle we please, and thus from an incredible distance we may read even the smallest letters, and number the grains of dust and sand, on account of the greatness of the angle under which we see them; and we may manage so as hardly to see bodies when near

us, on account of the smallness of the angle under which we cause them to be seen; for vision of this sort is not a consequence of distance, except as that affects the magnitude of the angle. And thus a boy may seem a giant, and a man a mountain.

3. *Medieval Science*

EARLY medieval science had been a curious mixture of superstition and magic. Roger Bacon had influenced scientific thinking in the thirteenth century, but there were also other influences at work. Something has already been said of the early contributions of the Arabs to science. They had inherited some of the ancient Greek knowledge, for Arabic translations of Greek scientific works had been made long before the latter were known in western Europe. The works of Galen, for instance, the Greek physician of the second century, were well known to the Arabs, but it was only when Latin translations of the Arabic version were made for the use of students at the university of Salerno in the eleventh century, that western men of science knew anything about him or his work.

Between the years 750 and 1100 Arab scientists had done notable work not only in medicine, but as alchemists and chemists, in optics, mathematics, and astronomy. The Arabs had astronomical observatories at Bagdad, Damascus, Cairo, Samarcand and Cordova, and they had calculated the latitude and longitude of every great city in the Islamic world.

With the translation of many of the Arab writings into Latin, western science began to develop. The two orders of friars, in particular, interested themselves in scientific thinking. The Dominicans were always the more conservative (St. Thomas Aquinas was a Dominican), the Franciscans (Roger Bacon was a Franciscan), were more adventurous and critical. They made great advance in physics, chemistry, astronomy and mathematics.

These medieval scientists were not as ignorant as is often supposed. None of them believed that the world was flat; they understood eclipses and could predict them accurately. They had a knowledge of optics, Roger Bacon in particular. He wrote of the lens that it was "a useful instrument for the old who have impaired eyesight," and a little later it was said of it: "When the reader who looks at the writing of any book, however difficult it may seem to read to the naked eye, uses a lens, the letters appear greater, so that even the old can read with ease." The wonder of the work of medieval scientists is not that they knew so little, but that with so little in the way of scientific instruments or equipment they advanced so far.

4. The Making of a Medieval Book

IN the Middle Ages every book had to be made by hand. The parchment that was used, the cutting of the sheets into the size wanted for the leaves, the binding of the book and the copying of the script were all hand work. In the early Middle Ages the chief makers of books were monks and in every large monastery there was a room, called the *Scriptorium*, where the work was done. Later, scribes were found in all places where education was carried on, especially in university towns where there was a demand for books, and the work of the scribe became a profession.

A scribe had to copy carefully and accurately the text that was set before him. This may have been a Missal, a Psalter, a Book of Hours or the Gospels; it may have been a book about the lives of the Saints; it may have been a copy of an ancient classic or one of the writings of a Father of the Church; it may have been some of the poetry or prose, songs or chronicles that were being written during the Middle Ages. The work was slow and infinite patience was needed to transcribe the pages, word by word and letter by letter. In a monastery there were strict rules for all who worked in the scriptorium. No candles might be used, for the manuscripts that were being copied were very precious and the danger from fire was great. No one was allowed to speak and generally no one might enter the room unless he were a scribe.

The handwriting that was used was varied. The older script was larger, with letters not unlike modern capitals; as the centuries went by the form of the letters changed, they became smaller and narrower. Parchment was more expensive than papyrus had been and scribes found it necessary to put more on a page. In the time of Charlemagne a particularly beautiful script was used. It was simple, clear and dignified and was soon adopted by most schools.

For about four hundred years there was comparatively little change in the character of the script used, then a difference appeared. The architecture was changing from the grave dignity and rounded arch of the romanesque period to the soaring height and pointed arch of the Gothic buildings. At the same time the handwriting changed from the simpler script of the early Middle Ages to the Gothic script of the later period. It became more angular, the vertical strokes were heavy and the general form was pointed. Both forms of medieval writing were developed by men whose work was influenced by that of those who fashioned in stone.

The work of the scribe was laborious, it took a long

time and needed endless patience. Many of the medieval manuscripts have a note added at the end, in which the scribe expressed his relief at having finished a weary task.

> I have made an end at last,
> And my weary hand can rest,

wrote one tired worker, and another, copying books for a livelihood, scribbled at the end,

> Now that I an end have made,
> See that what I'm owed is paid.

Occasionally such notes appear in the margin. Sometimes they are comments on the work copied, or ideas that have suddenly flitted through the mind of the scribe. Sometimes they are irrelevant remarks about the scribe himself or his companions; sometimes they are scraps of poetry. In the eighth century an Irish monk once stopped his work long enough to write a poem about his cat.

PANGUR BAN

> I and Pangur Ban, my cat,
> 'Tis a like task we are at;
> Hunting mice is his delight,
> Hunting words I sit all night.
>
> Better far than praise of men
> 'Tis to sit with book and pen;
> Pangur bears me no ill-will,
> He, too, plies his simple skill.
>
> 'Tis a merry thing to see
> At our tasks how glad are we,
> When at home we sit and find
> Entertainment to our mind.

Oftentimes a mouse will stray
In the hero Pangur's way;
Oftentimes my keen thought set
Takes a meaning in his net.

'Gainst the wall he sets his eye
Full and fierce, and sharp and sly;
'Gainst the wall of knowledge I
All my little wisdom try.

When a mouse darts from its den,
Oh! how glad is Pangur then;
Oh! what gladness do I prove
When I solve the doubts I love.

So in peace our task we ply,
Pangur Ban, my cat, and I;
In our arts we find our bliss,
I have mine, and he has his.

Practice every day has made
Pangur perfect in his trade;
I get wisdom day and night,
Turning darkness into light.[1]

Closely allied to the work of the scribe was that of the illuminator, and illuminated manuscripts are amongst the most beautiful examples of medieval art that exist. Just as the script varied, so did the kind of illumination, and different schools developed characteristics of their own. Initial letters of paragraphs were made large, they were coloured and ornamented both with designs and with small pictures. Margins were highly decorated in the same way, sometimes even a whole page was taken up by an illustration.

In the early Middle Ages nearly all illuminated manu-

[1] Translated by Robin Flower.

scripts were made by monks. Later, the work was done outside the monastery, and other books besides Missals and Service-Books, the Psalter and the Gospels were illustrated and illuminated. In some towns illuminators were organized in craft gilds and their work was as strictly regulated as that of any other craft. In the earlier manuscripts the chief colours used were gold, red and blue; later, green and other colours appeared, so that it is possible to date a manuscript not only by the form of the script, but also by the colours.

Many of the books made in the monasteries were for the use of the monks, but those made outside were generally ordered by wealthy patrons to be given as gifts to some great personage. A Book of Hours was a favourite gift. It generally began with a calendar containing all the feasts to be observed during the year. Such a book gave the artist a wide choice of subjects for his illustrations, and in some of the calendars in these books the occupations of the year are represented. Sometimes it is country life with the toil characteristic of the different seasons, others show the life of the castle and the different occupations during the year of knights and ladies.

The work of the illuminator, like that of the scribe, was one in which every detail was finished and perfected with skill and care. The manuscripts are amongst the important sources for our knowledge of all kinds of medieval customs, for, no matter what the subject of the illustrations may be, they are all placed in a medieval setting.

5. *Medieval Libraries*

MOST medieval libraries were in monasteries or universities. Monastic rules and chronicles make a good many references to books and reading, and study was an important part of a monk's life. The Benedictine Rule provided for time every day for reading and study, and at the beginning of Lent every monk was expected to take a book from the library and read it through.

In some monasteries a day was appointed on which all the monks went to the chapter house, book in hand. The librarian would then read out the name of each monk and the book he had received, and when he heard his name, the monk would rise from his seat and return his book. If he had not read it, he was expected to fall on his face and ask for pardon.

In the early Middle Ages books were kept in cupboards in the cloister, but as the number of books increased special rooms were set apart where they were kept. After the fourteenth century, universities sometimes even had separate buildings as libraries. In these medieval libraries each book was chained to a desk and the student had to stand while he read. When a room became too crowded, the method of keeping books on shelves was adopted, but always the books were chained to the shelves.

It would seem that it has always been difficult to care for books in libraries. The rules for a fourteenth century library in Oxford are still in existence. Every book was to be chained, there were to be two librarians and one was always to be present whenever the library was open. He was required to see that no one brought either a pen or a knife into the room, and readers seem also to have been refused admittance if they appeared in wet clothes. It was not easy to obtain permission to use the library, and when it had been gained, the student had to take an oath that he would not in any way mutilate a book.

In these libraries there were always the Bible, the service books of the Church, the writings of the Fathers, especially of St. Augustine and of Gregory the Great, and in English libraries copies of the works of Bede. History, chronicles, occasionally some of the classical writers of Rome, lives of the saints, books on law, some of the early Christian Latin poetry, and as time went on the writings of the great medieval scholars were to be found in most libraries. The number of books varied according to the size or the wealth of the monastery, cathedral or university. Some had less than fifty volumes, others had several hundred and in a few cases even a thousand or more.

Books were so costly that it was almost impossible for private individuals to possess many, but in the later Middle Ages kings and princes began collecting books and the foundations were laid of what are now amongst the great libraries of Europe. The fifteenth century popes, Nicholas V and Sixtus IV began the collection of books that is now the library of the Vatican, and a little later Francis I of France possessed a library that became part of the Bibliothèque Nationale in Paris. With the invention of printing, books became less costly, and so their number increased. The work of the scribe and the illuminator was no longer needed, but the men who could print and the people who could collect books for themselves were no longer living in the Middle Ages, but in the period that is called that of the Renaissance.

PART III

THE LATER MIDDLE AGES

CHAPTER XX

ADVENTURES IN GOVERNMENT

WHENEVER men live together in communities, no matter how small the communities may be, so that order may be maintained and that there may be justice between man and his neighbour, some form of law has to be observed. The form that this law takes in different places, in different communities or countries is what is called government.

Communities or countries are always governed in one of three ways: either by one man, or by a few men, or by many men. In the early Middle Ages, though in most countries there were kings at the head of the government, they were not always very powerful, for the great feudal lords had their own armed retainers and administered justice in their own courts. In the later Middle Ages especially after the Crusades, the feudal system grew gradually weaker and the kings and the central government became stronger. But all governments were not alike. In some the king ruled almost alone and was called absolute; in some he had an elected parliament which he was expected to consult on all important occasions; in Italy and Flanders the chief cities were independent of any central royal authority and governed themselves; the Holy Roman Empire was a group of German states, self-governing for all domestic affairs, but loosely joined together under an elected Emperor. He had little more power over the states of the empire than certain feudal rights, but he was important in the Middle Ages because he claimed the right to have a voice in the election of the pope.

The two countries in the Middle Ages which developed important forms of government, both for themselves and for their influence on the future, were England and France.

1. *England and Parliament*

IT has already been seen that the early Anglo-Saxons in England governed themselves by assemblies called Folk-Moots, and that when England became united under a king, there developed a larger assembly called the Witan. In 1066 William of Normandy conquered England, but though he introduced many new Norman customs, he did not destroy the old institutions he found in England, when these institutions were good. In Anglo-Saxon England the Witan consisted of the bishops, some of the more important abbots, and such thegns (a thegn was the Anglo-Saxon *companion* of the king), as the king chose to invite. Under William I and the Norman kings who succeeded him, the Witan became known as the Great Council, but there was a real difference between the two. The thegns who attended the Witan were chosen by the King, whereas all those who held land from the King, all who were his tenants, had the right to attend the Great Council.

In the thirteenth century the barons were the strongest class in England. They had already had some experience in government, for the Shire Courts were under their control. Henry II (1154-1189) had been a strong king. He had organized the courts of the country, developed the work of the judges, and introduced the jury system. But he was succeeded first by Richard I (1189-1199) who was out of England on a Crusade for the greater part of his reign, and then by John (1199-1216).

John had quarrelled with the pope, spent a great deal of money, some of it in fighting, and lost nearly all the lands in France ruled by the English kings. He ruled so badly that the barons refused to grant him any more money. In 1215, led by the archbishop of Canterbury, Stephen Langton, they forced him to sign Magna Carta. This was a charter which contained the ancient rights of the English concerning justice, taxation, and the liberties of England.

In the year of our Lord 1215, which was the seventeenth year of the reign of King John, he held his court at Winchester at Christmas for one day, after which he hurried to London, and took up his abode at the New Temple; and at that place the nobles came to him in gay military array, and demanded the confirmation of the liberties and laws of King Edward (the Confessor), with such other liberties granted to them and to the kingdom and church of England as were contained in the charter and the above-mentioned laws of Henry I. They also asserted that at the time of his absolution at Winchester he had promised to restore those laws and ancient liberties, and was bound by his own oath to observe them. The king, hearing the bold tone of the barons in making this demand, much feared an attack from them, as he saw that they were prepared for battle; he however made answer that their demands were a matter of importance and difficulty, and he therefore asked a truce till the end of Easter, that he might, after due deliberation, be able to satisfy them as well as the dignity of the crown.[1]

[1] Roger of Wendover. James Harvey Robinson, *Readings in European History*, Vol. I. Ginn and Company, Boston.

The barons granted this delay, and after Easter they again assembled and made the same demands of the king. He sent messengers to the barons asking them what it was they demanded of him.

The barons then delivered to the messengers a paper, containing in great measure the laws and ancient customs of the kingdom, and declared that unless the king immediately granted them and confirmed them under his own seal they would, by taking possession of his fortresses, force him to give them sufficient satisfaction as to their before-named demands.

The archbishop with his fellow-messengers then carried the paper to the king and read to him all the heads of the paper, one by one. The king, when he heard the purport of these heads, derisively said, with the greatest indignation, "Why, amongst all these unjust demands, did not the barons ask for my kingdom also? their demands are vain and visionary, and are unsupported by any plea of reason whatever." And at length he angrily declared, with an oath, that he would never grant them such liberties as would render him their slave.[1]

But John found that he stood almost alone, and he was forced at last to meet the barons and to grant their demands. On the 15th of June 1215 they met at Runnymede, an island in the Thames near Windsor, and John signed the charter.

Some of the more important of the clauses of Magna Carta were:

No scutage or aid shall be imposed in our kingdom save by the common council of our kingdom, except for the ransoming of our body, for the making of our oldest son a knight, and for once marrying our oldest daughter; and for these purposes it shall be only a reasonable aid. (Article 12.)

No free man shall be taken, or imprisoned, or dispossessed, or outlawed, or banished, or in any way injured, nor will we go

[1] Roger of Wendover.

upon him, nor send upon him, except by the legal judgment of his peers, or by the law of the land. (Article 39.)

To no one will we sell, to no one will we deny or delay, right or justice. (Article 40.)

In Magna Carta the King also promised to send a writ summoning each of the greater barons to the Great Council by name. This was the origin of the House of Lords.

And for holding a common council of the kingdom concerning the assessment of an aid otherwise than in the three cases mentioned above, or concerning the assessment of a scutage, we shall cause to be summoned the archbishops, bishops, abbots, earls, and greater barons by our letters under seal; and, besides, we shall cause to be summoned generally, by our sheriffs and bailiffs, all those who hold from us in chief, for a certain day, at the end of at least forty days, and for a certain place; and in all the letters of that summons we will state the cause of the summons, and when the summons has thus been given the business shall proceed on the appointed day, on the advice of those who shall be present, even if not all of those who were summoned have come. (Article 14.)[1]

Fifty years after Magna Carta there was another controversy between the king (Henry III) and the barons. Henry III was a good man, but a very weak ruler. The chronicler calls him the king with the waxen heart. He had married a French princess, Eleanor of Provence, and with her had come to England a host of French relations and friends who were given positions of importance in England in both church and state. As a result of John's controversy with the pope, papal exactions had increased in England. A popular song of the day said:

[1] James Harvey Robinson, *Readings in European History*, Vol. I. Ginn and Company, Boston.

King and Pope, alike in this, to one purpose hold,
How to make the clergy yield their silver and their gold.[1]

By 1258 the misgovernment of the king had reached
the point where the barons began to resist openly. Led by
Simon de Montfort they fought against the king and took
him prisoner. By 1265 Simon was in a strong enough position to call a parliament from which in addition to the
barons and clergy, two burghers from each town were to
be elected *ad parlamentum* (i.e., to have a discussion). But
in the same year Simon de Montfort fought another battle, this time against Prince Edward, and he was killed.

The cause for which Simon de Montfort had given his
life did not die with him. In 1272 Henry III died and
was succeeded by his son Edward I. Since fighting against
the barons Edward, accompanied by his wife, Eleanor of
Castile, had been to the Holy Land on a Crusade. Edward
I was one of the great medieval kings. He was a statesman and his legislation earned for him the name of the
English Justinian. He believed that England, Wales and
Scotland would be better ruled under one king and he
succeeded in bringing Wales under English government,
but he was not successful in Scotland. The motto of this
king of England sums up his ideals and character: *Pactum
serva,* Keep troth.

We are concerned here with Edward I and the development of Parliament. Like all medieval kings he was
largely dependent on his barons for the raising of money.
He had needed an army for his campaigns in Wales and
Scotland, and to keep order on the Welsh marches (the
border between England and Wales) he had built strong
castles. The towns were growing in importance and in

---

[1] R. B. Mowat, *A New History of Great Britain.* Oxford University Press, London and New York.

wealth, but according to Magna Carta their consent was necessary if they were to be taxed. In 1295 Edward I summoned what has since been called the Model Parliament. To it were summoned the greater barons (the Lords), the Bishops and Abbots (the Clergy), knights from the shires and burghers from the towns (the Commons).

A Summons to Parliament by Edward I, A.D. 1295.

The King to the Sheriff of Northamptonshire:

Since we intend to have a consultation and meeting with the earls, barons and other principal men of our kingdom with regard to providing remedies against the dangers which are in these days threatening the same kingdom, and on that account have commanded them to be with us on the Lord's day next after the feast of St. Martin in the approaching winter, at Westminster, to consider, ordain, and do as may be necessary for the avoidance of those dangers, we strictly require you to cause two knights from the aforesaid county, two citizens from each city in the same county, and two burgesses from each borough, of those who are especially discreet and capable of labouring, to be elected without delay, and to cause them to come to us at the aforesaid time and place.

Moreover, the said knights are to have full and sufficient power for themselves and for the community of the aforesaid county, and the said citizens and burgesses for themselves, and the communities of the aforesaid cities and boroughs separately, then and there, for doing what shall then be ordained according to the common council in the premises; so that the aforesaid business shall not remain unfinished in any way for defect of this power. And you shall have there the names of the knights, citizens, and burgesses, together with this writ.

Witness the King, at Canterbury, on the 3rd of October.

Though this parliament of 1295 was the model for succeeding parliaments, its duties were very different from those of a parliament or of other legislative bodies today. To the barons the king explained his policy and he expected that they would agree with it; from the knights and burghers he expected money to carry on the government and to carry out whatever policy he had decided on. Parliament could, however, present petitions to the king. If he refused what was asked, he said, *Le roi s'avisera;* if he granted the request he said, *Le roi le veult,* and the petition became law. Nearly all medieval legislation in England was passed in this way.

After the thirteenth century, Parliament grew in importance and added to its powers. By the fifteenth century it controlled the finances of England, both Houses had a share in the making and passing of laws, Parliament could act as judge of the royal ministers and debates were free. Under strong kings Parliament was apt to be of little importance, under weak kings, it was very powerful; but under all conditions, from the thirteenth century onwards, it was an essential part of the English government.

2. *France and Absolute Monarchy*

a. Philip Augustus, 1180-1223

In 1180 Philip II, called Philip Augustus, became king of France. He inherited a country in which the king of England ruled more land than the king of France and in which in spite of the work of Louis VI, the feudal lords were still powerful and menacing. Philip Augustus was only fifteen years old when he became king, but he was intelligent and able, vigorous and ambitious. "I desire," he said, "that at the end of my reign the monarchy shall be as powerful as in the time of Charlemagne."

Philip II reigned from 1180 to 1223 and during this time he came into conflict with three kings of England:

Henry II and his two sons Richard I and John. Philip supported Richard and John when they were plotting against their father in France, and though he had been outwardly friendly to the king of England, Philip invaded his territory and Henry was forced to retreat. Defeated and disappointed, Henry asked for the names of those who had been fighting against him.

He therefore sent Master Roger, the Keeper of the Seal, to the King of France to demand the promised list. Master Roger sent to Tours where he copied the list of those who had promised to help the French. On his return Henry asked him the names: "Sire," replied he with a sigh, "the first name on the roll is that of your son Count John."

If that were so, he had nothing left to live for. John was his favourite son. "Now," he said, "let things go as they will. I care no more for myself or for the world." He died soon after, murmuring to himself, "Shame, shame, on a conquered king."

In the meantime Richard I had joined Philip II in the Third Crusade. Philip had returned to France in 1191, Richard was not back till 1194. In his absence Philip had taken Normandy from him and for five years after the return of Richard the two kings fought. Sometimes one was successful, sometimes the other. Near Les Andelys on the Seine Richard had built a castle, despite a treaty he had made with Philip. It was one of the strongest fortresses of the Middle Ages, and built to defy the French king. Richard called it Chateau Gaillard. Philip determined to capture it. "I will take it," he said, "even if its walls are of iron." Quickly came back the retort, "I will hold it, were its walls of butter." The castle was taken by Philip, but not until the reign of John.

In 1199 Richard was attacking the castle of the Viscount of Limoges when an arrow shot by an archer on the battlements wounded him. He was told that the wound was serious and he asked to see the archer.

"What evil had I done to thee that thou shouldst kill me?"

"Thou hast slain with thine own hand my father and my two brothers, and wouldst have killed me also. Take what vengeance thou wouldst; I am ready to suffer all the cruelties thou canst invent, provided that thou thyself art to die, thou who hast done so many and so great evils in the world."

Richard replied to the archer that he would pardon him.

"I want not thy pardon. I am happy to die."

"Thou shalt live in spite of thyself," replied the king, "a living witness of my humaneness."

And after seeing that he was given a hundred sous in English money, the King had him set at liberty.

A few days later, Richard died, but the man who had killed him was taken and cruelly put to death. Richard's chivalry was not always shared by those who served him. Minstrels lamented for Cœur de Lion and his deeds and prowess passed into tale and song.

ON THE DEATH OF KING RICHARD OF ENGLAND

Alas! the greatest ill that I have known,
    The bitterest woe that time can ever bring,
Woe that I needs must endlessly bemoan,
    Must e'en by me be sung, by me proclaimed;
    For Valour's sire and chief, of deeds far-famed—
The mighty Richard, England's noble king,
Is dead. Ah, God! that death what voice can sing!
    How terrible that word! How cruel its sound!
    How cold were he whom all unmoved it found!

Dead is the king. A thousand years and more
    Have passed since e'er his like on earth was seen;
Yet such a man there never lived before,
    Of bounty and of bravery so vaunted,

E'en Alexander, who Darius daunted,
Ne'er gave so freely as my lord, I ween;
Nor Charles nor Arthur braver knights have been;
　　And of a truth, in half the world he waked
　　A mighty love—the rest in terror quaked.

Alas, Sir King! how will without thee fare
　　Tourneys and arms, and many a noble fight,
Many a rich feast, and gallant gift and rare,
　　Since thou, their founder, desolate dost leave us?
　　And how will all they fare of fortune grievous,
Who, serving thee, were raised from hapless plight,
And hope that thou their toils wouldst rich requite?
　　How will those fare, to whom thou e'er didst give
　　Great wealth and power? Such now should scorn to live.

Such now will suffer grievous want and woe,
　　And endless tears for thee will dim their eyes.
Pagans and Turks for death of their dread foe,
　　Whom more than any mother's son they feared,
　　Down-trodden erst, their haughty heads have reared,
That hard it were to win the Tomb for prize.
So God doth will, but willed He otherwise,
　　And thou, my lord, didst live, I nothing doubt
　　That soon from Syria thou wouldst drive them out.

That kings and princes Syria regain,
　　Thereof, alack! all hope is long since dead;
But those that now do in thy place remain,
　　Should mind them of the fame thou hadst before them,
　　And of thy brothers, who full stoutly bore them,
(The young king and Earl Geoffrey, Bretagne's head)
And certes be he that ruleth in their stead,
　　A constant heart should bear, and turn his face
　　From all things ill, and do the deeds of grace.

Great Lord and God, to whom belongeth pardon,
　　Thou that art God, and Man, and Life indeed,
　　Grant him that pardon that his sins do need,

His faults and failings mercifully o'erlook,
Remember that for Thee the Cross he took.[1]

The struggle with the English king continued after the death of Richard. In 1202 King John was summoned to Paris.

The Court of France declared that the King of England should be deprived of all the fiefs which he held from the King of France, for not having fulfilled the conditions on which the said fiefs were held, and for having disobeyed his suzerain in almost every way.[2]

For two years Philip and John fought and besieged each other's castles, until in 1204 Philip captured Chateau Gaillard and Normandy was lost to England. During the next ten years Philip gradually won for the French monarchy Anjou, Touraine and Maine, but during the same period his enemies were plotting against him. In 1214 John joined the Emperor and the Count of Flanders and gave battle to Philip at Bouvines. The result was a victory for Philip, and a treaty was made with John by which only part of the south of Aquitaine was left to England.

France received the news with rejoicing.

"Who could describe in writing the hymns of victory, the innumerable dances, the songs of the clerics, the chimes of the bells under the golden cocks, the adornment of the sanctuaries, the white hangings of the houses draped in cendal and silk, the strewing of roads and streets in which brightly coloured flowers and green branches were spread.[3]

Under Philip II France prospered. Paris became a great city. He strengthened its defences, he added to its build-

[1] Gaucelm Faidit (Troubadour of the 12th century).
[2] Raoul, Abbot of Coggeshall.
[3] William le Breton.

ings, it was in his reign that Notre Dame was begun; he encouraged schools and learning; he brought to Paris merchants from all parts of northern France. Outside Paris Philip Augustus showed himself a friend of the towns which were growing up in all parts of France and he fostered trade and commerce.

Philip Augustus found that the old feudal officials of the courts of his predecessors did not suffice for the administration of a whole kingdom, and he instituted a new office, that of the *bailli*. A bailli was in charge of a certain district and he was responsible to the king for the order kept, the justice administered and the taxes collected. A chronicler of the time said of Philip Augustus:

No one could deny that for our time Philip was a good prince. Under him the kingdom was strengthened and the royal power was greatly increased. Only—if he had been more gentle and moderate, the kingdom would have been all the better.[1]

But when he died in 1223 Philip Augustus in fact, as well as in name, was king of France.

b. St. Louis
1226-1270

In 1226 the grandson of Philip Augustus, Louis IX, called St. Louis, came to the throne. He was only twelve years old and until he came of age, France was ruled by his mother, Blanche of Castile. He inherited a well-knit kingdom and because of his personality and character, his reign was one of the great periods in medieval French history. He loved justice, he refused to give bribes, forbade the barons to tax the people on their land too heavily, and transformed the ruthless ambition of Philip Augustus

[1] Gille of Paris.

into a policy that brought a greater contentment to the French people.

The picture of St. Louis given us by Joinville shows us a man of sincere and deep piety. He attended Mass every day, he observed all the obligations of the Church, his charity was boundless. He lived very simply and it was easy for all to approach him.

Ofttimes it happened that he would go, after his mass, and seat himself in the wood of Vincennes, and lean against an oak, and make us sit round him. And all those who had any cause in hand came and spoke to him without hindrance of usher, or of any other person. Then would he ask, out of his own mouth, "Is there any one who has a cause in hand?" And those who had a cause in hand stood up. Then would he say, "Keep silence all, and, you shall be heard in turn, one after the other." Then he would call my Lord Peter of Fontaines and my Lord Geoffrey of Villette, and say to one of them, "Settle me this cause."

And when he saw that there was anything to amend in the words of those who spoke on behalf of any other person, he would himself, out of his own mouth, amend what they had said. Sometimes have I seen him, in summer, go to do justice among his people in the garden of Paris, clothed in a tunic of camlet, a surcoat of tartan without sleeves, and a mantle of black taffeta about his neck, his hair well combed, no cap, and a hat of white peacock's feathers upon his head. And he would cause a carpet to be laid down, so that we might sit round him, and all the people who had any cause to bring before him stood around. And then would he have their causes settled, as I have told you afore he was wont to do in the wood of Vincennes.[1]

As a soldier St. Louis was brave. "Never was there so fine a man under arms," said Joinville, "and the finest knight that was ever seen."

The advice given by St. Louis to his son who was to

[1] Joinville's *Chronicle of the Crusade of St. Louis.*

become king after him, showed what his ideals of kingship were:

Fair son, the first thing I would teach thee is to set thine heart to love God; for unless he love God none can be saved. Keep thyself from doing aught that is displeasing to God, that is to say from mortal sin.

If God send thee adversity, receive it in patience, and give thanks to our Saviour, and bethink thee that thou hast deserved it, and that He will make it turn to thine advantage. If He send thee prosperity, then thank Him humbly, so that thou become not worse from pride, or any other cause, when thou oughtest to be better.

Maintain the good customs of thy realm, and abolish the bad. Be not covetous against thy people; and do not burden them with taxes and imposts save when thou art in great need.

Let none be so bold as to say before thee any word that would draw and move to sin, or so bold as to speak evil behind another's back for pleasure's sake; nor do thou suffer any word in disparagement of God and of His saints to be spoken in thy presence. Give often thanks to God for all the good things He has bestowed upon thee, so that thou be accounted worthy to receive more.

In order to do justice and right to thy subjects, be upright and firm, turning neither to the right hand nor to the left, but always to what is just; and do thou maintain the cause of the poor until such time as the truth is made clear.

If thou holdest aught that belongeth to another, whether by thine own act or the act of thy predecessors, and the matter be certain, make restoration without delay. If the matter be doubtful, cause inquiry to be made by wise men, diligently and promptly.

Give heed that thy servants and thy subjects live under thee in peace and uprightness. Especially maintain the good cities and commons of thy realm in the same estate and with the same franchises as they enjoyed under thy predecessors; and if there be aught to amend, amend and set it right, and keep them in thy favour and love. For because of the power and wealth of the great cities, thine own subjects, and specially thy peers and thy barons, and foreigners also, will fear to undertake aught against thee.

Beware of undertaking a war against any Christian prince without great deliberation; and if it has to be undertaken, see that thou do no hurt to holy Church, and to those who have done thee no injury. If wars and dissensions arise among thy subjects, see that thou appease them as soon as thou art able.

Fair dear son, I give thee all the blessings that a good father can give to his son. And may the blessed Trinity and all the saints keep and defend thee from all evils; and God give thee grace to do His will always, so that He be honoured in thee, and that thou and I may both, after this mortal life is ended, be with Him together, and praise Him everlastingly. Amen.[1]

In 987 Hugh Capet ruled little more than the land round Paris. Three hundred years later, when Philip IV, called the Fair, became king (1285), he ruled over the whole land of France except some parts of the north and east. By this time the king was aided by ministers and councils, but France had not the same kind of assembly that was developing in England. There was, however, a council in France consisting of the Three Estates, the Lords, Clergy and Commons. This council was called the Estates-General. These men did not meet to pass laws, but as a rule only to authorize money grants to the king. Philip IV summoned them three times, the last time in 1314. But though it was an elected, representative assembly, it was allowed no share in the government, and whereas at the end of the Middle Ages the English government was on a road that was to lead in the seventeenth century to a constitutional monarchy, the French government followed the road that was to lead to complete absolutism.

[1] Joinville's *Chronicle of the Crusade of St. Louis.*

CHAPTER XXI

THE HUNDRED YEARS' WAR

THERE had been much warfare during the early Middle Ages. Alfred the Great had fought to keep invaders out of England. William the Conqueror had fought, and successfully, to conquer England. On the continent Charles Martel had fought to keep the Moors out of France. Charlemagne had fought in order to unite vast lands in one empire. Later, kings, barons and knights of western Christendom had joined together in the crusading movement, and all through the period there had been constant petty warfare amongst the feudal lords themselves.

By the fourteenth century the countries of Europe were more clearly defined than in the earlier periods. The kings of England had lost their lands in France, and England was developing as an English land. The kings of France were no longer weaker than their feudal vassals and France was a country with a character of its own and its own interests and ambitions. Where conflicts had once been between rival barons, they now developed between rival countries, and in the fourteenth century a great war broke out between England and France which lasted for a century. This war has been called the Hundred Years' War, but as a matter of fact it was a number of different wars, fought at different periods, with stretches of peace in between.

Medieval warfare gave opportunity for deeds of hero-ism and of self-sacrifice, and many tales of chivalry have come down to us from this period. But in spite of this, the war was the great catastrophe of the later Middle Ages. France and England had begun to develop relations with each other that should have led to friendly intercourse and friendly rivalry. But the wars put a stop to all that, and instead of friendly relations, France and England de-veloped antagonisms and jealousy of each other which had far-reaching consequences for later periods. The kings who carried on the wars tended to become more despotic and the lords who fought with them became greedy for lands and plunder. The war was fought in France. It began in 1338 and ten years later a terrible plague, known as the Black Death, swept over Europe. What the war began in devastation and slaughter, the Black Death con-tinued, and the peasants and country people in France were left at the end of the war in a miserable condition.

Medieval warfare did not touch every one, as modern wars do, and on the whole the towns, especially in Eng-land, took little part and they carried on their business as if no warfare were going on about them. In many ways this may have been good for the towns, but it tended to keep them self-centred and aloof from the affairs of the country as a whole.

The English won most of the battles in the Hundred Years' War, but in the end they were driven out of France, and they had gained little or nothing by the long years of fighting. France, on the other hand, in spite of many defeats, had in the end rallied round a leader who did more, perhaps, than any other one person to give to the

French of the fifteenth century a sense of patriotism and of a common nationality. That leader was Jeanne d'Arc.

There were several causes for the war. For a long time whenever the English had been fighting in France, the Scotch had taken the part of the latter, or if the English were fighting in Scotland, then France had helped the Scotch. There was an old saying that ran:

> "If that you will France win,
> Then with Scotland first begin,"

and there was enough truth in it for it to be one of the causes of friction between England and France. Then the French had interfered with the English wool trade in Flanders, a trade which England was inclined to look upon as her monopoly. And lastly, Edward III claimed that he was the lawful king of France. The claim was based on the fact that the mother of Edward III was the sister of Charles IV of France who had died leaving no son to succeed him. But the ancient tradition of the Salic Law did not consider a claim to the throne made through a woman to be valid, and so a cousin of Charles was made king. Edward III had no right to the French throne but the claim was made because of an alliance he had made with the burghers of Flanders.

1. The Black Prince and Crécy

THE war began in 1338. The Count of Flanders was allied with France, but the Flemish burghers opposed this policy because the interests of the Flemish wool trade were more closely bound up with England. Jacques van Artevelde, a rich wool merchant of Ghent, headed the

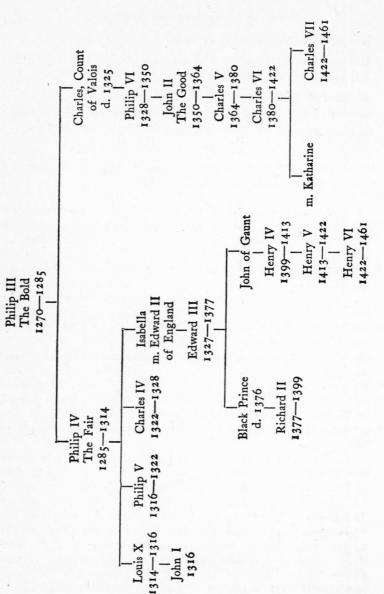

ENGLAND AND THE CLAIMS TO THE FRENCH THRONE

Philip III
The Bold
1270—1285

Philip IV
The Fair
1285—1314

Louis X
1314—1316

John I
1316

Philip V
1316—1322

Charles IV
1322—1328

Isabella
m. Edward II
of England

Edward III
1327—1377

Black Prince
d. 1376

Richard II
1377—1399

John of Gaunt

Henry IV
1399—1413

Henry V
1413—1422

Henry VI
1422—1461

Charles, Count
of Valois
d. 1325

Philip VI
1328—1350

John II
The Good
1350—1364

Charles V
1364—1380

Charles VI
1380—1422

m. Katharine

Charles VII
1422—1461

burghers against the count. The pope gave his support to the count and France, and he threatened the rebellious Flemings with an interdict unless they paid a large sum of money to the king of France. At the same time Edward III was trying to gain the support of the Flemings against France. If they would help him, he promised to get back for them certain of their towns that the French had taken. By assuming the title of king of France, he solved the difficulty of the Flemings.

This request was well heard of the Flemings, and thereupon they desired to take counsel among themselves; and so they took counsel at good leisure, and then they said to the king: "Sir, or this time you have made to us request in this behalf: sir, if we might well do this, saving your honour and to save ourselves, we would gladly do this; but, sir, we be bound by faith and oath and on the sum of two millions of florins in the pope's chamber, that we may make nor move no war against the king of France, whosoever it be, on pain to lose the said sum and beside that to run in the sentence of cursing. But, sir, if ye will take on you the arms of France and quarter them with the arms of England and call yourself king of France, as ye ought to be of right, then we will take you for rightful king of France and demand of you quittance of our bonds, and so ye to give us pardon thereof as king of France: by this means we shall be assured and dispensed withal, and so then we will go with you whithersoever ye will have us."

Then the king took counsel, for he thought it was a sore matter to take on him the arms of France and the name, and as then had conquered nothing thereof, nor could not tell what should fall thereof, nor whether he should conquer it or not; and on the other side, loth he was to refuse the comfort and aid of the Flemings, who might do him more aid than any other. So the king took counsel of the lords of the Empire and of the lord Robert d'Artois and with other of his special friends; so that finally, the good and the evil weighed, he answered to the Flemings that if they would swear and seal to this accord, and to promise to maintain his war, how he would do all this with a good will, and promised to get them again Lille, Douay and Bethune: and all they answered how they were content.[1]

Edward III agreed to this. He called himself king of France, quartered the lilies of France on the shield of England, and took as his motto Dieu et mon Droit.

The first battle was fought in 1340. It was the battle of Sluys and was fought at sea.

The king of England and his came sailing till he came before Sluys: and when he saw so great a number of ships that their masts seemed to be like a great wood, he demanded of the master of his ship what people he thought they were. He answered and said, "Sir, I think they be Normans laid here by the French king, and hath done great displeasure in England, brent your town of Hampton and taken your great ship the Christofer." "Ah," quoth the king, "I have long desired to fight with the Frenchmen, and now shall I fight with some of them by the grace of God and Saint George; for truly they have done me so many displeasures, that I shall be revenged, an I may."

Then there began a sore battle on both parts: archers and cross-bows began to shoot, and men of arms approached and fought hand to hand: and the better to come together they had great hooks and grappers of iron, to cast out of one ship into another, and so tied them fast together. There were many deeds of arms done, taking and rescuing again, and at last the great Christofer was first won by the Englishmen, and all that were within it taken or slain. Then there was great noise and cry, and the Englishmen approached and fortified the Christofer with archers, and made him to pass on before to fight with the Genoways. This battle was right fierce and terrible; for the battles on the sea are more dangerous and fiercer than the battles by land: for on the sea there is no reculing nor fleeing; there is no remedy but to fight and to abide fortune, and every man to show his prowess. This battle endured from the morning till it was noon, and the Englishmen endured much pain, for their enemies were four against one, and all good men on the sea.

[1] *The Chronicles of Froissart.*

But in the end the English prevailed. The Frenchmen, Normans and others were discomfited, slain and drowned; there was not one that scaped, but all were slain.[1]

A truce was made and for several years there was peace, but in 1346 Edward III set out again for France. He was accompanied by his young son, Edward Prince of Wales, later to be known as the Black Prince, and at Crécy they met the French. The French outnumbered the English, but they lost the battle. Crécy was one of the great battles of medieval history. During the Crusades, except for Richard Cœur de Lion, it was the French whose prowess in arms was most celebrated; for over a hundred years France had been growing more powerful and in 1214 the victory of Philip Augustus at Bouvines had established her military prestige. Now, a smaller army, fighting on foreign soil, had defeated the chivalry of France. But the French were still fighting as they had fought in the Crusades. Knights on horseback, clad in armour and armed with the lance, together with Genoese cross-bowmen formed the bulk of the French army. The English army, on the other hand, was chiefly made up of yeomen, fighting on foot with the terrible long-bow. They had learnt the use of this weapon in the wars of Edward I against the Welsh and Scotch. A long-bow was made the height of the man who used it, and the steel-pointed arrow shot from it carried for a hundred yards and would penetrate the armour of knight or horse.

When the Genoways were assembled together and began to approach, they made a great leap and cry to abash the Englishmen, but they stood still and stirred not for all that: then the Genoways again the second time made another leap and a fell cry, and stept forward a little, and the Englishmen removed not

[1] *Chronicles of Froissart.*

one foot: thirdly, again they leapt and cried, and went forth till they came within shot; then they shot fiercely with their cross-bows. Then the English archers stept forth one pace and let fly their arrows so wholly (together) and so thick, that it seemed snow. When the Genoways felt the arrows piercing through heads, arms and breasts, many of them cast down their cross-bows and did cut their strings and returned discomfited.

The battle of Crécy was the beginning of the end of feudal fighting. It is said that gunpowder was used at it, probably for the first time in a medieval battle.

The young Prince of Wales had not yet been knighted. Edward III was not fighting himself, but was watching the battle from a near-by windmill. A message came to him that the prince was hard pressed.

Then the knight said to the king: "Sir, the earl of Warwick and the earl of Oxford, Sir Raynold Cobham and other, such as be about the prince your son, are fiercely fought withal and are sore handled; wherefore they desire you that you and your battle will come and aid them; for if the Frenchmen increase, as they doubt they will, your son and they shall have much ado." Then the king said: "Is my son dead or hurt or on the earth felled?" "No, sir," quoth the knight, "but he is hardly matched; wherefore he hath need of your aid." "Well," said the king, "return to him and to them that sent you hither, and say to them that they send no more to me for any adventure that falleth, as long as my son is alive: and also say to them that they suffer him this day to win his spurs; for if God be pleased, I will this journey be his and the honour thereof, and to them that be about him." [1]

The French losses were great and amongst them was King John, the old and blind king of Bohemia.

The valiant king of Bohemia called Charles of Luxembourg, son to the noble Emperor Henry of Luxembourg, for all that he

[1] *The Chronicles of Froissart.*

was nigh blind, when he understood the order of the battle, he said to them about him: "Where is the lord Charles my son?" His men said: "Sir, we cannot tell; we think he be fighting." Then he said: "Sirs, ye are my men, my companions and friends in this journey: I require you bring me so far forward, that I may strike one stroke with my sword." They said they would do his commandment, and to the intent that they should not lose him in the press, they tied all their reins of their bridles each to other and set the king before to accomplish his desire, and so they went on their enemies. The lord Charles of Bohemia his son, who wrote himself king of Almaine and bare the arms, he came in good order to the battle; but when he saw that the matter went awry on their party, he departed, I cannot tell you which way. The king his father was so far forward that he strake a stroke with his sword, yea and more than four, and fought valiantly and so did his company: and they adventured themselves so forward, that they were there all slain, and the next day they were found in the place about the king and all their horses tied each to other.[1]

From Crécy Edward marched to Calais which he besieged.

In the town of Calais there was captain a knight of Burgoyne called sir John de Vienne, and with him was sir Arnold d'Audrehem, sir John de Surie, sir Baldwin de Bellebrune, sir Geoffrey de la Motte, sir Pepin de Wierre and divers other knights and squires. When the king of England was come before Calais, he laid his siege and ordained bastides between the town and the river: he made carpenters to make houses and lodgings of great timber, and set the houses like streets and covered them with reed and broom, so that it was like a little town; and there was everything to sell, and a marketplace to be kept every Tuesday and Saturday for flesh and fish, mercery ware, houses for cloth, for bread, wine and all other things necessary, such as came out of England or out of Flanders; there they might buy what they list. The Englishmen ran oftentimes into the country of Guines, and into Ternois, and to the gates of Saint-Omer's, and sometimes

[1] *The Chronicles of Froissart.*

to Boulogne; they brought into their host great preys. The king would not assail the town of Calais, for he thought it but a lost labour: he spared his people and his artillery, and said how he would famish them in the town with long siege, without the French king come and raise his siege perforce.

When the captain of Calais saw the manner and the order of the Englishmen, then he constrained all poor and mean people to issue out of the town, and on a Wednesday there issued out of men, women and children more than seventeen hundred; and as they passed through the host, they were demanded why they departed, and they answered and said because they had nothing to live on: then the king did them that grace that he suffered them to pass through his host without danger, and gave them meat and drink to dinner, and every person two pence sterling in alms, for the which divers many of them prayed for the king's prosperity.[1]

After standing the siege for eleven months, Calais surrendered. (August 3rd, 1347.) The captain of Calais "went to the walls of the town and made sign to speak with some person of the host," and two English knights were sent to him. He pleaded with them for mercy on the inhabitants of the town. They told him that it was Edward's intention to "ransom all such as pleased him and to put to death such as he would." To which the captain replied:

"We pray that of your humility, yet that ye will go and speak to the king of England and desire him to have pity of us: for we trust in him so much gentleness, that by the grace of God his purpose shall change."

Sir Gaultier of Manny and sir Basset returned to the king and declared to him all that had been said. The king said he would none otherwise but that they should yield them up simply his pleasure. Then sir Gaultier said: "Sir, saving your displeasure, in this ye may be in the wrong, for ye shall give by this an evil

[1] *The Chronicles of Froissart.*

ensample: if ye send any of us your servants into any fortress, we will not be very glad to go, if ye put any of them in the town to death after they be yielded; for in like wise they will deal with us, if the case fell like." The which words divers other lords that were there present sustained and maintained. Then the king said: "Sirs, I will not be alone against you all; therefore, sir Gaultier of Manny, ye shall go and say to the captain that all the grace that he shall find now in me is that they let six of the chief burgesses of the town come out bare-headed, bare-footed, and bare-legged, and in their shirts, with halters about their necks with the keys of the town and castle in their hands, and let them six yield themselves purely to my will, and the residue I will take to mercy."

Then sir Gaultier returned and found sir John of Vienne still on the wall, abiding for an answer. Then Sir Gaultier shewed him all the grace that he could get of the king. "Well," quoth sir John, "sir, I require you tarry here a certain space, till I go into the town and shew this to the commons of the town, who sent me hither." Then sir John went unto the market-place and sounded the common bell: then incontinent men and women assembled there: then the captain made report of all that he had done, and said, "Sirs, it will be none otherwise; therefore now take advice and make a short answer." Then all the people began to weep and to make such sorrow, that there was not so hard a heart, if they had seen them, but that would have had great pity of them; the captain himself wept piteously. At last the most rich burgess of all the town, called Eustace of Saint-Pierre, rose up and said openly: "Sirs, great and small, great mischief it should be to suffer to die such people as be in this town, other by famine or otherwise, when there is a mean to save them. I think he or they should have great merit of our Lord God that might keep them from such mischief. As for my part, I have so good trust in our Lord God, that if I die in the quarrel to save the residue, that God would pardon me: wherefore to save them I will be the first to put my life in jeopardy." When he had thus said, every man worshipped him and divers kneeled down at his feet with sore weeping and sore sighs. Then another honest burgess rose and said: "I will keep company with my gossip Eustace." He was called John d'Aire. Then rose up Jaques of Wissant, who was rich in goods and heritage; he said also that he would hold company with his two cousins. In like wise so did Peter of Wissant his brother: and then rose two other; they said they would do the same. Then they went and apparelled them as the king desired.

Then the captain went with them to the gate: there was great lamentation made of men, women and children at their departing: then the gate was opened and he issued out with the six burgesses and closed the gate again, so that they were between the gate and the barriers. Then he said to sir Gaultier of Manny: "Sir, I deliver here to you as captain of Calais by the whole consent of all the people of the town these six burgesses, and I swear to you truly that they be and were today most honourable, rich and most notable burgesses of all the town of Calais. Wherefore, gentle knight, I require you pray the king to have mercy on them, that they die not." Quoth sir Gaultier: "I cannot say what the king will do, but I shall do for them the best I can." Then the barriers were opened, the six burgesses went towards the king, and the captain entered again into the town.

When sir Gaultier presented these burgesses to the king, they kneeled down and held up their hands and said: "Gentle king, behold here we six, who were burgesses of Calais and great merchants; we have brought to you the keys of the town and of the castle and we submit ourselves clearly into your will and pleasure, to save the residue of the people of Calais, who have suffered great pain. Sir, we beseech your grace to have mercy and pity on us through your high nobles." Then all the earls and barons and other that were there wept for pity. The king looked felly on them, for greatly he hated the people of Calais for the great damages and displeasures they had done him on the sea before. Then he commanded their heads to be stricken off: then every man required the king for mercy, but he would hear no man in that behalf: then sir Gaultier of Manny said: "Ah, noble king, for God's sake refrain your courage: ye have the name of sovereign nobless: therefore now do not a thing that should blemish your renown, nor to give cause to some to speak of you villainy. Every man will say it is a great cruelty to put to death such honest persons, who by their own wills put themselves into your grace to save their company." Then the king scowled at him and commanded to send for the hangman, and said: "They of Calais have caused many of my men to be slain, wherefore these shall die in like wise." Then the queen, being great with child, kneeled down and sore weeping said: "Ah, gentle sir, sith I passed the sea in great peril, I have desired nothing of you; therefore now I humbly require you in the honour of the Son of the Virgin Mary and for the love of me that ye will take mercy of these six burgesses." The king beheld the queen and stood still in a study a space, and then said: "Ah, dame, I would ye had been as now in some other place; ye make such request to me that I cannot deny you. Wherefore I give them to you, to do your pleasure with them." Then the queen caused them to be brought into her chamber, and made the halters to be taken from their necks, and caused them to be new clothed, and gave them their dinner at their leisure: and then she gave each of them six nobles and made them to be brought out of the host in safeguard and set at their liberty.[1]

The year after the surrender of Calais, France was ravaged by the Black Death and the following year the plague spread to England. But in 1356 the Black Prince was in France again, and in the autumn another great battle was fought at Poitiers. Again the English were successful, and John the Good, king of France, was prisoner.

And as it was reported, there was slain all the flower of France, and there was taken with the king and the lord Philip his son a seventeen earls, beside barons, knights and squires, and slain a five or six thousand of one and other. When every man was come from the chase, they had twice as many prisoners as they were in number in all. Then it was counselled among them because of the great charge and doubt to keep so many, that they should put many of them to ransom incontinent in the field, and so they did: and the prisoners found the Englishmen and Gascons right courteous; there were many that day put to ransom and let go only on their promise of faith and truth to return again between that and Christmas to Bordeaux with their

[1] *The Chronicles of Froissart.*

ransoms. Then that night they lay in the field where the battle had been: some unarmed them, but not all, and unarmed all their prisoners, and every man made good cheer to his prisoner; for that day whosoever took any prisoner, he was clear his and might quit or ransom him at his pleasure. All such as were there with the prince were all made rich with honour and goods, as well by ransoming of prisoners as by winning of gold, silver, plate, jewels, that was there found: there was no man that did set anything by rich harness, whereof there was great plenty, for the Frenchmen came thither richly beseen, weening to have had the journey for them.

The same day of the battle at night the prince made a supper in his lodging to the French king and to the most part of the great lords that were prisoners. The prince made the king and his son, the lord James of Bourbon, the lord John d'Artois, the earl of Tancarville, the earl of Estampes, the earl Dammartin, the earl of Joinville and the lord of Partenay to sit all at one board, and other lords, knights and squires at other tables; and always the prince served before the king as humbly as he could, and would not sit at the king's board for any desire that the king could make, but he said he was not sufficient to sit at the table with so great a prince as the king was. But then he said to the king: "Sir, for God's sake make none evil nor heavy cheer, though God this day did not consent to follow your will; for, sir, surely the king my father shall bear you as much honour and amity as he may do, and shall accord with you so reasonably that ye shall ever be friends together after. And, sir, methink ye ought to rejoice, though the journey be not as ye would have had it, for this day ye have won the high renown of prowess and have passed this day in valiantness all other of your party. Sir, I say not this to mock you, for all that be on our party, that saw every man's deeds, are plainly accorded by true sentence to give you the prize and chaplet." Therewith the Frenchmen began to murmur and said among themselves how the prince had spoken nobly, and that by all estimation he should prove a noble man, if God send him life and to persevere in such good fortune.[1]

[1] *The Chronicles of Froissart.*

The Black Prince took his royal prisoner to Bordeaux and from there he sailed to England.

The French king was in a vessel by himself, to be the more at his ease, accompanied with two hundred men of arms and two thousand archers; for it was showed the prince that the three estates by whom the realm of France was governed had laid in Normandy and Crotoy two great armies, to the intent to meet with him and to get the French king out of his hands, if they might; but there were no such that appeared, and yet they were on the sea eleven days, and on the twelfth day they arrived at Sandwich. Then they issued out of their ship and lay there all that night and tarried there two days to refresh them, and on the third day they rode to Canterbury. When the king of England knew of their coming, he commanded them of London to prepare them and their city to receive such a man as the French king was. Then they of London arrayed themselves by companies and the chief mesters (with) clothing different (each) from the other. At Saint Thomas of Canterbury the French king and the prince made their offerings and there tarried a day, and then rode to Rochester and tarried there that day, and the next day to Dartford and the fourth day to London, where they were honourably received, and so they were in every good town as they passed. The French king rode through London on a white courser well apparelled, and the prince on a little black hobby by him. Thus he was conveyed along the city, till he came to the Savoy, the which house pertained to the heritage of the duke of Lancaster. There the French king kept his house a long season, and thither came to see him the king and the queen oftentimes and made him great feast and cheer.

Anon after the French king was removed from the Savoy to the castle of Windsor, and all his household, and went a-hunting and a-hawking thereabout at his pleasure, and the lord Philip his son with him: and all the other prisoners abode still at London and went to see the king at their pleasure and were received all only on their faiths.[1]

[1] *The Chronicles of Froissart.*

The French had lost a great many men, large numbers had been taken prisoner and either remained in captivity or were ransomed, but the actual battles had done but little harm to the land of France. It had, however, been wasted and made desolate by the armies that for ten years had marched to and fro. Sometimes the French had ravaged a district themselves in order that the English, when they came, should find nothing on which they could live; more often it was the English who wasted it, sometimes to punish a rebellious lord, sometimes to force peasants into submission and to give them food, sometimes just to give a show of power. Petrarch, the Italian poet, said of this time:

I could not believe that this was the same France which I had seen so rich and flourishing. Nothing presented itself to my eyes but a fearful solitude, an utter poverty, land uncultivated, houses in ruins. Even the neighbourhood of Paris showed everywhere marks of desolation and conflagration. The streets are deserted, the roads overgrown with weeds, the whole is a vast solitude.

In 1360 peace was made and a treaty signed at Bretigny. Edward gave up his claim to the French crown; in the north he kept Calais, and in the south, the duchy of Guienne was recognized as his, not as a fief for which he must do homage to the king of France, but it was to be his in full sovereignty. King John was set at liberty after he had paid a ransom.

2. *Limoges*

THE peace made in 1360 ended for a time the English invasions of France. But France was not at peace. The years of fighting had made large numbers of men, both French and English, disinclined to settle down again to a peaceable life, and these formed themselves into what became known as *free companies*. Under chosen leaders these bands raided France, wasted and plundered and pillaged and became a serious menace. Bertrand Du Guesclin, a Breton knight, did good service for the French during these years. He ably supported the king, Charles V (son of John the Good, who had died), he attempted to restore the shattered power of France and to drive out the English in the south.

Since the Treaty of Bretigny the Black Prince had been governing in Guienne, but his rule was unpopular. He gave most of the administrative positions to Englishmen, a reversal of the earlier English policy in the south of France, which had encouraged the appointment of trained and experienced Frenchmen. Complaints from Gascon nobles were taken to the king of France, and Charles V summoned the Black Prince to Paris as his vassal to answer for his misgovernment. The Black Prince sent back as answer: "I will gladly go to Paris, but it shall be with helmet on my head and sixty thousand men in my company." Rebellions broke out against him, but though he was ill, he invaded the neighbouring territory and, carried on a litter, he besieged Limoges (1371). The city surrendered. Froissart described the Black Prince as being "courageous and cruel as a lion." At Limoges he justified the description.

It was a great pity to see the men, women and children that kneeled down on their knees before the prince for mercy: but he was so inflamed with ire, that he took no heed to them, so that none was heard, but all put to death, as they were met withal, and such as were nothing culpable. There was no pity taken of the poor people, who wrought never no manner of treason, yet they bought it dearer than the great personages, such as had done the evil and trespass. There was not so hard a heart within the city of Limoges, an if he had any remembrance of God, but that wept piteously for the great mischief that they saw before their eye: for more than three thousand men, women and children were slain and beheaded that day. God have mercy on their souls, for I trow they were martyrs.[1]

Two years later the Black Prince returned to England. He was ill and in 1376 he died. His death was followed the next year by that of Edward III. The new king of England, Richard II, was a boy, and for a time, though England and France were hardly at peace, there was at least a truce to violent hostilities.

3. *Henry V and Agincourt*

THE opening of the fifteenth century found France torn and weakened by party strife. The king, Charles VI, suffered from fits of insanity and the great dukes of Burgundy and Orleans quarrelled and fought for power. In 1415 Henry V of England took the opportunity of renewing the claim of the English kings to the crown of France. He crossed the Channel, besieged and captured Harfleur and then set out for Calais. On October 25th, St. Crispin's Day, a French army, larger than the English, barred his way at Agincourt. The English were tired and hungry, and when in the king's hearing, some one wished for more men, he said: "I would not have a single man more. If God give us the victory, it will be plain that we owe it to His grace. If not, the fewer we are, the less loss for England."

The French were defeated. The courage of Henry V in the face of tremendous odds against him and the confidence he inspired in his men gave him the victory and

[1] *The Chronicles of Froissart.*

made of Agincourt one of the great battles in English history. But war is not all glory. It does give opportunity, as all crises in which there is danger give, for chivalry, for deeds of heroism and of sacrifice for others, but there is another side of it. During these wars the French peasant suffered untold misery.

Alas! when a poor man shall have paid his impost, his villein tax, his salt tax, his hearth money, his fourth, the King's spurs, the customs, the road tax, the tolls—not much remains to him. Then will come another levy newly created, and sergeants to come and take in pledge his pots and his store. The poor man will have no bread to eat, except by chance some little rye or barley; his poor wife will be in child-birth, and will have four or six little children round the hearth—or by the oven, if it chance to be warm—asking for bread and crying with the desperation of hunger. The poor mother will have nothing to put into their mouths but a little bread, even if she has this. This should be sufficient misery; but then will come ruffians who will ransack everything. They will find, perhaps, a hen with four chickens, which the wife was nourishing to sell and pay the remainder of the tax, or a new one just levied—everything will be taken or seized, and who shall pay? And if the man or woman protest, they will be abused, fined, or maltreated. If they sue for payment they will lose their time, spend double, and get nothing in the end: or sometimes, by chance, a note stating that to such a person so much is owing.

"Very well," says the debtor.

And he goes on owing.

How could it be worse for a poor fellow? It could hardly be worse. But still worse is to come ... soldiers fighting with each other who are not content to take nothing where there is nothing, but threaten and beat the man and his wife, and set fire to the house unless they pay ransom, and make people pay them in unjust and crooked ways, with money or provisions. ... And there are thousands and thousands, and more than ten thousand, in the land in a worse state than I have described.[1]

[1] Gerson.

Among the French prisoners taken after the battle of Agincourt was the young French poet, Charles d'Orléans. He was sent to England and whilst living there in exile, knowing something of what war had brought, he prayed for peace.

BALLADE

Priez pour paix, doulce Vierge Marie,
Royne des cieulx et du monde maistresse;
Faictes prier, par vostre courtoisie,
Saincts et sainctes, et prenez vostre adresse
Vers vostre Filz, requerant sa haultesse
Qu'il Lui plaise son peuple regarder
Que de son sang a voulu racheter,
En desboutant guerre qui tout desvoye.
De prieres ne vous vueilliez lasser,
Priez pour paix, le vray tresor de joye.

Priez, prelatz et gens de saincte vie,
Religieux, ne dormez en paresse;
Priez, maistres et tous suivans clergie,
Car par guerre fault que l'estude cesse;
Moustiers destruis sont sans qu'on les redresse,
Le service de Dieu vous fault laissier,
Quant ne pouvez en repos demourer.
Priez si fort que briefment Dieu vous oye:
L'Eglise voult a ce vous ordonner;
Priez pour paix, le vray tresor de joye.

Priez, princes qui avez seigneurie,
Rois, ducs, contes, barons plains de noblesse,
Gentilz hommes avec chevalerie
Car meschans gens surmontent gentillesse.
En leurs mains ont toute vostre richesse,
Debatz les font en hault estat monter,
Vous le pouvez chascun jour veoir au clair,
Et sont riches de voz biens et monnoye,
Dont vous deussiez le peuple supporter.
Priez pour paix, le vray tresor de joye.

Priez, peuple qui souffrez tirannie:
Car voz seigneurs sont en telle foiblesse
Qu'ilz ne peuvent vous garder par mestrie,
Ne vous aidier en vostre grant destresse.
Loyaulx marchans, la selle si vous blesse
Fort sur le dos: chascun vous vient presser
Et ne pouvez marchandise mener,
Car vous n'avez seur passage ne voye
Et maint peril vous convient il passer:
Priez pour paix, le vray tresor de joye.

Dieu tout puissant nous vueille conforter
Toutes choses en terre, ciel et mer!
Priez vers lui que brief en tout pourvoye,
En lui seul est de tous maulx amender:
Priez pour paix, le vray tresor de joye!

CHARLES D'ORLÉANS

"PRIEZ POUR PAIX"

Pray thou for peace, thou gentle Maid Marie,
Queen of the Heavens, that over earth has sway;
Summon all Saints, of thy great charity,
That they to thy Almighty Son may pray.
Do thou before him our petition lay;
Pray Him, who did consent for us to die,
To turn on us, His folk, a pitying eye,
And from His ransomed banish war's distress,
Whose fell confusion setteth all awry.
Pray thou for Peace, true fount of happiness.

Pray ye, O bishops, men of sanctity;
Ye monks, spend not in idle dream the day;
Ye who in learning have the mastery
Pray well, that God may hear without delay.
How shall ye then God's service duly say,
When in the wars both prayer and study fly,
And all is in confusion far and nigh,
And convents are destroyed without redress?
Lest ye the word of Holy Church deny,
Pray ye for Peace, true fount of happiness.

Pray ye, my lords, who wield your sovranty,
Kings, dukes, counts, barons, in your fine array,
And all ye gentle knights of chivalry.
Villains on your nobility do prey,
For their ill deeds compelling you to pay.
They reach high state, so cunningly they lie,
As ye yourselves may every day descry.
How shall ye use your wealth the poor to bless,
When these do both despoil you and defy?
Pray ye for Peace, true fount of happiness.

Pray, all ye nations suffering tyranny,
Which feeble rulers can no more allay,
Nor can protect you, as their charge should be,
Nor help you, when distresses on you weigh,
Ye honest merchants, struggle as ye may,
See how your laden back is piled more high
By war; for then ye cannot sell nor buy,
Nor find safe passage for your business,
So many a deadly peril ye espy.
Pray ye for Peace, true fount of happiness.

Envoi

To God Almighty now for help we cry,
Praying the Lord of earth and sea and sky
To free us soon from all this bitterness.
Who else for all our ills can health supply?
Pray we for Peace, true fount of happiness.[1]

Soon after Agincourt England regained Normandy, and then in 1420 peace was made at Troyes. By the treaty Henry V was to marry Katharine, daughter of Charles VI, and on the death of the king of France he was to be recognized as the heir. In August 1422 Henry V died and in October, Charles VI. In England the son of Henry V and Katharine of France, a baby of eighteen months, was pro-

[1] Translated by Mr. B. C. Boulter.

claimed "by the grace of God King of France and England." In France it was said, "No Englishman was ever King of France or shall be."

4. *Jeanne d'Arc*

THREE years before the battle of Agincourt there was born at Domremy in Lorraine, a little peasant girl, Jeanne d'Arc. She was brought up in a home that was deeply religious, she learned to sew and spin, she was known by her neighbours as tender and kind to all who were ill or in any trouble.

As Jeanne grew up she heard of the wars and the fighting and whenever the quiet country-side resounded to the noise of passing soldiers, she shared the anxiety of the villagers as to whether they were friend or foe. And from the passing stranger, seeking in the quiet village a refuge from the dangers of the road, she learnt of the desolate lands and wasted fields of the fair land of France, and as she grew older, "pity for the fair realm of France" filled her every thought.

When Jeanne was about thirteen years old, the English were again invading France, and it was then that she began to hear her Voices. Day after day as she sat under a tree, visions came to her. Sometimes it was St. Michael, sometimes St. Catherine or St. Margaret, but always the message was the same: she was to go to the Dauphin Charles, who had not yet been crowned king and help him to recover his land. "There was pity in heaven," said her Voices, "for the fair realm of France." She pleaded with them that she was but a maiden and knew nothing about war. But always the Voices bade her go. She told her father, who said he would rather drown her than let her go on any such errand. By the time she was seventeen, Jeanne had determined that nothing should stand in her way. The English were besieging Orleans, and at last she persuaded her uncle to take her to the castle of Vaucouleurs, which was under the command of Robert de Baudricourt. She succeeded so well in her pleading that Baudricourt undertook to take her to Chinon to see the Dauphin. She saw him and convinced him. "Gentle Dauphin," said Jeanne, "my name is Jeanne the Maid. The Heavenly King sends me to tell you that you shall be anointed and crowned in the town of Reims, and you shall be lieutenant of the Heavenly King who is the King of France."

Jeanne was sent with an army that was to relieve Orleans, and inspired by her presence and her confidence the siege was raised, and on May 3rd, 1429, the English were forced to withdraw. Orleans was saved. It was the beginning of the end of the war, for from that time on the English power in France grew weaker.

In the meantime Jeanne had led the Dauphin to Reims where he was crowned. She felt then that she had fulfilled her mission for she had done what her Voices had bade her do, but in spite of her entreaties she was not allowed to go home. She was forced to take the field again, but while defending Compiègne against the Duke of Burgundy, she was captured by a Burgundian soldier. Her captor delivered her up to the duke of Burgundy who sold her to the English and she was imprisoned at Rouen.

Jeanne was kept in prison for a year, and the country girl must have suffered from the confinement and above all from the loneliness. The Dauphin had been crowned because of Jeanne, but never during the months of her weary imprisonment did he send any word or make any effort to save her. The English were afraid of her influence and to destroy it she was tried as a witch. Brought before an ecclesiastical court presided over by the bishop of Beauvais, every effort was made to trick her into saying that she had been mistaken in her Voices, and that they came from the devil and not from God. Worn out by questioning and weakened by the close confinement she acknowledged that she had been mistaken, but finding that imprisonment for life awaited her, her courage returned, and she declared that her Voices were of God and had never deceived her.

The court condemned her to death. On May 29th, 1431, Jeanne d'Arc was burnt at the stake as a witch and heretic. Before she died she asked for a cross and a soldier made one for her with two bits of wood. When all was over, an English soldier, as he was turning away, whispered to his neighbour: "We are lost; we have burnt a saint."

The war was practically at an end. Desultory fighting went on for another twenty years. One after another castles, cities and provinces were lost to England, until in 1453 nothing was left of all that England had once ruled in France but Calais, which was not taken by the French until 1558, and the Channel Islands, described by Victor Hugo as "those bits of France fallen into the sea and picked up by England," which are still English.

CHAPTER XXII

THE CLOSE OF THE MIDDLE AGES

T
HE thirteenth century was one of the great centuries in the history of the world. It was a century not only rich in its own splendour, but one which held within it the seeds from which the modern world was to develop. The Church grew powerful under great popes; England and France developed forms of government that still influence political life; in the towns of the Netherlands, Germany and Italy there grew up a rich and prosperous civic life; universities were founded; great cathedrals were built; it was the age of Chartres and Canterbury and Amiens; Europe had been united in the enthusiasm of the Crusades; the friars, Franciscan and Dominican, had shown the way to a more spiritual interpretation of religion; superstition and magic were beginning to give way before a more critical and scientific habit of thinking. Great personages stride across this century: Popes and emperors like Innocent III and Frederick II; kings like St. Louis of France and Edward I of England; scholars and thinkers like Peter Abelard, St. Thomas Aquinas and Roger Bacon; poets like Dante; friars like St. Francis and St. Dominic; travellers like Marco Polo.

To this great century there succeeded the fourteenth, an age of lesser men, an age when enthusiasm was less buoyant, when ideals seem to have been lower, when the Hundred Years' War that was disastrous in so many ways began. The Middle Ages were dominated by two ideas: a society based on feudalism and the unquestioned authority of the Church. It was when these two principles were seriously challenged that the Middle Ages came to an end, and it was the fourteenth century that saw the first challenge thrown down to them both.

1. *The Black Death and the Passing of Feudalism*

As has been seen, in the Middle Ages every man was attached in some way or other to the land; he was either the lord who owned it, or the serf who worked on it. Under the feudal system land had been given by the king to certain great lords in return for their military services, but the military aspect of feudalism had been seriously weakened during the period of the Crusades. Feudalism with all that it implied was still, however, the dominating principle of all agricultural life, and in the fourteenth century the serf or peasant was as much tied to the land as he had been in the twelfth or thirteenth centuries.

In 1348 a plague, known as the Black Death, swept over Europe. The pestilence spared no class of society, but the death rate was much higher wherever men lived closely together in communities, and the greatest sufferers were the monasteries and the manors. It has been estimated that in England, France and Italy at least one third of the population died. The result to the manor was that there were not nearly enough serfs to do the work, and the lords were only too glad to get any one to work for them on any terms whatever. The old prohibition that the serf might not move from one manor to another was disregarded; serfs went wherever there was plenty of work, and they began to demand money for wages. This new condition of things put a hope into the serf that he might materially better his condition and live in greater comfort, and in several places revolts of the serfs broke out.

In 1358 the peasants in northern France banded together in a revolt known as the *Jacquerie*. They plundered the houses of the nobles and seemed at first to be successful. But they were untrained and unused to arms, and the soldiers of the nobles soon quelled them, though not without much bloodshed and cruelty. Other revolts broke out in other parts of Europe, in Germany, in Hungary and in Denmark, but the result was defeat for the peasants and a return to the old feudal principles of serfdom. It was not until 1789 that serfdom was abolished in France, 1807 in Prussia and 1861 in Russia.

In England the abolition of serfdom came sooner and in a different way. No edict was ever passed as in France, Prussia and Russia, but serfdom disappeared of itself during the fourteenth century.

The Black Death affected the English manors just as it had those on the continent. Serfs fled to the towns, then returned to the manors demanding high wages and freedom, and so great was the need of agricultural labourers that in most cases they got what they wanted. But the lords were poor, and the wages demanded by the serfs were so high that laws were passed regulating both labour and wages. In 1349 it was decreed that "every man shall serve the master requiring him."

Because a great part of the people, and especially of workmen and servants, lately died of the Pestilence, many seeing the necessity of the masters of great scarcity of servants, will not serve unless they receive excessive wages, and some rather willing to beg in idleness than by labour to get their living. We considering the grievous incommodities, which of the lack, especially of ploughmen and such labourers may hereafter come, have upon deliberation and treaty with the prelates and nobles, and the learned men assisting us, ordained that every man and woman in England of whatever condition they may be, bond or free, able in body and under sixty years of age, not living by merchandise, or being an artificer, and not having property whereby they may live, shall serve the master requiring him or her.

Two years later a statute was passed regulating wages and fixing them at the low standard customary before the Black Death. Discontent grew greater and greater, but no solution of the difficulties was found. For more than twenty years agitation was carried on amongst the peasants by John Ball, a Lollard preacher who went up and down England trying to stir up opposition to the inequality of serfs and lords. He preached in villages, in the fields, at street corners, wherever he could get a hearing. He used to begin by saying,

> When Adam delved and Eve span
> Who was then the gentleman?

and the chronicler gives us some of his sermons. He would say thus to the people:

Ah, ye good people, the matters goeth not well to pass in England, nor shall not do till everything be common, and that there be no villeins nor gentlemen, but that we may be all united together, and that the lords be no greater masters than we be. What have we deserved, or why should we be thus kept in servage? We be all come from one father and mother, Adam and Eve: whereby can they say or show that they be greater lords than we be, saving by that they cause us to win and labour for that they dispend? They are clothed in velvet and camlet furred with grise, and we be vestured with poor cloth: they have their wines, spices and good bread, and we have the drawing out of the chaff and drink water: they dwell in fair houses, and we have the pain and travail, rain and wind in the fields; and by that cometh of our labours they keep and maintain their estates: we be called their bondmen, and without we do them service, we be beaten; and we have no sovereign to whom we may complain, nor that will hear us nor do us right. Let us go to the king, he is young, and show what servage we be in, and show him how we will have it otherwise, or else we will provide us of some remedy, either by fairness or otherwise.[1]

The king was Richard II. He was young, only fourteen years old, and his uncles, more powerful than he, had been ruling in his name. In 1381 the discontent of the peasants came to a head in the Peasants' Revolt. Under Wat Tyler, a Kentish leader, they marched on London, doing a good deal of damage, robbing and pillaging and committing deeds of violence. They attacked and burnt the palace of John of Gaunt, one of the king's uncles, they took prisoner and then beheaded the archbishop of Canterbury, and then at last they agreed to meet the king at Smithfield outside the walls of London and hold a parley with him. The king rode out to meet them and Wat Tyler and he began to talk. But one of the king's courtiers considered that the peasant leader was too bold in the way he behaved before the king. "Ha, thou knave," he said, "how art thou so hardy in the king's presence to speak such words? It is too much for thee to do so," and he drew his sword and struck him so that he fell down dead. For a moment there was horror-struck silence. Then some of the peasants said:

"Our captain is slain, let us go and slay them all." Then the king departed from all his company and all alone he rode to these people, and said to his own men: "Sirs, none of you follow me; let me alone." ... And when he came to the people, the

[1] *The Chronicles of Froissart.*

king said to them: "Sirs, what aileth you? Ye shall have no captain but me: I am your king: be all in rest and peace." [1]

Richard made them some promises, but he did not keep his word. He was too young then to be given full control of the government and his uncles were more powerful and dominating than he. But though in 1381 the revolt failed, the cause of the peasants was not lost. Slowly they gained more independence, statutes were passed bettering their condition, especially in the matter of wages, until by the end of the fifteenth century, nearly all labour had become free. The peasants still worked for landlords, they were still dependent on the landowner, they were still poor, but they were no longer serfs. A long period was to go by before they were regarded as citizens with equal rights with the townsmen and before they were allowed to vote. But with the passing of the serf from English life, one of the distinctively medieval characteristics had disappeared.

2. John Wycliffe

FEUDALISM was one of the characteristics of the Middle Ages. The unquestioned authority of the Church was another.

The Christian Church had had a long and splendid history. From being a small group of Christians, forced to worship in secret, persecuted, seemingly unimportant, it had grown in numbers until the Christian religion became first the religion of the Roman Empire and then of western Europe. It has been seen how the Church was organized, how it came about that the Bishop of Rome became the recognized Head of the Church and was called the

[1] *The Chronicles of Froissart.*

pope, how the Church was drawn into the feudal system and became a great temporal power as well as a spiritual society, and how the popes came into conflict with emperors and kings. By the fourteenth century the Church was very powerful, and she had spoken for so long with a voice of authority that was seldom questioned, that her leaders had grown to believe that she should never be questioned, and people all over Europe were taught to regard her authority as representing the voice of God to them on earth.

The climax of the political conflicts into which the Church was drawn came at the beginning of the fourteenth century. Philip the Fair of France refused to obey the pope when he ordered him to set free one of his subjects who was imprisoned for political reasons. Philip was supported by his nobles and they defied the pope. The latter died soon after and to prevent any further trouble of this kind, Philip so dominated the election of the next pope that a Frenchman was elected and the seat of the papacy was transferred from Rome to Avignon in France. This state of affairs lasted from 1305 to 1377 and was called *The Babylonian Captivity of the Church*. The popes during this period were nearly all Frenchmen, they lived in great luxury and magnificence, and gradually every one came to believe that they were completely under the influence of the French king. Having left Rome, they lost some of the revenues of the papal lands, and as they needed a great deal of money to maintain their court, they sent orders to all the archbishops and bishops of the Church that they should tax their people and send the money to Avignon.

The Church in England had always been independent in character, and had resented any attempt on the part of the popes to control English affairs. From 1066 onwards laws had been passed and agreements arrived at by which the pope's power to interfere in English affairs was curtailed. These taxes ordered by the pope in Avignon were bitterly resented. They were much higher than any levied by the king, and they went to a foreign pope. When in 1338 the Hundred Years' War began the resentment grew greater, for the papal taxes went to a pope who was living in France and whose policy was dominated by the enemy of England. Another cause of friction between England and the Papacy at this time was the increasing tendency of the pope to make appointments in England. In order to stop this Edward III had passed two laws, one forbidding the pope to make any appointments in England without the king's consent, and the other forbidding any appeal from an English court to the papal court.

The scholasticism of the thirteenth century had endeavoured to make theology agree with philosophy, and the results of the studies of the Schoolmen had tended to prevent much original thinking in matters concerning philosophy, and their conclusions were held as final. But in the thirteenth century Roger Bacon had taught that the way to study was by observation, by experiment and a critical mind, and now in the fourteenth century a scholar of Oxford dared to criticize the Church.

The Black Death had caused a good deal of questioning in men's minds. The relentlessness of the pestilence, the way in which all suffered alike, the rich and poor, the good and the bad, the saint and the sinner, made many people question the value of some of the religious observances and of the prayers and pilgrimages. It was a restless and unsettled time not only in material ways. The temporal power of the Church had been criticized and resisted by

Englishmen, but not until the time of John Wycliffe had any one in England seriously challenged the pope or the teaching of the Church.

John Wycliffe was born about 1320, but not much is known of his life until about 1355 when he went to Oxford. He soon made a name for himself there and was known as a man "strong and effective in disputations." Wycliffe was at Oxford for forty years. He had studied the Bible and like later reformers he believed that it should be the standard by which the truth of doctrines and belief should be judged. He was a man of strong convictions and of unflinching courage, and as he began to be convinced that there was a good deal in the Church that ought to be remedied, he gave voice unfalteringly to his criticisms.

He attacked the clergy for what he saw to be their weaknesses, criticizing the worldly lives of many of them, saying that the parish priests neglected their duty, that the friars were lazy and ignorant, and that the bishops were generally so busy looking after their lands, that they had no time for their religious duties. He was very outspoken about the land held by the Church, and said that the Church had no right to own land if it were not obeying the laws of God. Wycliffe then challenged the authority of the pope in England, maintaining that John had had no power or right to surrender England as a fief to Rome, and that even if he had had such right, a feudal relationship had obligations on both sides, and that the pope was failing in his as he gave no protection of any kind to England. He challenged the power of the pope to excommunicate. Then he went even further and maintained that every priest in the Church had the right to teach and preach what he chose, and he openly attacked some of the doctrines of the Church.

Wycliffe soon gathered some followers, men who were eager to follow a leader who had the courage to voice these protests, though later it was found that they had not always the same courage as Wycliffe in maintaining them in the face of persecution. These men were called the Poor Preachers, and they went about the country wearing simple clothes, eating poor fare and preaching in the open air. They were nicknamed Lollards and made fun of, but their numbers increased and their influence seemed to be growing. This alarmed the bishops of the Church, for the teaching of Wycliffe was considered by them to be heresy, and Wycliffe was summoned to London to answer in St. Paul's for his opinions. He arrived accompanied by four friars and John of Gaunt, but the trial ended in a riot. Then the pope issued five bulls against him; three were sent to the archbishop of Canterbury and the bishop of London, one to the king, and one to the University of Oxford. All five demanded that Wycliffe should be arrested and imprisoned. The bulls were not obeyed, but the following year a trial of Wycliffe was held at which he was convicted of teaching heretical doctrines, deprived of his position at Oxford, and forced to retire to Lutterworth, a country parish where he lived until his death in 1384. Certain in his convictions that he had been teaching only what was right, he stood openly by what he had said, and ended his defence with the words: "I believe that in the end truth will conquer."

Though his public teaching was over, a great work was still accomplished by Wycliffe. Believing that people who knew no Latin should be able to read the Bible for themselves, he began, and with the help of some of his pupils completed the translation of the Bible into English. Every copy was made by hand. It was the first complete translation of the whole Bible into English and it probably circulated widely. This translation influenced not only those who read it as a religious book, but it left a mark on the literature of the period. Before Wycliffe, English literature had been chiefly poetry. Wycliffe created a prose style of such quality that he profoundly influenced the writers who followed him, and because of this he has sometimes been called the father of English prose.

Wycliffe died in 1384. The Lollard movement did not die with him, but grew to such importance that the Church began to be seriously alarmed. The authorities had already ordered Wycliffe's Bibles to be burnt wherever they might be found and in 1401 a law was passed for the "burning of heretics," and a cruel persecution of Lollards began. Some of them had the courage to maintain their opinions in the face of persecution, and to be burnt at the stake for them, others were afraid and hid, others, and there were many of these, renounced them. The law had the effect desired and the work of Wycliffe seemed to have been stamped out.

In 1381 the Peasants' Revolt had ended in apparent failure, in 1384 Wycliffe died in his country parish, but both the struggles of the peasants and the teaching of Wycliffe had sown seeds that were to bear fruit later. With the passing of feudalism, the beginning of a questioning mind and the demand that men should have the right to think for themselves, the Middle Ages were passing away. Wycliffe was one of those men born ahead of their time who pointed to a path that men of a later age could tread. He has been called the *Morning Star of the Reformation*, for though living and teaching in the Middle Ages, he was a herald of the new world that was to come in the period of the Reformation and the Renaissance.

TIME CHART
OF THE
EVENTS AND PERSONAGES
OF THIS BOOK

═══════════════

Note. 1. The names of the Eastern Emperors are in italics.
2. The dates given for rulers are those of the reign.

Emperors	Popes	Kings of England	Kings of the Franks	Events	Islam	Norsemen	Great Men
				313 Edict of Milan			St. Martin 316
Constantine the Great 323 —— 337				325 Council of Nicæa			
				330 Constantinople becomes eastern capital			St. Basil 330 —— 379
							St. Ambrose c-340 —— 397
							St. Jerome c-340 —— 420
							St. Augustine of Hippo 354
Valens 364 —— 378				375 Goths cross the Danube			St. Patrick c-389
Theodosius 378 —— 395				378 Battle of Adrianople			

Emperors	Popes	Kings of England	Kings of the Franks	Events	Islam	Norsemen	Great Men
	Leo I, the Great 440 —— 461		Clovis 481	410 Sack of Rome by Alaric			St. Benedict c-480
				415 Visigoths in Spain			
				445 Decree recognizing supremacy of Bishop of Rome			
				449 Anglo-Saxon invasion of England			
				451 Battle of Chalons			
				452 Attila invades Italy			
				476 Fall of Rome			
				493 Theodoric, King of the Ostrogoths			

420

430

461

Emperors	Popes	Kings of England	Kings of the Franks	Events	Islam	Norsemen	Great Men
			Clovis 511	Frankish kingdom established by Clovis			St. Benedict
Justinian 527				529 Benedictine Monastery founded at Monte Cassino			St. Columba 521
				532 Sta. Sophia in Constantinople begun			
		Ethelbert, King of Kent 560		563 Monastery at Iona founded by St. Columba			c-544
565							
	Gregory I, the Great 590			597 St. Augustine arrives in Canterbury			St. Augustine of Canterbury
							597
							Mohammed c-569
							St. Aidan

Emperors	Popes	Kings of England	Kings of the Franks	Events	Islam	Norsemen	Great Men
	604	616		626 Paulinus in Northumbria	622 The Hejira		632
				635 Monastery at Lindisfarne founded by St. Aidan	630 Mohammed captures Mecca		613 St. Hilda 614
				642 Earliest charter for holding a fair. St. Denis in Paris	634 Conquest of 40 Egypt		680
				657 Monastery at Whitby founded by St. Hilda	636 Conquest of Persia		651
				664 Synod of Whitby	648 Conquest of Cyprus		Bede 673
				668 Theodore of Tarsus, archbishop of Canterbury	653 Conquest of Rhodes		St. Boniface 680
				674 Monastery at Wearmouth founded by Benedict Biscop			

EMPERORS	POPES	KINGS of ENGLAND	KINGS of the FRANKS	EVENTS	ISLAM	NORSEMEN	GREAT MEN	
Leo III, the Isaurian 718 ——— 741	Leo III. 795 ———		Charles Martel Mayor 714	718 St. Boniface in Germany	711 Conquest of Spain		Bede	St. Boniface
			Pepin the Short 741	726 Edict against Images				
				732 Battle of Tours				Alcuin 735
							735	754
				756 Donation of Pepin				
			Charlemagne 768 ——— 800	772 Charlemagne in Saxony				
				773 Charlemagne invades Italy				
				778 Charlemagne invades Spain				
					Haroun-al-Raschid in Bagdad 786	787 Invasions of England		
						793 Danes attack Lindisfarne		

Emperors	Popes	Kings of England	Kings of the Franks	Events	Islam	Norsemen	Great Men
Charlemagne 800 — 814	816	830 Egbert, King of Wessex, overlord of all England	Sons of Charlemagne 814 ——— 843	800 Charlemagne crowned Emperor	809		804
					821 Conquest of Crete		
						834 Norsemen in Ireland	
				843 Treaty of Verdun			
		Alfred the Great 871				869 Edmund, king of East Anglia, killed by Danes	
						874 Norsemen in Iceland	
				878 Battle of Ethandun, Treaty of Wedmore		882 Norsemen in Russia	
						886 Norsemen besiege Paris	

Emperors	Popes	Kings of England	Kings of France	Events	Crusades	Norsemen	Great Men
		Alfred the Great 901					
						Rollo in Normandy 911 — 930	
		Athelstan 925 — 940		937 Battle of Brunanburgh			
Otto I, the Great 962 — 973		Edgar the Peaceful 959 — 975					Dunstan, Archbishop 960 — 988
		Ethelred the Redeless 979	Hugh Capet 987 — 996			985 Eric the Red in Greenland	
				991 Danegeld levied in England			

Emperors	Popes	Kings of England	Kings of France	Events	Crusades	Norsemen	Great Men
						1002 LEIF ERICSON in America	
				1002 Massacre of Danes by ETHELRED the Redless			
						1014-16 Danish Conquest of England	
		EDMUND IRONSIDE 1016					
		CANUTE 1035					
		EDWARD the Confessor 1042					
				1054 Separation of Eastern and Western Churches			
HENRY IV 1056						1060-90 Norman Conquest of Sicily	
		HAROLD WILLIAM I 1066		1066 Norman Conquest of England Battle of Hastings		1066 Harold Hardrada of Norway invades North of England	
							LANFRANC Archbishop 1070
	GREGORY VII (Hildebrand) 1073			1077 Submission of HENRY IV at Canossa Beginning of Canterbury Cathedral by Normans.			ABELARD 1079
				1084 Carthusian Order founded by St. Bruno			
	1085 URBAN II 1087	1087					ST. BERNARD 1091 ANSELM Archbishop 1093
				1095 Council of Clermont	1096 First Crusade -99		
				1098 Monastery founded at Citeaux	1097 Siege of Antioch		1093
	1099				1099 Jerusalem taken GODFREY de BOUILLON		

EMPERORS	POPES	KINGS OF ENGLAND	KINGS OF FRANCE	EVENTS	CRUSADES	GREAT MEN
		HENRY I 1100		1107 Settlement of Investiture Conflict.		ABELARD · ST. BERNARD · ANSELM 1109
			LOUIS VI, the Fat 1108	1113 Order of Knights Hospitaller founded.		
				1115 Cistercian Order founded at Clairvaux by St. Bernard. Chartres Cathedral begun.		
				1118 Order of the Templars founded.		
CONRAD III 1138		1135	LOUIS VII 1137		SALADIN 1138	
FREDERICK I, Barbarossa 1152		HENRY II 1154			1145 Edessa captured by Saracens	1142
					1147 Second Crusade	1153
				1163 Notre Dame at Paris begun.		BECKET Archbishop 1162
				1164 Constitutions of Clarendon.		1170 ST. DOMINIC 1170
				1170 Murder of Becket.		
			PHILIP II AUGUSTUS 1180		1187 Capture of Jerusalem by SALADIN	ST. FRANCIS 1182
		RICHARD I 1189			1189 Third Crusade	
1190				1192 Bourges Cathedral begun.	1191 Crusaders take Acre	1193
		JOHN 1199			1192 Richard I's truce with SALADIN	
	INNOCENT III 1198					

Timeline chart (read top to bottom). Columns from left to right:

Emperors	Popes	Kings of England	Kings of France	Events	Crusades	Great Men
Frederick II 1212 — 1246	1216; Innocent IV 1243 — 1254	Henry III 1216; Edward I 1272	1223 St. Louis IX 1226 — 1270; Philip IV, the Fair 1285	c-1200 Universities of Oxford and Paris founded.	1204 Fourth Crusade	Stephen Langton Archbishop 1207 — 1229
				1204 Normandy lost to England.	1212 Children's Crusade	St. Thomas Aquinas 1227 — 1274
				1211 Reims Cathedral begun.		Roger Bacon 1214 — 1292
				1214 Battle of Bouvines.		1221 — 1226
				1215 Magna Carta. Lateran Council.	1227 Fifth Crusade	Marco Polo c-1254 — 1294
				1220 Dominican Rule authorized. Amiens Cathedral begun.		Kublai Kahn 1259 — 1292
				1223 Franciscan Rule authorized.	1244 Jerusalem lost	Dante 1265 — 1294
				1227 Beauvais Cathedral begun.	1248 Crusade of St. Louis	
				c-1230 University of Cambridge founded.		
				c-1240 Hanseatic League begun.		
				1265 Simon de Montfort's Parliament.		
				1266 Roger Bacon's Opus Majus; 1271 Marco Polo started for China.		
				1295 Model Parliament.		

Emperors	Popes	Kings of England	Kings of France	Events	Hundred Years' War	Great Men
		Edward I	Philip IV, the Fair	1302 First Summons of the Estates—General		Marco Polo · Dante
		Edward II 1307	1314	1305 Babylonian Captivity of the Church		1321
		Edward III 1327	Philip VI 1328	77 Seat of the Papacy at Avignon	1338 Beginning of the War	1324
					1340 Battle of Sluys	Froissart 1337
				1346 Gunpowder probably used at Crécy	1346 Battle of Crécy	Chaucer c-1340
			John 1350	1348 The Black Death	1347 Siege of Calais	Langland 1332
				1351 Statute of Labourers in England		Black Prince 1330
				1351 Anti-papal legislation of 53 Edward III	1356 Battle of Poitiers	Wycliffe c-1320
			Charles V 1364	1358 Revolt of the Jacquerie	1360 Treaty of Bretigny	
		Richard II 1377	Charles VI 1380	1362 Langland's *Vision of Piers the Plowman*	1371 Sack of Limoges	1376
				1380 Wycliffe's *Translation of the New Testament*		1384
				1381 Peasants' Revolt in England		1400

Emperors	Popes	Kings of England	Kings of France	Events	Hundred Years' War	Great Men
		1399 HENRY IV		1401 Law passed in England for the burning of heretics.		
		HENRY V 1413			1415 Battle of Agincourt	
		HENRY VI 1422	CHARLES VII 1422		1420 Treaty of Troyes	
					1429 Siege of Orleans	
					1431 JEANNE d'ARC put to death	The great men of the XV Century belong to the period of the Renaissance.
				1447 Library of the Vatican founded		
				c-1450 Invention of Printing	1453 End of the War	
				1453 Fall of Constantinople		
		EDWARD IV 1461	LOUIS XI 1461			
		RICHARD III 1483 — 1485	— 1483	1492 Discovery of America. Moors driven out of Spain		
				1497 VASCO da GAMA discovers Cape Route to India		

1410

INDEX

INDEX